IN THEIR VOICES

In Their Voices

BLACK AMERICANS ON TRANSRACIAL ADOPTION

Rhonda M. Roorda

Columbia University Press *New York*

Columbia University Press
Publishers Since 1893
New York   Chichester, West Sussex
cup.columbia.edu
Copyright © 2015 Columbia University Press
All rights reserved

Introduction, afterword, and appendix adapted with permission from Javier et al., *Handbook of adoption: Implications for researchers, practitioners, and families* (Thousand Oaks, CA: Sage Publishing, 2007).

Library of Congress Cataloging-in-Publication Data

Roorda, Rhonda M., 1969–
    In their voices : Black Americans on transracial adoption / Rhonda M. Roorda.
        pages cm
    Includes bibliographical references.
    ISBN 978-0-231-17220-2 (cloth : alk. paper) — ISBN 978-0-231-17221-9 (pbk. : alk. paper) —
ISBN 978-0-231-54048-3 (e-book)
    1. Interracial adoption—United States.   2. Adoptees—Family relationships—United States.
3. African Americans—Race identity.   I. Title.

HV875.64.R66 2015
362.734089'00973—DC23

2015011197

Columbia University Press books are printed on permanent and durable acid-free paper.
This book is printed on paper with recycled content.
Printed in the United States of America

c 10 9 8 7 6 5 4 3 2 1
p 10 9 8 7 6 5 4 3 2 1

COVER PHOTO: © Getty Images / Image Source
COVER DESIGN: Milenda Nan Ok Lee

References to websites (URLs) were accurate at the time of writing. Neither the author nor Columbia University Press is responsible for URLs that may have expired or changed since the manuscript was prepared.

This book is dedicated to the loving memory of Rita J. Simon, whose extensive scholarship and tireless advocacy in support of transracial adoption added voice to the many adoptees and families embarking on this journey. The partnership that I enjoyed with Rita for nearly twenty years produced the Simon-Roorda trilogy of books on transracial adoption and stretched my thinking on this fascinating and complex subject. I dearly treasured our friendship, her openness, and her generosity of time and spirit.

Thank you, Rita. Your work will not be forgotten.

Contents

PART III. POST–CIVIL RIGHTS ERA (1973–PRESENT)

Foreword

IN THE LATE 1960S and the early 1970s black people from all across the country, spurred by the death of Martin Luther King Jr., became acutely aware of, and sensitive to, the disparities they faced in American society. Before his death King had eloquently raised the issues of the injustices faced by black Americans. King's was among the most notable, but his voice was joined by others', such as those of Malcolm X, Stokely Carmichael, and Lerone Bennett, to name only a few of the most prominent leaders of the civil rights movement of the time. African Americans of almost every stripe—people on the streets, clergy, people in the halls of the academy, and professional people in almost every discipline—took to their pens, raised their voices, published books and essays, spoke from soap boxes on street corners, and shouted from their pulpits, declaring that injustice in American society must end. Their demands echoed the words of the Supreme Court almost a decade earlier when it urged that the end of injustice must proceed "with all deliberate speed."

In this context many black professional social workers began to question an emerging effort in their field to address the disproportionate and overwhelming numbers of black children who were languishing in foster care. That new effort was placing black children in white families for adoption. But other considerations influenced the nature of the discussion. The practice we now call transracial adoption had its earliest beginnings at a time when African Americans were developing anew their sense of personal identity, self-esteem, self-concept, and personal pride in their relationship with their native land of Africa. To be sure, these social workers were deeply concerned about the welfare of children in foster care, but they were also concerned about the effect of transracial placements on these children's emerging sense of self.

What had begun as a discussion with the potential to be an examination of a new trend in adoption practice was transformed in short order to a debate about the rightness of this new effort, the motivations of those who welcomed these children into their homes, and the potential, if not the certain, deleterious effects of sending black children to live with white families. These were not small matters. Those on both sides of the debate felt strongly about their positions.

Proponents of the practice of placing black children in white homes considered it reasonable, humane, and even progressive. For the proponents the questions were, Is it better to leave these children in the limbo and doubtfulness of an underfunded and understaffed foster care system with no promise of finding a permanent home for them before they reached their majority? Or should they be given the opportunity for a more promising future, even with a white family? Is it not immoral to deny white parents who clearly desired a child the opportunity to provide these children with a safe haven and the protection of a loving family during their tender childhood years? Or should these children be required to remain in foster care until more abundant black adoptive families could be recruited?

Opponents of transracial adoption raised significant questions challenging a practice that they believed threatened the development of wholesome identities, eroded competent senses of self-esteem, and jeopardized the emergence of robust self-concepts. The more strident among the opponents of transracial adoption raised the specter of a conspiracy to commit genocide among black children. These were tumultuous times indeed. Both sides were convinced of the rightness of their position, and both sides argued largely without evidence. For more than a decade the debate continued with seething hotness. The embers continue to smolder even now.

Even as I write this, emotions that I thought had quieted long ago arise in me anew, threatening to overtake my scholarly objectivity and revive my thoughts and feelings of that period. I almost tremble when I recall my frustration at the letters I received from people in Minneapolis that criticized me, based on an article I had published, for what they believed to be my position *against* transracial adoption. I am equally frustrated by the criticisms I received from colleagues in the National Association of Black Social Workers for what they believed to be my position *favoring* transracial adoption. Both criticisms were wrong, of course, for in the article I took the middle ground, recognizing that both sides had raised important issues. In my thinking at the time deciding the wisdom of this approach to adoption would be left to the future. I did suggest that if this practice succeeded, it had the potential to benefit society as a whole. My early observations on this subject did not end the debate.

Now forty-five years later, we take up the subject of transracial adoption yet again. This time we are fortunate to have the wise leadership of Rhonda M. Roorda, herself a transracially adopted child, to lead us through the complex and multifaceted territory of transracial adoption. Roorda and her colleague Rita J. Simon have examined almost every facet of this type of adoption in an earlier trilogy on the matter. Having talked to white parents who adopted black children, and to members of African American communities, this time she adds another dimension to her important subject. She not only speaks to transracially adopted children, she speaks *with* them, not as an intermediary but as a skilled facilitator who brings out the depth and the best of what these children have to say. And what they have to say is at once highly emotional and insightful. By turns their revelations are moving and critical. When they speak of the pain they suffered when the external world challenged their sense of self or their identity, one is compelled to think more seriously about any previous assumptions made about them. When they speak of the love they received in their adoptive families, a thoughtful person cannot help rethinking notions about the damage they had erroneously expected these children would suffer because of their adoptive experience. At the same time the adoptees' reports of the lack of knowledge possessed by some white adoptive parents make clear the need for these parents to reach out to the black community and to find ways to facilitate the development of connections between transracially adopted children and their heritage.

Perhaps the great contribution of this work is Roorda's insight that by allowing these brave individuals to speak through their own voices, we are given passage into a world of emotions, feelings, predictions, thoughts, and frustrations sorely needed by all who hope to help these individuals and future transracial adoptees.

The great takeaway from this work is that children, whether transracially adopted or living in birth families, and regardless of their ethnicity, still need a loving family, supportive communities, and an environment that prepares them for the taunts and erroneous assumptions that will inevitably be thrust at them by a world inclined to challenge their worth and dignity. They will also need the help of caring adults and an accepting society that recognizes not only the diversity of ethnicity but also the diversity of human experience. In the presence of such support not only will transracially adopted children develop optimally, but all children, whatever their childhood experiences, can be expected to thrive. This work moves us a great way toward that goal.

Leon W. Chestang, Ph.D.
Distinguished Professor Emeritus
Wayne State University

Preface

IT HAS BEEN MORE THAN FORTY YEARS since the National Association of Black Social Workers (NABSW) went on record as strongly opposing transracial adoption, particularly the adoption of black and biracial children by white parents. In 1972 the organization declared in an official position statement that "the National Association of Black Social Workers has taken a vehement stand against the placement of black children in white homes for any reason. We affirm the inviolable position of black children in black families where they belong physically, psychologically and culturally in order that they receive the total sense of themselves and develop a sound projection of their future" (Reid-Merritt, 2010, p. 167). Today academics, child welfare and adoption professionals, and concerned families throughout the United States still question whether this policy is effective long term for children of color. (While transracial adoption encompasses all kinds of parent-and-child racial combinations, this book focuses mainly on the adoption of black and biracial children by white parents, given the history of contentious race relations in this country.)

On December 28, 2013, the MSNBC host Melissa Harris-Perry called attention to transracial adoption when she invited comedians to appear on her show for a segment designed to make fun of events that had occurred during the year. Harris-Perry showed her guests a photo of former governor Mitt Romney, his wife, and their twenty-one grandchildren, all of whom are white except for Kieran, a transracial adoptee who is black. Harris-Perry asked her guests to come up with captions for the photo. Pia Glenn sang a popular Sesame Street song, "One of These Things Is Not Like the Others." Another guest, Dean Obeidallah, joked that the photo reflected the diversity of the

Republican Party. Harris-Perry interjected, saying, "My goal is that in 2040, the biggest thing of the year will be the wedding between Kieran Romney and North West. Can you imagine Mitt Romney and [hip-hop mogul] Kanye West as in-laws?" (Ghatt, 2014; Burke, 2013). Later Harris-Perry apologized multiple times on air and in social media for her statements, and for the segment itself, which ultimately belittled a family made through transracial adoption.

The Harris-Perry debacle shows that even in the twenty-first century issues relating to race, identity, and adoption can become fodder for awkward, demeaning, and superficial banter, even in mainstream media. Many young transracial adoptees are living in predominately white environments as the children of white parents, many of whom are convinced that love is enough and that a child's color is of no consequence. While the latter is a nice sentiment, it has no bearing on social reality in the United States. But as a result of their parents' policy of color-blindness, many transracial adoptees have learned to minimize their racial difference and accept the values and norms taught by their white parents. These adoptees seem to have found comfortable lives until tasteless and offensive comments, such as those made on MSNBC, force them to confront the duality and contradictions of their lives. And they are then often left to grapple on their own with issues of racial and cultural identity, as well as self-worth, and figure out where they fit within their white adoptive families and communities.

Identity formation is, as Erik Erikson pointed out almost fifty years ago, the most important developmental task of adolescence. Moreover, "a central part of identity development, especially for those who are not in the white-Anglo majority, is ethnic identity. The process of ethnic identity development, according to researchers (Phinney, 1990), in some respects follows the process of identity development in general — in short, an unquestioning view of oneself is altered during a period of 'crisis'" ("Identity Formation," 2002, p. 2). Now imagine that a person in the midst of such a crisis is coping not only with the usual adolescent angst but with having been imbued with the norms of white culture and little or no access to black culture. Furthermore, they are struck at the same time with the imperative that they also learn to navigate in a world in which racism and discrimination remain everyday problems.

Langston Hughes refers to a similar conflicting reality in his poem "I, Too, Sing America," when he envisions a time when he, the darker brother, considered unequal in the eyes of white America, will also "be at the table when company comes." He ends the poem with these powerful words: "I, too, am America" (Hughes, 1992, p. 326).

"I, too, am America." In this volume I argue that transracial adoptees who are living in two (or more) different worlds must be specifically and thoroughly taught how to navigate effectively in black or brown skin; otherwise, their self-worth, identity, compassion, and curiosity for learning about other people's diverse journeys, and the adoptees' ability to create a vibrant life, will be significantly compromised. Also compromised, and vitally important, will be the authentic relationships transracial adoptees can form and maintain with family members, friends, and eventually spouses and colleagues across socioeconomic, biological, adoptive, and racial lines. Like Langston Hughes, who pleaded that he, too, be embraced as America, I plead with white adoptive parents, social workers, therapists, educators, adoption policy groups, and Americans in general to understand that transracial adoptees are also America and deserve a seat at the table of inclusion and equality instead of having to suffer isolation, lack of preparation, and inequality.

In a recent working paper, "Contexts of Racial Socialization: Are Transracial Adoptive Families More Like Multiracial or White Monoracial Families?" Rose M. Kreider and Elizabeth Raleigh use restricted data from the 2009 American Community Survey (ACS) to compare the racial socialization of three groups: children who were adopted transracially by white parents, children in white monoracial families, and biological children of interracial couples. Kreider and Raleigh define *racial socialization* as two core components: how children feel about their racial and ethnic identity, and how they are taught to deal with discrimination and prejudice. The authors note that because "white adoptive parents may lack the individual experiences and resources to transmit positive racial socialization messages to their children, the role of community and social environment becomes even more important" (Kreider & Raleigh, 2011, p. 3). What makes their study compelling is that when Kreider and Raleigh looked at the residential patterns or social environments of all three groups, they found that transracially adoptive families were living in less racially diverse areas than children of interracial couples and in areas more similar to those of children in white monoracial families. In fact Kreider and Raleigh's study showed that Asian or Pacific Islander children who were transracially adopted lived in counties even less diverse racially than the average white child with white parents.

While adoption, including transracial adoption, is a regular occurrence, statistics tracking actual numbers of adoption placements in the United States remain frustratingly sketchy. According to the 2007 National Survey of Adoptive Parents, one out of four adopted children came from other nations; of the remaining children adopted domestically, half were adopted from foster care and half from private sources (Vandivere, Malm, & Radel, 2009). About 4 percent of Americans are adopted, and about half were adopted by people not related to them by blood (Fisher, 2003). The 2007 survey data also show that "adopted children are less likely to be White or of Hispanic origin than children in the general U.S. population, and they are more likely to be Black." Further, "the race and ethnic distribution of adopted children is different from that of adoptive parents. Whereas a majority of adopted children are nonwhite, the majority of these children's parents are White (73 percent)" (Vandivere et al., 2009, p. 13). We also know, based on data as of November 2013 from the Adoption and Foster Care Analysis and Reporting System (AFCARS), that during the 2012 fiscal year 397,122 children were in foster care; 101,915 (26 percent) of those children were black, and of those black children in foster care, 26,135 were available for adoption (U.S. Department of Health and Human Services, 2013). It is reasonable to believe that with a disproportionate number of black children in foster care desperately awaiting homes, there will be more transracial adoptive placements in the future.

Despite decades of so-called progress in the desegregation of U.S. society, most transracial adoptive families are still living in racially white homogeneous communities, apart from the adopted children's ethnic communities of origin and often, I fear, without a multifaceted, multiracial-cultural, and inclusive plan for integrating their family identity. My previous books on transracial adoption, coauthored with Rita J. Simon (Simon & Roorda, 2000, 2007, 2009), document the unintended challenges and pain experienced by adult transracial adoptees (as well as their adoptive parents and nonadopted white siblings) when the adoptees did not develop meaningful and sustainable relationships with friends, role models, godparents, and mentors from diverse ethnic and racial communities to guide and enrich their journeys. At the root of the pain are both the fragile racial and ethnic identities the supposedly color-blind behavior of the parents perpetuates for transracial adoptees and the adoptees' lonely struggle to navigate the harsh and institutional realities of racism and discrimination (Samuels, 2009; Smith, 2013; Simon & Roorda, 2000).

In Their Voices: Black Americans on Transracial Adoption is offered to readers—especially transracial adoptees, white adoptive parents, nonadopted siblings, social workers, therapists, adoption policy groups, educators, and mainstream America—as chance to hear the desperately needed voices of black Americans on transracial adoption, particularly as their thoughts relate to the challenges faced by black and biracial transracial adoptees raised by white parents, and to appreciate the values, cultural nuances, and inner strength that helped guide these interviewees. Fifty years of data and qualitative studies have shown that the gap between transracial adoptive families and children's ethnic communities of origin is real, and that if strong ties to communities of color are not developed and nurtured, this void can cause psychological and emotional damage to adopted children of color and their adoptive families, with generational consequences (Simon & Roorda, 2000, 2007, 2009; Smith, 2013; Kreider & Raleigh, 2011; Samuels, 2009). For that reason the thoughtful voices of the black men and women within these chapters are offered to help narrow the knowledge and experiential gap that is evident in the discussion and study of transracial adoption.

About the Interviews

I interviewed the sixteen individuals featured in *In Their Voices*. Their perspectives are based on their unique personal, educational, socioeconomic, and professional experiences, yet they share common experiences as black Americans and have a stake in the betterment of black and biracial transracial adoptees and families. These men and women became involved in this project after I connected with them through Facebook, LinkedIn, the Internet, and/or personal friendships; a few individuals reached out to me because they wanted to share their experiences. All but one of the interviews were conducted over the telephone. Each interview lasted at least one and a half hours. I taped the interviews, transcribed them, and then sent them to the interviewees for their approval. I also asked participants how they wanted to be identified. One participant, "Lora Kay," requested a pseudonym, another one preferred to be identified by first name only, and the others wanted their real names used in full. I honored the wishes of every interviewee. The interviews and my questions were lightly edited; they remain colloquial, but I have smoothed out some of the more tortuous constructions and grammatical errors to which we are all prone in conversation.

The participants (eight men and eight women) work in a wide array of fields. They range in age as well, from twenty-one through ninety-two. Three participants grew up during the Jim Crow era, four during the civil rights era, and nine during the post–civil rights era. The interviews in this collection are organized according to this rough chronology, so readers can better understand how race has affected black Americans from the era of Jim Crow to the present day and, more specifically, how the participants' lives were shaped by the era in which they lived. From these perspectives they share their views on the adoption and raising of black and biracial children by white American parents.

Most participants grew up in inner cities throughout the United States, including Washington, D.C.; New York City; Memphis, Tennessee; Hollywood, Florida; Toledo, Ohio; Chicago; Denver; and Sacramento. Three participants grew up in rural areas of North Carolina, Georgia, and Oklahoma.

In terms of their education, twelve of the sixteen participants have achieved at least a bachelor's degree, and of those seven have completed, or are in the process of completing, graduate degrees. Of the remaining four participants, one completed ninth grade, two earned their high school diplomas, and one completed an associate's degree. Three of the sixteen participants graduated from a historically black college.

Their family lives varied greatly as well. Ten of the sixteen participants were raised in a two-parent household. The other six were raised by single mothers. Three of the sixteen participants were formally adopted, two by black parents and one by white parents. One participant who was adopted by black parents did not learn until he was thirty-two that he was adopted. And another participant who was transracially adopted spent a significant number of years in the foster care system before being placed in an adoptive home. Three of the participants from single mother households, and even three from two-parent households, were informally adopted by grandparents, aunts, uncles, and church members. In addition two of the sixteen participants formally adopted a child themselves, and another participant has discussed formal adoption with her husband as a desirable option for their family. Finally, most of the participants have interacted with transracial adoptive families on some level, whether in their professional careers or because they have taken it upon themselves to mentor a black or biracial adoptee or contribute their expertise to the transracial adoptive community.

The interviews were designed to offer a structured yet compelling and intimate conversation on race, adoption, and identity. I was particularly interested in discussing certain topics with the interviewees: how they address racial discrimination and injustice in their own lives; what it means for them to be black in America; as parents, how they help prepare their children emotionally and psychologically for the society in which we live; their suggestions and words of encouragement for white adoptive parents committed to nurturing their black and biracial children to their full potential; and much, much more. I hope that from these pages readers will gain a cultural and adoptive intelligence that can help them better understand and navigate the realities of transracial adoption.

About the Author

My conviction to move forward on this project stems from my personal investment in the transracial adoptive community and the desire for adopted children of color raised transracially to absorb that they are beautiful, worthy, connected to their historical story, and full of promise. It also stems from my personal history as a transracial adoptee. In 1969, shortly after my birth, I entered the New York foster care system and survived there for two years before being placed in a home with white parents of Dutch heritage. At the time, given the many black and biracial children waiting for placement in adoptive homes, my adoption was nothing short of a miracle. However, the physical and emotional separation from my biological family (and community) left me feeling deep pain, loss, instability, powerlessness, and fear. I was fortunate to gain an adoptive family that provided me with a solid foundation, so I could plant my limp and fragile roots and have the chance to dream and grow. By being a part of my adoptive family, I learned through trial and error, and sometimes through fire, how to love, forgive, fall down, get back up, and pay it forward. Not a day goes by that I do not recognize that my path in life, and the privileges I have enjoyed that come from living in a white family, have guided me with comfort, flexibility, and confidence through the doors of higher education, social networks, and employment opportunities. As a result of my life's journey, and the many transracial adoptive parents I have met who love and care for their children and are working hard to do right by them, I endorse the practice of transracial adoption, fully aware that this remains a complex, bold, and controversial experience for families and especially for the transracial adoptee.

Recently I had the opportunity to speak at an African American heritage camp for transracial adoptive families. The goals of this particular camp (and others like it around the country) are for transracially adopted children to become connected to their rich heritage, in the hope that they will become well-adjusted individuals with high self-esteem and for their white adoptive parents to develop more knowledge and comfort around the issues of race, culture, and adoption that inevitably affect their families. At this camp the transracial adoptive families ate foods traditional to the African American community and celebrated African American culture through dance, art, and hair-care activities. For many of these children and parents, a camp like this is the only opportunity they have each year to really immerse themselves in aspects of the African American experience and connect with African Americans.

Still, it is difficult for the transracial adoptive families who attend to translate their new knowledge to their day-to-day lives. At one camp activity I attended, the parents broke into groups to discuss particular topics specific to transracial adoption. One of the most popular topics, with roughly forty people in the group, was building relationships in the black community. Group members agreed that, because few of them had black friends, or knew how to make connections in the black community, expecting to develop relationships in the black community was unrealistic. In my experience this is a common response. I think it is easier for transracial adoptive families to live in white communities and deny that race matters—until they become consciously aware that their children are judged or treated poorly because of the color of their skin. When that happens, the parents can no longer hold to a color-blind worldview. It takes tremendous courage and introspection for these parents to examine their own thoughts about their children's ethnic communities of origin, as well as the privileges that come for no other reason than being white in America. Doing so also requires transracial adoptive parents to push beyond their racial and socioeconomic comfort zones and take tangible risks to build equal and sustainable relationships with people who look like their children.

As I left the camp that morning almost in tears, I was reminded of the parallel but separate worlds—one white and one black or brown—that are separated by discomfort, fear, stereotypes, anxieties, and lack of awareness. Just as I was feeling most disheartened, a group of eight-year-old transracially adopted African American girls ran toward me to greet me. They had just had their hair braided at a hair-care workshop organized by African American women in the local community. These children wrapped their arms around me with hope in their eyes and excitement shining through their beautiful faces. They shrieked in unison and with great delight: "Ms. Rhonda, do you like my hair?!

Look at my colorful beads! It took a long time to get my hair done, but I didn't cry. I feel pretty!" I felt hope that this new generation of girls and boys would became aware of the history and present state of race in this country and learn how to rise above it to understand their true worth and that they are powerful beyond measure. I hope they will give this gift of empowerment to the generation of transracial adoptees behind them.

About the Book

The introduction, Moving Beyond the Controversy of the Transracial Adoption of Black and Biracial Children (which has been adapted from the version originally published in 2007 by Sage), covers the general history of transracial adoption, its ramifications for black and biracial adoptees, and the controversies surrounding it. The introduction also addresses the importance of the voices of black Americans in conversations about transracial adoption.

Conversations with the interviewees are organized roughly chronologically to illustrate how race has affected black Americans from the era of Jim Crow to the present day. From that platform the participants share their perspectives on transracial adoption, specifically, the adoption of black and biracial children by white American parents. In the conclusion I identify the key themes raised by the participants in this book that specifically address the needs of black and biracial transracial adoptees. In the afterword I examine current adoption policy. I make suggestions, based largely on the interviews here and from the findings in the Simon-Roorda trilogy of books on transracial adoption, about how to amend that policy for the betterment of children and families. Finally, in the appendix I describe a multicultural adoption plan that I hope will offer white adoptive parents in particular concrete guidelines for encouraging their child of color to develop a healthy racial identity and self-esteem. (Both the appendix and the afterword have been adapted from the version originally published in 2007 by Sage.)

Acknowledgments

In Their Voices is a labor of love that came about with the unwavering support of amazing people, including friends and family, who saw the importance of and urgent need for a book on transracial adoption and race. Thank you to everyone who helped me—you know who you are—for your time, insight, and encouragement. Your imprint is on every page.

I would like to especially thank the following individuals:

My husband, Floyd J. Brumfield Jr., for his love, wise counsel in the development of this book, and most of all for putting up with me during the ups and downs of the writing process.

Laurie Goff, one of my closest friends and a transracial adoptee, who was available, even when I called at unspeakable hours of the night, to lend an ear and hold me accountable for providing a book that gives transracial adoptive parents the tools to help them raise confident children of color with healthy self-esteem.

Vonja Kirkland, whose faith in me began in my childhood days in Takoma Park, Maryland, lifted my spirits in the tough times, celebrated with me during the good times, and reminded me along the way of my purpose.

Kathy Yates, transracial adoptive parent and veteran social worker extraordinaire, who made "all things adoption" a little bit more clear over a plate of Korean food.

W. Wilson Goode Jr., whose policy acumen, incredible patience, and ability to learn about transracial adoption and "get it" helped lend credibility to this book.

Anton Armstrong, Rose, Hassan A. Latif, Henry M., Kirkland Murray, Marvin Davis, and Lindsay Huddleston II for their powerful stories and support for this project. Although space limitations did not permit their interviews to appear, their experiences and thoughts on race and adoption gave me a deeper appreciation of the strength of the human spirit and the impact of racial discrimination on people of color in the United States. I carry their stories in my soul.

Finally, I would like to thank Columbia University Press, namely Jennifer Perillo, Stephen Wesley, Anne McCoy, and Polly Kummel, for their impeccable work on this project.

IN THEIR VOICES

Introduction

WHAT ARE THE IMPLICATIONS for children who are adopted by parents who are racially and ethnically different? Do these children grow up to be psychologically healthy? With which ethnic group will they identify? Will these children be able to fully function in dual societies when they become adults? Does race even matter? These are vital questions and concerns that have spawned intense discussion in the public arena and among social work professionals, politicians, scholars, and families for more than four decades.

The issue of transracial adoption, particularly the adoption of black and biracial children into white homes in this nation, is a fascinating subject. The issue ignites great curiosity about the development of adoptees in this situation and the responsibilities and roles of the adoptive parents, siblings, extended family, and community in guiding transracially adopted children into healthy adulthoods. This type of adoption brings the issues of race, identity, love, belonging, forgiveness, and racial reconciliation to the forefront for adoptees and their adoptive families.

Transracial adoptees who were adopted in infancy or early childhood have come into adulthood in the past several decades and have generated numerous contributions to our understanding of the outcomes of transracial adoption. Through the personal accounts of adult transracial adoptees and the books, films, and scholarly work done by transracial adoptees or other adoption participants, knowledge, awareness, and familiarity with the issues linked to transracial adoption have grown substantially, but much more territory remains to be covered. For the sake of those directly involved—transracial adoptive families and children—studying the results and impact of transracial adoption needs to be a higher priority among academics.

This introduction examines some of the groundbreaking research and critical thought at the heart of the transracial adoption controversy, which centers primarily on the identity formation of black and biracial children adopted by white parents. I also will discuss what the children themselves told me and my coauthor, Rita J. Simon, about their struggles with identity formation for *In Their Own Voices: Transracial Adoptees Tell Their Stories* (Simon & Roorda, 2000). What do the reports of older transracial adoptees and the transracial adoption controversy mean for black and biracial children adopted by white parents today? One useful way to answer this is to extract key information from some of the pioneering studies of transracial adoption in the 1970s, 1980s, and early 1990s that set the stage for more recent studies as well as the development of current federal policy on transracial adoption. Another way is to listen to the stories of those adoptees who are struggling with their identity and to learn from them. By using the perspectives offered in both the empirical and personal literature, researchers, practitioners, and leaders in ethnically diverse communities can better assist adoptive parents in creating strategic avenues through which transracial adoptees (children, adolescents, and adults) can most effectively develop a knowledge base that enables them to embrace their ethnic heritage(s) and communities, their adoptive families, and, most important, themselves. In addition to providing a critical review of the early literature and theory relevant to transracial adoption as it relates to the adoption of black children by white parents, my goal is to highlight the importance to this discussion of the voices of black Americans. Research, theory, and practice, as well as my own experience as an adoptee and with adult adoptees, tell me that those involved in transracial adoption, as well as society at large, need a greater understanding of the issues that affect transracial adoptees—and their adoptive families—to help these young people become dynamic citizens able to move fluidly within and between racially, ethnically, economically, and socially diverse worlds.

Lessons Learned: The Viewpoint of a Transracially Adopted Adult

As an African American woman who was adopted across the color line, someone whose identity was significantly influenced by her genetic makeup, foster care, and her own journey of transracial adoption, I recognize and appreciate the complexities and challenges inherent in finding a balance within oneself. I have worked to integrate psychologically and be proud of being both African American and the product of a white family. This combination has created unique talents and abilities that have enabled me to move effectively within different racial, cultural, and socioeconomic groups and to look at the world from not just a black or white perspective. I've done all this while nurturing the love I've developed for myself within a society that too often defines a person based on race. Developing self-confidence and my own identity truly were contingent on my honoring all of who I am. This is hard work, and at moments I feel as though the slightest thing could throw me off balance. Yet I have seen excellent examples of maintaining balance, through my own experiences as an adoptee as well as through listening to adoptive families throughout the country. Many parents are raising children of color cross-culturally and are successfully creating bridges to their children's ethnic communities—efforts that are clearly in the best interest of their children and their blended family. This investment yields unbelievable dividends. These parents are why I see transracial adoption as a viable option for building families. But I believe this choice must be viewed realistically, as a long-term commitment that requires awareness, intentionality, planning, flexibility, and humility on the part of the adoptive parents, (nonadopted) siblings, and the adoptees themselves. It also requires the guidance of thorough research on transracial adoption and comprehensive training or counseling for adoptive families conducted by social work and mental health professionals.

Every child needs and deserves to be loved, to have shelter and nourishment. Every child deserves to grow roots in a family. But how do white adoptive parents raise black and biracial children to be culturally and racially confident and psychologically strong? The answer should expand the meaning of love to include empowering transracial adoptees to successfully navigate, and feel comfortable in, different worlds simultaneously.

Transracial adoptees should be raised not only to be comfortable in their adoptive homes but also to be able to enter and thrive in a society that still perceives or judges individuals and their abilities on the basis of their skin color. Given this reality, how transracial adoptees choose to address the bias and complexities of racial relations will influence how they negotiate who they are, their personal and professional relationships and their worldview, and ultimately their success. Therefore, in addition to love, providing transracial adoptees early in their lives with the tools that will teach them to value who they are as adoptees and people with a rich cultural heritage is essential.

When I think about identity, race, and culture, I compare it to a poetry-jazz improvisation of unique and colorful sounds, all playing significant parts that rely on each other but ultimately transform each other. To me the beauty of a jazz and poetry ensemble is that its parts cannot be fully felt or appreciated in isolation. It needs to be heard in its entirety. So when looking for deeper understanding of the black experience, transracial adoptive families might look to the rich oral histories of African American culture, including songs, stories, and poetry. The poet Mari Evans (1992) wrote about the importance of poetry as a gateway to the African American cultural experience and describes poetry as traditionally the essence of a people's culture; it showcases who they are, what they feel, and how they view their surroundings. "We are," she said, "the sum and substance of all that is past. Racial and ethnic identities and histories have significantly shaped the climate in which we presently move, determining not only how we appear physically, but why we live as we do and, most importantly, why we think as we do." Evans continues: "Who we are, then, becomes a complexity of past and present, and when we go in search of ourselves, we often find the keys to ourselves in the poetry that reflects the culture of our people" (1992, p. 644).

My story and the stories of other transracial adoptees are part of a mosaic that includes the poetic voice inside each of us, in concert with the beat of our racial or ethnic histories and the chord that is instrumental in binding us to our adoptive families. For that reason I believe that social work professionals, policy makers, and researchers who seek to determine the ways in which white adoptive parents can successfully raise black and biracial children will find that the answer lies in a qualitative and holistic approach to research and practice that focuses on these adoptees, their experiences, and the relationship they (and their adoptive families) have with members of the adoptees' ethnic communities. If the hope is to promote healthy self-identities and self-esteem among black and biracial transracial adoptees, a qualitative and inclusive methodology, not quantitative research, may prove to be the more flexible and effective approach for exploring the long-term impact of transracial adoption on the identities of these adoptees.

History of the Transracial Adoption Controversy

To get to the heart of the transracial adoption controversy, it is necessary to understand what shaped the fear and concern for black and biracial children who were being raised by white parents in the early 1960s. The practice of transracial adoption would change the trajectory and the rhythm of these children's struggle to form their identities.

During the civil rights movement of the 1960s society became aware of the acute needs of parentless black children in America. An increasing number of organized groups committed to meeting the needs of these children began to pressure public and private agencies to permit adoption placements with white adults (Kennedy, 2003). By the late 1960s many progressive adoption professionals, and agencies that once had adhered to a strict race-matching policy in placing available children, became open to transracial placements, as reflected in the Standards for Adoption Service enunciated by the Child Welfare League of America in 1968 (Macaulay & Macaulay, 1978). In fact, as Kennedy (2003) observed, the Child Welfare League changed its position to both advocate for transracial placements and to be mindful of problems that might arise with transracial placements. This led to a 1971 surge in transracial adoption placements of black and biracial children in white homes in the United States (Simon, Altstein, & Melli, 1994). While the numbers of same-race and transracial adoptions that occurred annually before 1975 are difficult to determine accurately because of incomplete census data, it is estimated that twelve thousand black children were placed with white families between 1968 and 1975 (Simon et al., 1994). Within this seven-year period the greatest number of black children to be transracially adopted (2,574) were adopted in 1971 (Simon et al., 1994); one result was that placement of black children in white homes became a public controversy. Then in 1972, a year later, the National Association of Black Social Workers (NABSW) declared its strong opposition to the practice.

African Americans were deeply concerned about the loss of black children from their communities and mobilized to reclaim them (Townsend, 1995). Fueled largely by the NABSW's position, opposition to transracial adoptions gained ground. The controversy garnered further national attention when in 1972 the NABSW's president, William T. Merritt, declared at the organization's national conference that "Black children should be placed only with Black families, whether in foster care or for adoption" (Simon et al., 1994). His speech embodied concern for the identity of black children who were removed from their cultural heritage:

Black children belong physically, psychologically and culturally in Black families in order that they receive the total sense of themselves and develop a sound projection of their future. . . . Black children in white homes are cut off from the healthy development of themselves as Black people. The socialization process for every child begins at birth. Included in the socialization process is the child's cultural heritage which is an important segment of the total process. This must begin at the earliest moment; otherwise our children will not have the background and knowledge which is necessary to survive in a racist society. This is impossible if the child is placed with white parents in a white environment. . . . We [the members of the NABSW] have committed ourselves to go back to our communities and work to end this particular form of genocide [transracial adoption].

(SIMON ET AL., 1994, P. 40)

During that same period Leon Chestang (1972) became interested in the phenomenon of transracial adoption and its effects on the identities of black and biracial children. He acknowledged the dilemma posed by transracial adoption: the need to get African American children out of the foster care system and into permanent homes, even though white parents are less well equipped to help African American children gain a healthy sense of racial identity. He posed a series of questions designed to help social workers identify the white parents best suited for transracial adoption:

> The central focus of concern in biracial adoption should be the prospective adoptive parents. Are they aware of what they are getting into? Do they view their act as purely humanitarian, divorced from its social consequences? Such a response leaves the adoptive parents open to an overwhelming shock when friends and family reject and condemn them. Are they only interested in building world brotherhood without recognizing the personal consequences for the child placed in such circumstances? Such people are likely to be well meaning but unable to relate to the child's individual needs. Are the applicants attempting to solve a personal or social problem through biracial adoption? Such individuals are likely to place an undue burden on the child in resolving their problems.
>
> (CHESTANG, 1972, P. 104)

Chestang then went on to describe the problems that black children raised by white families are likely to experience and the probable outcomes of these adoptions. He predicted that if these children survived, they would have the potential to become catalysts for change in society (Chestang, 1972).

In response to the deep-seated concerns for transracially adopted children expressed by critics like Chestang and the NABSW, researchers and professionals, primarily in the field of social work and child development, set out to determine whether such worries were legitimate. Much of their work in the 1970s, 1980s, and early 1990s was empirical and looked at the extent to which black and biracial children adapted to their white adoptive families (compared with black children adopted into black families and white children adopted into white families).

These researchers also attempted to measure whether these children had a healthy sense of racial self-identity. A few landmark studies set the course for this exploration.

In 1977 Charles Zastrow, a doctoral student, compared the responses of forty-four white couples who had adopted a black child with the responses of forty-four white couples who had adopted a white child. All these couples lived in Wisconsin and were grouped according to the age of their children and the socioeconomic status of the adoptive parents. All the children were reported to be preschoolers. Zastrow set out to measure the degree of satisfaction and difficulties both groups encountered with their adoption placements. Data were obtained through in-home interviews with the adoptive parents and by reviewing the adoption agencies' records on these families. The parents' overall satisfaction with their adoption experience was the key factor in the study's outcome assessment. Zastrow (1977) reported that these transracial adoption placements were as successful as the inracial placements. On a subtle but important note, many transracial adoptive parents in the study said they had opted to become "color blind" and accept their child as an individual and a member of their family (Zastrow, 1977, p. 81).

In the early 1980s Ruth McRoy, Louis Zurcher, Michael Lauderdale, and Rosalie Anderson conducted exploratory studies of the self-esteem and racial identity of black transracial adoptees compared with those of black inracial adoptees (1982). McRoy and colleagues also studied the adoptees' racial identities based on their adoptive parents' perceptions of their children's attitude toward their racial background (1984). In both studies the researchers chose respondents—thirty parents and thirty adoptees who were at least ten years old—from the Southwest, Midwest, and upper Midwest whom the researchers had identified through adoptive parents' groups and adoption agencies (McRoy et al., 1982, 1984). Teams of black and white researchers interviewed parents and children.

In their 1982 study McRoy and colleagues found that while the black parents who adopted black children lived in predominately black communities (70 percent) and the majority of white parents who adopted black children resided in predominately white communities

(87 percent), the adoptees in both groups exhibited similar levels of self-esteem, believing that they were people of value (McRoy et al., 1982). These findings suggested that these adoptees possessed healthy and positive feelings of self-regard regardless of the race of their adoptive parents. Yet when these same researchers looked at the racial identity formation of the black transracial adoptees, the data revealed a high correlation between the communities in which the adoptees lived and their perceptions of their identities (McRoy et al., 1984). For example, those transracial adoptees whose families lived in a racially diverse community and who were exposed to people who resembled them physically tended to identify themselves as black people and had positive self-images of their blackness (McRoy et al., 1984). But those adoptees who were raised apart from their ethnic communities tended to develop stereotyped impressions of blacks, and these adoptees believed that they were advantaged because they had been adopted into white families. In addition, those children of color who were segregated from their ethnic communities (as was true for the majority of the transracial adoptees in the study) reported an acute feeling of difference. To compensate for this alienation they tended to dismiss the importance of their racial identity and heritage and acted like their white peers and family members in order to fit in.

Another landmark study, conducted by Joan Shireman and Penny Johnson (1986), was designed to measure the racial identity of twenty-six black transracial adoptees whose parents were white; it compared this group (studied separately) with twenty-seven black adoptees from black adoptive families. All were studied at preschool age (four years old) and at eight years of age and were living with their families in Chicago. The researchers used the well-known Clark and Clark Doll Test to determine how these children viewed themselves racially.[1] At age four, Shireman and Johnson found, 71 percent of the transracially adopted children identified themselves as black, whereas 53 percent of the inracially adopted black children did so. At age eight equal percentages of both groups of children identified themselves as black and displayed positive images of their blackness. Inherent in the 1986 report of Shireman and Johnson, and contrary to the expectations of opponents of transracial adoption, was the message that black transracial adoptees developed and maintained a positive racial identity despite living in predominately white communities. In essence the four-year longitudinal study found only a small but insignificant difference between the ways in which black transracial and inracial adoptees viewed their racial identities. The racial identities of transracial adoptees who had a strong start in embracing their black identity and pride remained constant during the four years of the study, but the inracially adopted black children showed a noticeable developmental gain during this same period. Shireman and Johnson (1986) concluded that adoption, including transracial adoption, is a good solution for children and families.

In 1994 Rita J. Simon, Howard Altstein, and Marygold S. Melli published *The Case for Transracial Adoption* and announced the findings of their twenty-year longitudinal study, which attempted to determine whether transracial adoption is in the best interests of the child. From 1971 to 1991 Simon and colleagues surveyed 206 transracial adoptive families with white parents in the Midwest. Unlike the researchers discussed earlier, Simon and colleagues interviewed families with adopted black children as well as families that adopted other children of color, including Korean and Native American adoptees. The researchers examined how relationships developed, particularly between the adoptive parents and the adoptees, and how parents' perceptions of their adopted children's racial identities varied over time. The report conveyed a positive message for white prospective adoptive parents and policy makers—Simon and colleagues (1994) found transracial adoption a viable option for children and families. These researchers concluded that during adolescence and adulthood, the transracial adoptees in their study were aware of, and comfortable with, their black racial identity. These authors clearly advocated transracial adoption and asked policy makers and adoption professionals to provide permanent homes for children in foster care regardless of race.

Critique of the Empirical Research

Certainly the research conducted on transracial adoption has been useful in several ways. It has brought attention and resources to learning in greater depth about the effects of this type of adoption on families and adoptees over time. It also sought to evaluate transracial adoption as an opportunity to provide permanent placements for children in need of homes. As an African American transracial adoptee, I am particularly attentive to the studies that home in on the identity development of children of color adopted by white parents, the majority of whom settle within predominately white communities. These landmark studies suggest that most, if not all, transracial adoptees seem, at the point at which the particular study was conducted, to have the ability to successfully adapt to, and identify with, their adoptive families. Also these children seemingly learn to sacrifice their own racial and cultural difference, perhaps to their detriment, in order to create added comfort for their adoptive parents, siblings, and the communities in which they are raised.

However, these landmark studies were limited in several important ways. They primarily assessed these children during childhood and studied racial identity only in their early years, whereas researchers have recognized that racial identity formation is more crucial and of primary concern during late adolescence and adulthood (Baden & Steward, 2000; Smith, Jacobson, & Juàrez, 2011). As a result the conclusions of these studies made it easier for white adoptive parents (and other parties that supported transracial adoption policy) to feel comfortable with raising children of color in their world and without changing their approach to parenting—the studies seemingly confirmed that love is enough for setting adoptees on the path to a healthy and productive adulthood (Simon et al., 1994). However, the studies did not take into account the complexities of raising children of color (and nonadopted siblings) to be conscious of, and informed about, the adoptees' ethnic background. These studies in effect gave white adoptive parents a stamp of approval, without addressing the racial and cultural difficulties these adopted children face as they become teenagers and then adults. The studies did not explore the comfort level of the white parents with, or their knowledge of, their adopted children's racial and ethnic background, nor did these studies hold the parents accountable for considering, and incorporating in the fabric of their family, the racial and ethnic richness of their adoptive children. These studies (Zastrow, 1977; Shireman & Johnson, 1986) make it much easier for parents, educators, and society to minimize both the racial and physical differences between white parents and their transracially adopted children and any difficulties that transracial adoptees may face as they attempt to negotiate their racial identities after being raised to share their adoptive parents' belief in the legitimacy and value of being color blind. The message from this research to families is that they do not have to change their lifestyle or priorities to help their children of color develop their racial identity.

Another unintended consequence of the traditional empirical research is its potential for influencing how the identity development of black and biracial transracial adoptees is understood and viewed. The bulk of the research essentially is designed to examine these children's racial identity and self-esteem within a narrowly defined concept: how these children view themselves (based, for example, on the Clark and Clark Doll Test) and how their adoptive parents (who have convinced themselves they are color blind) view their transracially adopted children. Moreover, the researchers made their assessments while the children were so young that they lived solely within the confines of their adoptive families and within what their parents perceived to be a safe, nonthreatening environment. Further, the young age of the children studied meant that they were many years from their teens, long recognized by psychologists as the period crucial for identity formation. This research bias may provide parents with an excuse to avoid learning about racial identity processes that are part of their children's lives; instead, the parents believe that racial identity formation is static or fixed (e.g., "My child is an individual who is happy and happens to be black, end of story"). It would be reasonable to assume that black and biracial transracial adoptees, who have already suffered an overabundance of abandonment, would be invested in accepting the values and norms taught by their white parents. As a result the racial identities of black and biracial transracial adoptees take a backseat, even in their teenage years, when they are supposed to be exploring their identities by, among other things, challenging their parents. According to my conversations with more than a hundred young adult transracial adoptees from various racial and ethnic groups throughout the country, a significant number find it challenging to become comfortable and self-confident enough to explore and nurture their racial identities. They express fear that by exploring their racial identities, they will breach unspoken boundaries within their families or even jeopardize the love their adoptive families have for them (personal communications, 1999–2014).

Furthermore, these traditional studies do not consider the effects of subtle and overt forms of racism experienced by black and biracial transracial adoptees living in predominately white worlds (Smith, Jacobson, & Juàrez, 2011). That means these studies do not provide data on the psychological outcomes for transracial adoptees who experience racial incidents, an especially glaring gap in the literature, given that many such adoptees say brushes with racism plunged them into an identity crisis.

Moving beyond the limitations of the original research findings is integral to learning more about raising successful and competent black and biracial transracial adoptees. Since the early 1990s studies of transracial adoption have become more sophisticated and comprehensive in examining the strengths and challenges of this type of family placement as it relates to the racial and ethnic experiences of adoptees (Smith, Jacobson, & Juàrez, 2011; Smith, McRoy, et al., 2008). These newer studies show a direct correlation between the racial orientation of transracial adoptees and their parents' attitudes and behaviors in relation to racial socialization—rates of which have been shown to be low among white adoptive parents, that is, they are relatively uniformed about and have little experience with the black community (or other communities of color). The parents' racial socialization in turn affects these adoptees' psychological adjustment outcomes on such measures as happiness, good self-esteem or depression, interpersonal problems, and substance abuse (Smith, McRoy, et al., 2008). One such study (Smith, McRoy et al., 2008) found that most adolescent and young adult adoptees identified with the racial identity of their white adoptive parents, because doing so created less psychological stress for the adoptees (and better adjustment outcomes). However these same studies show conclusively that when white adoptive parents are proactive in helping their children to understand and become comfortable with their racial and ethnic backgrounds, and are able to tend to the children's race-related needs, these children show higher levels of self-esteem and racial and ethnic contentment, as well as a greater ability to achieve their fullest potential than do their counterparts whose parents are not proactive (Smith, Jacobson, & Juàrez, 2011;Smith, McRoy, et al., 2008). Additional scholarship in this area should be encouraged. The results of such research are likely to impress upon white parents the importance of exposing their black and biracial adoptees to their communities of origin and how empowering and unifying knowledge of the adoptees' cultural and ethnic history is to the entire family unit.

Federal Legislation

A significant addition to the discussion of transracial adoption was the introduction of two complementary pieces of federal legislation enacted in 1994 and 1996 based largely on the transracial adoption research conducted by social scientists in the 1970s, 1980s, and early 1990s; in effect, these two pieces of legislation changed national policy on adoption from strictly upholding same-race placements to accepting transracial placements (Alexander & Curtis, 1996). Written by former senator Howard M. Metzenbaum (D-Ohio) because of the need to address the disproportionate numbers of children of color in the U.S. child welfare system who were waiting and available to be adopted, the Multiethnic Placement Act of 1994 (P.L. 103-302) was enacted by the 104th Congress and signed into law by President Bill Clinton. MEPA was designed to prohibit agencies (those managing foster care and adoption placements and receiving federal assistance) from delaying and denying the placement of children based solely on the race or national origin of the adoptive or foster parents or of the children involved. However, vague language in the statute created confusion among child welfare agencies and practitioners regarding its implementation guidelines, so Congress passed an amendment, the 1996 Interethnic Adoption Provision Act (P.L. 104-188), to clarify the language in MEPA (Fenster, 2002).

The effect of both pieces of legislation was to make clear that "in-racial placement preference would no longer be legal except in those cases in which it was specifically justified by the needs of the individual child" (Fenster, 2002, p. 37). In other words, if a black child is available for adoption and a qualified white couple (or parent) that can meet the child's needs is available and willing to adopt this child, federal law requires that an adoption plan for both the child and the parent(s) be made expeditiously. The agency or case worker cannot stall placement indefinitely in anticipation that a black couple (or parent) will come forward to provide a home for the child. Although race cannot be a factor in determining placements for a child in the majority of cases, both laws were designed to encourage agencies to be creative and aggressive in their recruitment efforts in order to enlarge the pool of ethnically and racially diverse parental applicants to better reflect the ethnic and racial diversity of the children in the system (Hollinger & the ABA Center, 1998).

Nearly ten years after MEPA and IEPA became law, the Evan B. Donaldson Adoption Institute released a groundbreaking report, "Finding Families for African American Children," that examined the effectiveness of federal legislation in promoting the adoption of African American children from the U.S. child welfare system. The report found a modest increase (nearly 3 percent) in the number of transracial adoptions of black children from foster care between 1996 and 2003 but that federal policy had not led to placement of African American children in permanent homes as quickly as white children are placed (Smith, McRoy, et al., 2008). African American children, according to the report, were still staying in foster care an average of nine months longer than white children. Further, the report found that implementation of the color-blind approach to adoption, inherent in MEPA-IEPA, has inadvertently prevented adoption agencies and social workers from adequately preparing adoptive families for parenting outside their own race. Finally, Smith, McRoy, and colleagues (2008) found that efforts to recruit prospective parents from communities of color, as mandated by both laws, have not been well implemented or enforced. Clearly further studies are needed to monitor the effectiveness of this legislation and to ensure that these measures do what they are intended to do. Children awaiting adoption while in foster care desperately need to be placed in permanent, stable homes, whether the placement is with same-race or transracial parents. Since the report by Smith, McRoy, and colleagues in 2008, the U.S. Department of Health and Human Services (2013) has found that between 2008 and 2012 the number of children in foster care decreased slightly but steadily, from 463,792 children to 397,122 children, a 14.4 percent (66,670 children) drop during the five-year period. This is welcome news, but more progress is needed. The next step for children of color who are placed in transracial adoptive homes is learning to address the complexities of living within white families. The pressing issue then becomes how social work practitioners, mental health professionals, and parents can assist these children in this effort despite the imperfections in federal policy.

Complexities of Identity: Beyond Adjustment

No matter what federal law says, how its mandates are carried out ultimately depends on how case workers and agency professionals interpret the law as well as on their attitudes toward these laws. Fenster (2002) surveyed 363 social workers (158 African Americans and 205 Caucasians) throughout the United States and used their identification as members of either the National Association of Social Workers (NASW) or the NABSW to categorize them according to their attitudes about transracial adoption—in particular the adoption of black children by white parents. The goal of the study was to determine whether social workers generally favored transracial adoption as a social policy and whether race was a determining factor in their attitudes toward the policy. Although the study does not specify how many of the black (or white) social workers were in a position to make placement decisions within their agencies, the results did show that race and membership affiliation were key factors in how these social workers viewed transracial adoption. Black social workers who identified more strongly with the NABSW were more opposed to transracial adoption than were white social workers or even those black social workers who identified less strongly with the NABSW (Fenster, 2002). Thus, as the findings indicate, NABSW members were less supportive of transracial adoption placements, which is consistent with the NABSW's long-held concerns about transracial adoption, than were black nonmembers (Fenster, 2002). Fenster points out the need for additional studies to determine how these attitudes do or do not affect practice. With the pressing need to find permanent homes for the many children in the U.S. foster care system, how social workers, based on their race and affiliation, interpret the existing law on transracial adoption is of considerable interest. How will social workers decide what home is in the best interest of the black child in particular? Are social workers capable of preparing potential white adoptive parents to raise children of color by exposing these children to their cultural heritage and the rich black experience? If social workers do so, will they be operating appropriately within federal law? Or will these same social workers, out of fear of federal sanctions or personal discomfort, choose to achieve the easier task of not educating the parents about the racial or cultural sensitivities that the family may confront? Further, will black social workers who identify strongly with their own ethnic group overlook current federal law, which urges them to place children without considering their race, and deny placement of a black child in a white home? When I look at Fenster's study, my concern is that white social workers who are placing children of color in white homes have no frame of reference or adequate training for guiding white adoptive parents in raising children of color.

The case against transracial adoption, articulated for more than forty years by the NABSW and other opponents of transracial adoption, has not been supported within academia or in the halls of Congress because it has not been sustained by empirical data (Altstein, 2006; Turner & Taylor, 1996). The NABSW's argument has some merit in regard to how well white parents can consciously raise confident black children. The frustrating point is that for more than four decades the NABSW, some of whose members are charged with the responsibility of placing children, has failed to sit down with the transracial adoption community to discuss what can be done to help transracial adoptive families and their children. Transracial adoptive families, particularly white parents raising black and biracial adoptees, need to understand

the importance of black identity and pride in the black community—
and the NABSW could and should be instrumental in fostering that
understanding.

Transracial adoptees truly find it easy, in the short term, to deny their
blackness, especially when issues of racism, inequality, and injustice
become hot news. It is also easy for transracial adoptees to ignore in
the short term the challenges that affect black America. Clearly adoptive families and adoptees must do more work to incorporate in the
core values of the family African American history and experiences so
that these transracial adoptees can authentically identify, and become
comfortable, with the development of their identities both within their
homes and within society. And the black community, whether leaders or members, cannot stand on the sidelines, indifferent to learning more about transracial adoption and to building relationships with
black and biracial adoptees and their transracial adoptive families.

Black and biracial transracial adoptees, especially, need healthy and
sustainable relationships with people in the black community to help
strengthen their racial identities and find comfort in their own skin.
For members of the black community, connecting with black and biracial transracial adoptees can be a gateway to better understanding
the white community. My hope is that these groups will connect and
that those connections will bring about added understanding, empathy, and support for each other. As some of the interviews collected by
Simon and Roorda (2000) reflect, white transracial adoptive parents
need guidance from the black community. White adoptive parents and
the black community must hold each other accountable and do what
is difficult and responsible for the future of black and biracial adoptees, transracial adoptive families, communities of color, research, and
society.

The Significance of Overcoming Racial Stereotypes: My Journey

When I was about twelve years old, my adoptive family and I moved to
the city of Takoma Park, Maryland, a predominately black enclave. We
lived in a geodesic dome on top of a hill. During that time my brother
and I delivered newspapers for the *Washington Post*. Our paper route

took us through adjacent neighborhoods. The challenge for me, especially on Saturday mornings when I needed to walk down our street to get to my route, was to avoid the black males in our neighborhood because I was afraid of them. I thought I was good at avoiding them. I could usually dodge them from a distance. I willingly walked a mile or more out of my way so that I would not come in contact with these young black men. One morning, as I walked down the street as usual, I failed to notice the young black man in front of me until I could feel his breath on my face. In a panic I dropped my bag and my newspaper cart and ran up the street to my home. I was so shaken by what seemed to me his invasion of my world that I vomited in the bathroom.

In that poignant moment I knew I had a deep and potentially paralyzing fear of black men. Even though I lived in a black neighborhood, I had allowed myself to become insulated in a world of primarily white friends who attended my private Christian elementary school and our church. I had absorbed the values, experiences, and stereotypes about people of color from the people around me, without questioning whether their perspective conflicted with who I was. Although I was an African American, I had no understanding about how people of color were judged and ill treated based on quick and casual observation. This man, this black man who was in front of me that Saturday morning, had simply said hello, and I had reacted to him as if I had seen him on the nightly news as the suspect in a horrible crime. I was black, yet as I sat in the living room with my family, I took in the negative portrayals of black people from the broadcasts of news stories, ads, and dramatic series. My family was not aware that these images struck me in a more personal and negative way than they, and they did not provide any counterbalancing commentary about these images. Nor did I seek to aggressively find positive images of people who looked like me. I was too ready to digest the prepackaged images delivered by television and other media, in part because I was more concerned about not making waves in my family. The result was slow sacrifice of my self-identity. To attempt to reconcile these disparate realities, I overcompensated and rationalized that I was far removed from these negative images of black Americans I saw portrayed on television and in print.

Obviously those images set the trajectory for how I responded to black males in society and how mainstream America has pigeonholed this segment of the population. Nevertheless, because of that morning walk on the streets of Takoma Park, I realized that my journey would be longer and more complicated than my need to overcome my fear of black men. I came to a committed awareness that, for me to succeed in achieving my unique purpose, I needed to gradually develop relationships with people of color based on their character instead of a thirty-second sound bite on the nightly news. I would also have to replace the shallow and stereotypical images in my mind with more informed images of people who looked like me and were making lasting contributions to humankind. This challenge led me to reflect on myself as an adoptee, as a black female, and as someone who was and is blessed with God-given and genetically ingrained gifts and talents. From that process, through lonely moments, tears, anguish, and triumph, came a book; my painful labor helped to deliver a broader and deeper understanding of how race and identity affect the transracial adoptee.

Identity: In the Voice of Adult Transracial Adoptees

In the spring of 2000, with the support of transracial adoptees, adoptive parents, adoption groups, politicians, leaders, and caring people in the black and white communities, and those in the social work and legal professions, *In Their Own Voices: Transracial Adoptees Tell Their Stories* (Simon & Roorda, 2000) was published. This book used a narrative format and primarily provided a forum for young adult black and biracial adoptees to discuss in their own words, and in their own rhythm and style, their experiences of being raised in transracial homes. The text presented the history and legal status of transracial adoption as well as the controversy surrounding the practice. Those represented in the book are now adults approaching middle age. They told me and the prolific scholar Rita J. Simon their stories, which provided an insider's more informed understanding of how to most effectively raise psychologically strong and culturally confident black and biracial children adopted transracially.

Simon and I wanted to see whether black and biracial adoptees around the country experienced similar (or different) challenges and successes throughout their lives, particularly when moving into arenas of higher education, career, dating, and home ownership; how they developed their identities and attempted to juggle their divergent worlds; and whether, based on their experiences, they believed that love is enough (Simon & Roorda, 2000). As an adoptee I believed early on that within me is a depth and complexity that reaches far beyond the scope of the research models, questionnaires and surveys, and focus groups used in the traditional studies I discussed earlier. While those parameters are valuable in giving clinical researchers a snapshot in time for assessing the general thoughts and behavior of their respondents, they do not show the mental, emotional, or physical progression required for transracial adoptees to learn to accept their difference in their white family and what it takes to navigate as people of color in society. Simon and I sought the stories we believed we could obtain only because I could connect with other adult transracial adoptees.

The stories from the adult adoptees we interviewed revealed several interesting points. A recurring theme was their sincere expression of feelings of love and loyalty toward their adoptive parents and their appreciation for having the opportunity to grow within a family through adoption. The adoptees also identified with and embodied key character-building values taught to them by their adoptive parents and that clearly contributed to the children's inner confidence. These values included love, trust, honesty, and respect for one another, hard work, and education (Simon and Roorda, 2000). Tage Larsen, a classical trumpet player who at the time was a member of the President's Own U.S. Marine Band, said his parents taught him to "work hard and stay focused and determined" (Simon & Roorda, 2000, p. 252).

That first book made clear that the love, stability, and care provided by the majority of the adoptive parents to their black and biracial children, particularly during their childhood and adolescent years, was immeasurable and contributed to building a strong foundation for the adoptees. Yet what emerged from this project that had not come out in previous studies was that love, while essential to the development of a healthy self-esteem and identity, is not enough when white parents are raising adopted children of color. In fact race and ethnicity do matter—substantially—in the healthy upbringing of transracial adoptees. This realization was especially clear to many of the adoptees as they left their white adoptive homes and entered society as adults of color. They no longer were protected by the privileges of their white parents but rather were viewed by society based on the color of their skin. At that point society's view of black and biracial transracial adoptees became similar to its view of other black Americans. Transracial adoptees find that race and ethnicity issues become a priority in their lives as they go on to higher education, marry (whether their spouse is black or white), parent children of color, and work in corporate America. I believe that some transracial adoptees do perceive themselves to be capable and even confident. However, in my opinion far too many left their adoptive families with no tools for strategically negotiating the social terrain as people of color away from their safe adoptive family structure.

"Aaliyah," who was born and raised in a predominately white environment near Grand Rapids, Michigan, struggled throughout her adolescence and into adulthood with low self-esteem and feelings of differentness from her adoptive family. As a young adult she found herself desperately seeking answers in urban areas by recklessly partying on the weekends at seedy bars and bringing home any man who would tell her she looked good, at times putting herself at risk physically and psychologically. In her search for identity and happiness, she described herself as "going this way and that way and not knowing which way to turn" (Simon & Roorda, 2000, p. 193). While she wanted to remain close to her adoptive parents, she acknowledged that racial and cultural issues were starting to divide her and her parents. She stated, "I feel like we're [she and her adoptive parents] totally different. Since I've grown up from a teenager to an adult, I've changed a lot because I've lived in the city and have seen that side now. I lean toward that. I don't think my parents ever really liked my boyfriend (who's from the city). They thought all the decisions I made were wrong" (Simon & Roorda, 2000, p. 185).While most young people do not always see eye to eye with their parents, Aaliyah's story shows how issues of disagreement between a young adult and her parents become more complex when race, adoption, socioeconomic levels, and cultural differences become divisive factors.

Aaliyah struggled with not wanting to lose her parents' love and the values they taught her while having an inexplicable need to explore her black identity. Her search, which turned out to be both aimless and harmful to her at the time of the interview, kept her stuck, unable to navigate her course effectively in either the black or white community. And she was unable to truly realize her potential because she had lost her inner compass and confidence.

Unlike Aaliyah, Seth Himrod, who was raised in Evanston, Illinois, had parents who were more informed about the difficulties of race. When I interviewed him, he was a stockbroker and a single father living next door to his adoptive parents. Seth was a good and honest man with a high caliber of professionalism, but he experienced the harsh realities of society despite his fine qualities and his parents' best efforts to shield him. He explained:

As I got older, I stopped being this cute little boy and others perceived me as this black teenager and a menace to society. Apparently, I was liable to rape, kill, or whatever. I got pulled over by the cops; I got slammed against the wall with a flashlight up in my face. Questions were thrown at me, like what am I doing? Where am I going? You fit the description; come over here, we got to talk to you. Those things are what anger me. The fact that I was able to go to my dad and see his pain and outrage, the same way as I was feeling even though he never experienced it, was a support system for me. He never had a cop do that to him. Instead of asking me what I was doing, he'd tell me I should be upset about what happened. (SIMON & ROORDA, 2000, P. 296)

Raised in a predominately white suburb of Chicago and cut off from her ethnic community of origin, Rachel is an adult adoptee who is supportive of transracial adoption but carried a lingering air of sadness and confusion throughout the interview. She believed that this was in large part because she had little information about her ethnic heritage. Because she was experiencing a growing sense of insecurity, she had difficulty fitting into the predominately white community and with being totally comfortable in the black community. When asked about her view of transracial adoption, she said, "I think they [white adoptive parents] need to make sure that the children stay in touch with their roots. It's essential that they know the history and background of their people. I feel as though I've lost touch with who I am" (Simon & Roorda, 2000, p. 157).

When adoptive parents ask me for advice about raising black and biracial children (as well as other adoptees), I tell them it is helpful for the entire family to be exposed to the African American community through friendships made through church, school, and support groups. Also helpful are family discussions, and celebrations that can be included in "life books," records of family memories and life events before and during a child's adoptive placement. What was missing for most of the adoptees we interviewed (Simon & Roorda, 2000) were black and biracial role models and mentors during their adolescent and young adult years. Why is that important? Because too many of these adoptees were disillusioned when they entered the real world, and their disillusionment was magnified by not having the tools for maneuvering in life with dark skin. And far too many believed that once they recognized they needed the black community or that they shared a common bond, the black community at large would be immediately receptive and not suspicious of them. But black and biracial children raised in white homes are culturally different from black children raised in same-race homes; transracial adoptees need people familiar with both perspectives to patiently share their knowledge, love, and time to teach these adoptees about the world in which they live. Transracial adoption is still a controversial subject, and participating in such an adoption requires conscientious effort toward, and long-term focus on, the transracial adoptive family as a unit. Transracial adoptive parents and professionals working to support this form of adoption must be committed to nurturing these children to become grounded and secure adults of color who are connected with their ethnic communities.

The Importance of the Voices of Black Americans in
Discussions of Transracial Adoption

The discourse on transracial adoption is paying increased attention to
the importance of the racial identity and ethnic community or communities of origin of the adopted child of color. All parties with a stake
in transracial adoption—including progressive transracial adoption
researchers, policy group think tanks, transracial adoption support
groups, adoption agencies, white adoptive parents, and adult adoptees—wrestle with how to effectively prepare transracial adoptees to
build healthy racial identities. Paramount is the growing recognition
by these stakeholders that race and discrimination are real factors that
impede transracial adoptees (and by extension their white adoptive
families) and that white adoptive parents often have limited skills and
strategies for teaching their children of color about how to maneuver
between white privilege and institutional racism.

The purpose of this book is to bring the voices of black Americans
to the table on transracial adoption. Outside the emotionally charged
statements made by the National Association of Black Social Workers
(along with other black political groups) in opposition to the practice
of placing black children in white homes, the discussion of the merits
of, and problems with, transracial adoption has involved few members of the black community. Certainly the black perspective has had
little influence on current transracial adoption policy, which supports
a color-blind philosophy to expeditiously remove children (and they
are disproportionately children of color) from the foster care system to
permanent homes.

These children will grow up to be adults of color who have the
right, need, and responsibility to understand African American history,
culture, and experience. Research has shown that when transracial
adoptees are separated from their ethnic community, their self-identity
suffers (Baden & Steward, 2000). Those in favor of the color-blind
approach to adoption placement often do not fully acknowledge this.
There is a great need for cultural understanding and tools that can help
prepare white adoptive parents to raise culturally aware, self-confident,
and centered children of color.

I strongly believe that a productive way for black transracial adoptees who are raised in white families to understand their racial and cultural heritage is to regularly see a range of people who look like them. Yet I recognize that there is often a significant geographic gap between the neighborhoods where white adoptive parents raise black children and where the black community resides. This book offers the voices of black men and women who can shed light on the black-white tensions and disparities in America and the complex societal issues that plague black America.

My hope is that the varied voices of the black Americans in this book will benefit transracial adoptive families, influence adoption policy, and provide to scholars, adoption professionals, adoptive families, therapists, and the general public added understanding of this complex subject. The interviewees offer their best advice to help white adoptive parents gain insight into aspects of the black experience and to share ideas about how to prepare black and biracial children to function and thrive outside their white adoptive homes and communities. Also, all the interviewees understood that black and biracial children raised in white homes will eventually confront the problems of race and discrimination that most African Americans deal with on a daily basis. All the participants in this book recognize the urgent need for them to add to the conversation on transracial adoption, primarily for the benefit of black and biracial transracial adoptees but also for transracial adoptees from other ethnic backgrounds. Finally, for readers, especially those interested in learning more about transracial adoption and the growing number of transracial adoptive families, it is my hope that the stories shared by the men and women in this book will show how important it is for white transracial adoptive parents to take a proactive role in learning about the history and culture of their child of color.

PART I

Jim Crow Era (1877–1954)

THE LEGAL SYSTEM OF SLAVERY in the United States, which treated black people as property and therefore allowed children and parents to be separated, bought, and sold—ended in 1865 after the North won the Civil War and Congress ratified the Thirteenth Amendment to the Constitution. Yet many in the South refused to give up the economic caste system that greatly benefited whites, although at first southerners had little choice, as the federal government was administering the states of the former Confederacy. During that period, known as Reconstruction, "the newly freed men . . . could vote, marry, or go to school . . . and the more ambitious among them could enroll in black colleges . . . open businesses, and run for office under the protection of northern troops. . . . Some managed to become physicians, legislators, undertakers, insurance men. They assumed that the question of black citizens' rights had been settled for good and that all that confronted them was merely building on these new opportunities" (Wilkerson, 2010, p. 37).

But within ten years the federal government had given up on Reconstruction. As the writer Nicholas Lemann (2013) details:

> The Army was in the South to enforce the Fourteenth and Fifteen Amendments [civil rights and voting rights, respectively], and it became increasingly clear that without its presence, the white South would regionally nullify those amendments through terrorism. But the use of federal troops to confront the white militias was deeply unpopular, including in the North. . . . The country had never been entirely for full rights for African Americans in the first place, and it wanted to put the Civil War and its legacy behind it.

The Ku Klux Klan, which began in the immediate aftermath of the war
and was suppressed by federal troops, soon morphed into an archipelago
of secret organizations all over the South that were more explicitly devoted
to political terror. . . . In the aggregate, many more black Americans
died from white terrorist activities during Reconstruction than from many
decades of lynchings. Their effect was to nullify, through violence, the
Fifteenth Amendment, by turning black political activity and voting into
something that required taking one's life into one's hands.

Isabel Wilkerson picks up the story: "Around the turn of the twentieth century . . . southern state legislatures began devising with in-
ventiveness and precision laws that would regulate every aspect of
black people's lives, solidify the southern caste system, and prohibit
even the most casual and incidental contact between the races. They
would come to be called Jim Crow laws" (2010, p. 40). The Jim Crow
era lasted almost one hundred years.[1] By 1915 all southern states had
some form of Jim Crow laws. For example, blacks were prohibited
from eating in the same restaurants, drinking out of the same drinking
fountains, entering the same restrooms, going to the same schools, or
watching movies in the same theaters as whites. Common signage at
the time warned: "Whites Only"; "Restrooms for Colored"; "No Dogs,
Negroes or Mexicans"; "Colored Waiting Room"; and "Staff and Negroes Use Back Entrance" (Householder, 2012).

Punishment for blacks who defied Jim Crow laws (and even for
sympathetic whites) was severe. For infractions like attempting to register to vote, stealing a cow, talking back to a white person, or fighting
for justice, blacks could be lynched by white mobs that didn't even
bother to hold a sham trial (NAACP, 2000). And in the case of serious
felonies, many innocent people were hanged.

Compounding the strictures of the Jim Crow laws were the unwritten and rigid social expectations during this period. For example, a
black man was strongly discouraged from shaking hands with a white
man—and from making eye contact with a white woman, lest he be
accused of making sexual advances. Blacks were expected to address
whites as "Mister," "Sir," or "Ma'am," yet whites more often than not
spoke condescendingly to blacks. Such unwritten rules further rein-

forced the unequal relationship between blacks and whites. Black people were ever mindful of the need to not break a Jim Crow law, give the appearance of breaking a law, written or unwritten, or "cause" a white person to feel any discomfort for any unfathomable reason.

It wasn't until 1954 that the U.S. Supreme Court decision in *Brown v. Board of Education of Topeka, Kansas*, overturned separate-but-equal laws and declared segregation in public schools unconstitutional. By extension this ruling made segregation in other public facilities illegal. Subsequent decisions struck down similar kinds of Jim Crow legislation (Reid-Merritt, 2010).

During the Jim Crow era the idea that white American families might adopt black and biracial children would have been incomprehensible both socially and legally, especially in the South but in the North as well. After the end of World War II in 1945, some white American families intentionally set out to make their families interracial by adopting Asian children from Korea, Japan, and Vietnam and later through the Indian Adoption Project (Herman, 2012). As Ellen Herman (2012) notes, "Attitudes toward these transracial placements reproduced the historical color line in the United States. . . . White parents were more likely to accept 'yellow,' 'red,' or even 'brown' children. Those who took in 'black' children were considered the most transgressive."

The first interracial, or transracial, adoption on record involving an African American child placed in a white home occurred in Minnesota in 1948. Shortly thereafter campaigns to promote adoptions of African American children motivated other white couples to inquire about transracial adoption (Herman, 2012). Black adoptive families were in short supply because white social workers tended to regard them as "weak, ineffective, and culturally deficient" and therefore did not view "homes of color as the kinds of stable, healthy environments ideal for raising a child." But as the civil rights movement progressed, it helped to turn "national concern to the injustices suffered by black Americans. Child welfare professionals began to express concern with the disproportionate numbers of black children growing up in foster care" (Logan, 1996, 5, 7). A few agencies began cautiously placing mixed-race and African American children in white homes. Some of these families became targets of violence and harassment (Herman,

2012). Although only a few white couples adopted African American children at first, these adoptions began to define the debate on transracial adoption that continues today.

IN THIS SECTION three fascinating individuals discuss their lives during the latter part of the Jim Crow era. All three were born and raised in the South and have a tireless focus and determination that helped them to rise above the systematic racial, political, and socioeconomic disenfranchisement of black Americans. They fought to overcome racial segregation and discrimination in their own worlds in order to forge paths of economic, political, educational, and social opportunities for others. Their journeys were far from easy. But all three had parents and guardians who taught them to dig deep, carry themselves with a healthy sense of self-respect, and exemplify in their daily lives the values of hard work, education, perseverance, compassion for others, faith in God, and love of country. The skills and experiences they gained during their upbringing guided them into their adult years and influence their thoughts about transracial adoption and their hopes for children and families.

Evelyn Rhodes was born in 1920 in Memphis, Tennessee. She is a mother, grandmother, and great grandmother. Rhodes, a writer of poetry and short stories, is also a decades-long member of the Detroit Black Writers Guild. I sat down with Rhodes in her East Lansing living room for our discussion. I was interested in learning how she viewed herself while she was growing up, particularly since she was raised in a period when society devalued black families, especially black girls and women. I was especially curious about what values sustained her and her family through the civil rights era and into the present day. I wondered whether the racial cruelty of the era in which she grew up had made her bitter toward white people and whether it had adversely affected her intellectual, emotional, and spiritual growth.

W. Wilson Goode Sr. was born in 1938 in North Carolina. He was the son of a sharecropper, yet he rose to become the first black mayor of Philadelphia. In childhood he endured the dire economic realities resulting from the Jim Crow laws and witnessed the vulnerability of his own family. As a teenager his family migrated north to Philadelphia for better opportunities, but he soon discovered similar disenfranchisement in Philadelphia. Given these circumstances, I wanted to know how Goode found his inner strength and established a support network in such difficult circumstances. What gave him the audacity to believe that he could achieve academic success and lead a city? Goode's voice is crucial to the discussion of transracial adoption because he has also invested in the lives of transracial adoptees and interacted with white adoptive parents.

The final interviewee in this section, Cyril C. Pinder, was born in Fort Lauderdale, Florida, in 1946. His story vividly reveals what it was like to be black during a time when society could legally and overtly undervalue a person's talent, wit, social acceptance, and even character solely because of the color of his skin. I think Pinder's frank discussion of racism is important because one of the most traumatic experiences for many black transracial adoptees occurs when they leave their white adoptive homes, with all the attendant privileges, and confront the burden of race and discrimination in this country. Pinder's honest conversation will help adoptees understand why it is vital to know who you are. It is also important to note that Pinder has known a few transracial adoptees, most of whom led tormented lives because of their confused racial identity.

EVELYN RHODES
Great Grandmother and Matriarch
INTERVIEWED SEPTEMBER 29, 2012, EAST LANSING, MICHIGAN

Ms. Rhodes, I am thrilled to talk with you today. You were born on May 16, 1920, in Memphis, Tennessee. Tell me about your childhood, your family, and the values that were instilled in you at a very young age.

My brother and I were raised by our dear mother after my father passed. He was a World War I veteran. My grandparents also played a big part in raising us. We didn't have a kindergarten or day care. I learned how to read and write before I entered first grade. My grandparents said to me, "Here are five apples. You take four away. How many do you have left?" And that is how I learned how to add, divide, multiply, and subtract. And after my father died, we moved to Chicago. This was in 1929. We were children of the Depression. We didn't know that we were poor. We didn't consider ourselves poor. We lived in a big apartment building. We were the only two children there. My mother would give me two dimes and tell me to go to the store and take this dime and change it and get two nickels and take the other dime and get five cents' worth of potatoes and three cents' worth of sugar and bring home the remaining two cents. There were gangs in Chicago then, but, no, they didn't bother us. They would say as we passed by, "There goes skinny Evelyn and her brother." Still, I went to high school in Chicago. I graduated from Wendell Phillips Academy High School in 1938 and from Theodore Herzl Junior College in 1940. That college was later renamed to Malcolm X College. During World War II my brother entered the armed forces, and he went to [Great Britain and] landed on the beach [at] Normandy. My brother is ninety years old now and lives near me in Holt, Michigan.

But as I got older, in high school we lived in a tenement building, where we had just one room and everyone used the community kitchen. My mother worked on the railroad. Across the street I could see a big mansion. I would ask my mother, "Can I go out and play?" She said yes. The young lady across the street said to me, "Why don't you ask your mother if you can come over here?" This young lady's parents were beautiful people. Her father was the first black attorney to have an office building in downtown Chicago. And in 1923 there was a race riot in Chicago so he helped some of those who had been persecuted. Her mother was head of the National Association of Negro Women. From this family I learned about all of the wonderful things I read in books. I would go to the prestigious Goodman Theatre and to concerts. My dear mother was working, and she knew that I was in good hands with this family. So as the years passed, my girlfriend, she went to Northwestern University, and I went to the junior college. My girlfriend [oversaw black music programs in Chicago public schools]. Later on she was nationally known for her accomplishments. Although she has passed, we had a great time together. When I think back on my childhood in Chicago, my mother did wonderful things for my brother and me and made sure that we were open to cultural activities. My mother was happy that her children had a good childhood.

What was it like growing up as a black young girl and then young woman in Memphis and Chicago? Did you know that you were a beautiful and smart person? Or did race issues in society or within your own family obscure that?

In my family I did know that I was beautiful and smart. Although my mother and her sisters, my aunts, and uncles, they were all light complected, and my grandmother was part Irish, we didn't run into racial issues within my family.

Chicago had race riots again in 1968. What were your thoughts about it then, when you were older, especially given the fact that you did not experience racial tension within the boundaries of your own family? Or had you left Chicago by then?

As I got older we moved from Chicago to Detroit. Now in 1967 there was a racial riot in Detroit. I was a postal employee by then. I remember there were people complaining about the noise. The police came. People were killed. Houses were burned. But I never did have any racial upheaval with me as a person. And I am glad to say that!

I want to go back to the time of the Harlem Renaissance (1920–30). What was that period of time like for you?

When my friend was at Northwestern University, the late Langston Hughes was a guest speaker there [and] I attended. I was thrilled by being at his talk and meeting him. Langston Hughes autographed a book for me. And I gave the book to my niece. I am sorry that I gave it to her because it was signed by him. [*Laugh*] I have a lot of books on the Harlem Renaissance, and I love all of the writers during that time.

What is the importance to you of the Voting Rights Act of 1965 [which banned discriminatory voting practices designed to discourage black Americans from voting]?

The Voting Rights Act of 1965 means a lot to me. My grandfather, in the late 1930s and 1940s, who was living at that time in Tennessee, would regularly go to the city hall, and he even wrote to President Franklin Roosevelt about the poll taxes and how they were used to suppress black people from being able to register to vote or even voting if they didn't pay [the taxes]. My grandfather even went to the city-county building and demanded a streetlight and a post office box in his neighborhood. He would say to me, "If you want to learn about the laws impacting people and learn about the rights of the people, then go to the city hall during court days, and you can sit in the back, and you can learn so much about how the government is run and how the attorneys make their legal arguments on each case."

Then in the 1960s I did have friends that took part in the Southern Christian Leadership Conference [SCLC] which was first led by the Reverend Dr. Martin Luther King Jr. in the late 1950s. During the 1960s the SCLC worked very hard with other community groups in the South to fight for civil rights of all people, particularly for black people and for their voting rights. It has not been that many years since we as black people were able to vote. So, yes, the Voting Rights Act of 1965 means a lot to me.

In 1955 you were living in Detroit. That was the same year Rosa Parks boarded a bus in Montgomery, Alabama, and refused to give up her seat, for which she was later arrested. What did that mean to you?

[In the mid-1970s] my two grandchildren and I were waiting for the official opening of the People Mover in Detroit. The People Mover is an elevated transit system that operates in downtown Detroit. And Mrs. Rosa Parks was going to be one of the people that dedicated the building where the People Mover was stationed at. This lady walked over to us, and I said, "Mrs. Rosa Parks!" She replied, "Yes." I said, "You are going to be on the program." She explained to me that indeed she was going to be on the program, but the lady who was going to accompany her had not gotten there yet. So I met Mrs. Rosa Parks. And the lady came up to Mrs. Parks and said that she had been looking for her. . . . Then at a later date my grandson at school took part in a little program where they showed Mrs. Rosa Parks on a bus. And I think the actual bus she rode in is installed somewhere.

Yes. The Rosa Parks bus is at the Henry Ford Museum in Dearborn, Michigan.

And Mrs. Rosa Parks lived in an apartment building near where I lived in downtown Detroit. So I did meet her, and I have books about

Mrs. Parks. Mrs. Parks was a quiet lady but you don't have to be loud. You can be quiet and still a fighter.

What does *fighting* mean to you?

Fighting means just to stick to it or sticking to your guns. You don't have to be a rabble-rouser; you can just stick with it. That is the main thing.

Tell me about your work as a postal worker in Detroit.

I started in 1950 as a postal clerk and retired in 1982. I worked thirty-two years. The first day I worked, there was mail on the floor. I was not used to seeing mail on the floor. So I picked up the mail off the floor, and the foreman said to me in a firm voice, "Lady, what are you doing?" I said to him that the letters were getting dirty. He told me, "Get back to your case!" Back then we didn't have plastic trays. We had wooden trays. And in this one wooden tray were business-class letters. One of those letters was open with hundreds of dollar bills in it. After seeing this, I immediately raised my hand for a supervisor because I knew that it was a plant to see if I would take it. But during those thirty-two years I issued both mail permits for nonprofit organizations and I was acting District Women's Program coordinator. I worked for the postal newsletter called *Eve's Rib*. I worked in the Equal Employment Opportunity department of the post office. We hired the nonhearing. Even back then we didn't call them "deaf mutes" because they did excellent work on the computers. I had a wonderful career there. In fact I just returned from Detroit for the thirty-fifth annual women's luncheon. I was the oldest one there.

Along with your professional work, you were also a mother.

Yes. My son and I had a great time together. He is now deceased. My son's father and I did not stay together for long because of his life-style. He was a musician and played with all of the big bands, Jimmy Lunceford [a jazz saxophonist] and Cab Calloway.

. . . [My son's father] had a lot of women followers and I was not used to that. But he took care of my son and me for a while. I did not ask for childcare money because I always worked. And I took care of my son. My son had a great high school education. He didn't go to college. But he had many friends of all races and different backgrounds.

It was after high school that he became a truck driver in Michigan. He drove those big highway trucks.

Did your son have a talent for music?

Since his father was quite talented musically, my son started piano lessons at the Detroit Conservatory of Music. I bought a spinning piano. He played well. Then, when rock 'n' roll came, that was the end of that! But my son collected a lot of records. He went to a lot of concerts, including classical music concerts. After he got married, his children were raised on Mozart's musical work.

As a parent, what were the values that you instilled in your son? How did you parent?

My mother was working. I was working. And then there was a point when my mother had to go to Tennessee to pick up her mother, my grandmother, because her father had passed and her mother was by herself. So I made the decision to send my son off to a Catholic boarding school in Wisconsin. Unfortunately while he was at the boarding school, he broke his arm. I told him to come home, but the nuns there said no, so I listened to them. I knew that he did not like being there at the boarding school. Later on I was sorry that I sent him there, but it gave him a good background on how to be a good young man, which he was. From that he learned how to treat other people from all nationalities and races with respect, which he did. And certainly he was a music lover.

Your son was married and started a family. Can you share a bit about his family?

My son's wife, Peggy, is Caucasian. When he married my daughter-in-law she had a little girl named Cecilia. Now Cecilia is thirty-nine years old. My son had two children with Peggy: Eve, who is now thirty-seven, and Mark, who is thirty-six.

How did you feel about your son marrying a Caucasian woman?

I didn't have any hard feelings about my son marrying a Caucasian woman because my grandmother was a mulatto, as they called it back then; her father was white, and her mother was black. My mother was fair skinned and my father had dark skin. Many years ago this was something we did not have control over; white men had black women who were enslaved. That has changed. People can choose who they want to interact with. It is a different world today, even compared to when my son married his wife, Peggy. There are more mixed-race or multiracial people now. The world is getting smaller. People are going to mix forever.

Were you concerned for them as an interracial couple and how the community would accept them?

No. They were married in the early 1970s. At that time my son and Peggy were living in Detroit. I was also living in Detroit. There were white people and black people living in my building, as well as people from other racial and ethnic backgrounds. There were mayors and city employees who also lived there, people from many different walks of life. I don't think that Peggy or my son had problems with the community accepting them. I know that Peggy had white friends and black friends even before she met my son. Over the years both of our families have spent time together, so I don't think that her family has had bad feelings about the different races either. Love is important to us.

What values did you instill in your grandchildren?

I expected that they be strong and honest. I expected that they do good, always work hard, and do not hold any bad feelings against anybody. Those are the same values that my mother taught my brother and me.

What is it that you hope that your great grandsons and grandkids especially take from you and your commitment to each of them?

The main thing that I hope they take from me is the message of *love* and *understanding* no matter what the person's race or nationality. In the long run those traits don't matter because, if you are raised with a basic Christian attitude, it helps you to understand and communicate with people better. I have friends who are Polish, Chinese, African, Caucasian, and American. We all are going to leave here one day, so you might as well enjoy each day and treat each other good.

How did you develop friendships across racial and socioeconomic lines?

I lived in different communities and worked in Detroit as a postal employee, a real estate sales person, and a sales lady at Dayton Hudson's in Dearborn, Michigan, and Jacobson's clothing store in Grosse Pointe. Therefore I met people of all races and nationalities—and all incomes. I know wealthy people. I had lunch years ago with G. Mennen Williams [a six-term governor of Michigan] and his wife. I've danced at the prestigious Ford Auditorium in Detroit. I knew Mr. J. L. Hudson Jr. [president of the J. L. Hudson Company, which owned Hudson's department store] and other well-to-do people. You find out later that these people, no matter what their income or nationality, the basic thing they are interested in is, When do we eat? Where do we go now? It is that simple. Jesus said, "Love one another." That is the main rule I choose to live by.

What inspired you to compose words and develop your writing interests?

I think that my interest in writing started already way back in high school at the Wendell Phillips Academy. I always loved to read and write, and I had wonderful teachers, including my English teacher, that encouraged me to pursue my reading and writing skills. I could write a story in about one day. Back then I would write stories mostly around the people that I would see. Then in my later years, living in Detroit, I became a part of the Black Writers' Guild up to my recent years. It is a wonderful organization. I have some short stories and poems published. We would give readings and interviews at bookstores and other organizations.

You mentioned that you wrote a poem to the president of the United States. What does it mean to you to be alive to witness the first African American president?

First, President Obama is biracial, and there are a lot of biracial people in my own family. I think he is wonderful. I think the majority of the people in this country like him, but also there are those that don't like him because they say he is black. I think that because he is biracial, part white and black, his racial background should allow more people to personally identify with him.

As you know, I was adopted into a Caucasian family. With that came a lot of blessings but also struggles, especially trying to figure out who I was as a person with an African American heritage. There are other transracial adoptees who also struggle with the identity piece, given their situations. What words can you share with Caucasian parents who are raising multiracial children in this society?

I think the same basic principles that are important in my family are the same principles that I would share to other parents if I was asked. It is about learning to love and understand those that are like you and those that are different than you. I shop down the street at Meijers [a supermarket]. And almost every day when I go in Meijers, I see a Caucasian person with children, including two or three brown-skinned children. It appears that some of them are the biological children of the parent, and some have been adopted by this parent. I don't ask many questions but I always say hello. And the children say hello, and the parent says hello back to me. I think that it is wonderful when I see multiracial families. So, yes, I think that the main principles to teach children, especially in this society, are love and understanding.

Years ago when I was working at the Postal Service, this lady and her husband had a little girl in the store with them, and a woman approached the family and said to them, "Oh, what a pretty little girl. I wish I had a little girl like your daughter." And the little girl said to her in a happy voice, "You can. I am adopted." And I hope this beautiful girl is still living. I know she would be grown by now. Also, when I was living in Detroit I remember that our mail carrier and his wife adopted a little girl that had been fathered by a white gentleman and a black lady. I was told that the biological parents did not want this child, and so they decided to place her for adoption. That's when the postman and his wife adopted this little girl. This family did not tell the little girl that she was adopted. Sadly this little girl heard that she was adopted from her classmates after hearing it from their mothers. And some of these classmates teased this little girl and were awfully mean to her, saying that her parents were not her real parents because she was adopted. This girl had a very difficult time because of this and cried a lot. This then compelled her parents to finally tell her that she was adopted. . . . I am sure you know, Rhonda, and your readers, that it is very important that parents who are adopting children speak truthfully and tell them that they are adopted in a loving way.

We have established that love is so important in all families, racially and ethnically blended or not, and for those who choose to adopt to speak truthfully about the adoption with their child and, I would, add family members in an empowering and inclusive way.

So taking it a step further, for Caucasian parents who are adopting, for instance, a black child—how do they in your opinion reach out to the African American community, especially when these transracially adoptive families live in communities that are racially homogeneous Caucasian?

I think it is *very* important that these adoptive families reach out to the black community. Their black children and the rest of the family should know about black history, the black family, and ordinary black persons that they have access to, whether this person lives down the street or interacts within these families' social circles. It's important to know about the issues facing the black community and read the newspaper or stories on the Internet about black governors, politicians, community people, and et cetera. So, yes, I think that it is beneficial for black children adopted into white homes to know about their racial and ethnic background. They deserve to know where they came from and that story. Equally important is also for these families to know about white families and their diversity. It's just wonderful to know about your background, and I don't only study about the African American history and story; I study about many diverse groups and areas of interests. I study about Mozart, many of the politicians, the geniuses, et cetera. When you get to the basics you may discover that we are all humans and should be valued.

W. WILSON GOODE SR.
First Black Mayor of Philadelphia (1984–92)
INTERVIEWED BY TELEPHONE, FEBRUARY 25, 2012

What do being the first black mayor of Philadelphia and seeing in your lifetime the first black president of the United States mean to you?

There are two significant events in my life that I thought I would never see. The first is my election as Philadelphia's first African American mayor in 1983. To be elected mayor of the city where America started added significance beyond significance to this event. As a descendant of a grandfather who was born into slavery, and as a youngster who grew up as a sharecropper, rising to the top of city government in Philadelphia is beyond belief. I thought at that time about all the people who had sacrificed for me to be there. This was a tribute to them as much as it was a victory for me.

The second was twenty-five years later, in 2008, when Barack Obama was elected president. I recall being on my couch with tears streaming down my face and not able to speak for an hour. His election was a victory for every slave, every sharecropper, everyone who lost their lives in pursuit of freedom. The Obama election gave me renewed hope in this nation, which has meant so much to so many for so long, that at long last there could be a level playing field for all. For me these two events when joined together made me walk a little taller, hold my head a little higher, and be proud to be an American. In a sense some of the stain of slavery had been erased. [That] anyone born in America could be elected to the highest offices in this country was an incredible achievement. Even today tears flow when I think about those two miraculous accomplishments.

Dr. Goode, it is an honor to be able to talk with you about your work and about transracial adoption. What are you currently working on?

I am a senior fellow at Public/Private Ventures [a national nonprofit that researches the effectiveness of policies, programs, and community initiatives, especially as they affect vulnerable communities], where I work on administrative and policy issues for the entire organization. I spend the majority of my time running a program called Amachi, which finds mentors for children of incarcerated parents as well as children impacted by incarceration and now more recently for children who have parents in the military who are deployed.

Why are you so deeply committed to the work you do for Amachi, specifically for children of incarcerated parents?

Throughout my life I have had an interest in working with young people, particularly with children who are at risk. And over the years I have determined that the children in our society who are the *most* at risk are those who have a parent in prison and those who in some way are impacted by incarceration. For those who have a parent in prison have all of the poverty issues that all other children at risk have; but in addition to those issues, these children also have a parent who is incarcerated, which I believe makes them the most at-risk children in our society. And those who live in communities . . . where there is a high percentage of incarceration likewise are impacted by incarceration in almost to the same degree as a child of an incarcerated parent. We have to continue to work with these children to try to provide them with good role models so that they don't repeat the crimes committed by their parents.

Has Amachi shown measurable results?

Amachi is approaching its twelfth anniversary. Over the last ten years Amachi, through various programs across the country that it has been directly involved in, has served over 300,000 children. What we know from the research that we have conducted: two-thirds of those children will improve their grades; two-thirds of those children will improve their attendance at school; and two-thirds of those children will improve their behavior in school; and 90 percent of those young people and children will have a better relationship with their peers, with their siblings, and with the adults in their lives. Therefore we have concluded that, based upon a loving, caring adult relationship with a child one hour once a week—two hours twice a month for at least one year—and one year is critical—children will improve in the areas that I have indicated.

What is your hope or ultimate goal for the children who are impacted by the Amachi program?

The ultimate goal is to have them not follow their parents into prison. Based on research that has been done, we know that seven out of ten children with a parent in prison could end up in prison themselves. So the critical issue is, How do we avoid children with a parent in prison from ending up in prison? We believe, again, that involving a loving, caring adult in the life of a child for one hour once a week—two hours twice a month—can *improve* the child's grades, can *improve* the child's school attendance, can *improve* the child's behavior in school, and can *improve* the child's relationships with adults, siblings, and peers. We believe that children who have a role model like a Big

Brother or Big Sister, who can walk with them, who can guide them, who can direct them, and who can model for them positive attitudes and actions, that these children can end up going on to finishing high school and going on to attend colleges and universities and ultimately avoiding going to prison.

As you know, I was in the foster care system for two years and then was placed with an adoptive family. I certainly understand from my own experiences the importance of having love and stability from which to build. My question is, Have you come across children who are in the foster care system, and what are some of your concerns that you have for this segment of the population?

There are children in foster care who have parents that are incarcerated. Which means that it could be that for these children both parents are incarcerated; and it could be that those children in the foster care system have the same poverty issues that other children at risk have, and have the same issues that children of incarcerated parents have, but in addition to that they are also in foster care, and some of them even in residential homes, which is part of the foster care system. So what we know is that children with a parent in prison and in an impoverished condition are probably, of all the children, the most at risk. We found generally throughout that 10 to 15 percent of all the children we were working with were in the foster care system, whereas a high percentage of the children with a parent in prison lived with another parent or a grandparent or another relative.

Who guided you in your life that helped to nurture in you such a spirit of service?

I think that, as near as I can figure this out, it happened to me when I was about eleven years old, maybe twelve. I was living on a farm. One day near nightfall a hobo—

Hobo?

Yes, we called homeless persons *hobos* in the South. . . . A hobo came through our sharecropper's farm in North Carolina. This was a man who was a different race than ours. He was white, and we were black, living on a sharecropping farm. And he came up and knocked on the door. When my mother answered the door, he said to her, "I'm hungry." My mother invited him in without hesitation. She was fixing dinner for us, and she really took most of our dinner and fed this man all that he could eat. He kept asking for more. And when the man left, I remember being so struck by my mother's example that I ran into my room and looked under my mattress, where I kept a few coins. I don't recall how much it was, but I remember running down the path to the road, chasing after this man [and] yelling, "Mr. Hobo! Mr. Hobo!" I took every cent I had, which probably took a year for me to accumulate, and gave it to him and put it in his hand, feeling like I had done something tremendous by doing that. I felt good all over because I was able to share everything that I had with someone who had nothing. I knew that what I had would be replenished but what I gave him probably for a long time would not be replenished. And so ever since that time, I have had a desire to reach out and help others.

The specific issue of working with young people came because my father went to prison when I was fourteen years of age. He stayed in prison, and so our family relocated from the South to Philadelphia. While my father was in prison, the local church—the pastor and his wife—in essence became my mentors and guided me and directed me. Even though my high school counselor was saying to me that I was not college material, my pastor and his wife told me that I could be whatever I wanted to be! And after a year of [my] working in the back of a factory, they took up money in the church and sent me to college after I graduated from high school. So I had someone in my life at an early age who took an interest in me. In a neighborhood where no one had ever gone to college, the pastor and his wife saw to it that I went to college and sent me off to Morgan State University [a historically black college] in Baltimore, Maryland. I earned a bachelor of arts degree at Morgan State in history and political science; a master's degree in governmental administration at the Wharton School at the University of Pennsylvania; and a doctorate of ministry degree at the Palmer Theological Seminary, which is a part of Eastern University in Pennsylvania.

I know a young man who was adopted by a white couple as an infant. When this couple adopted their son, they immediately reached out to me because they knew me. When their son got to be five or six years of age, his parents said to me that they didn't know where they could take their son to get a haircut. So I walked through with them on how to get their son a haircut as well as talked about other things they could do to begin to give him a black experience. While I think living in this multicultural world is a good experience, there is something about his culture and his background that is essential. Even to this day—this is at least twenty years later—I still communicate with him.

This young man and I make time to have lunch together. It is an opportunity for us to talk and share. Although he is very much respectful of the culture that he grew up in, he also respects the black culture and the fact that he is an African American male living in a multicultural society. There is a desire, or thirst almost, on his part to reach across the racial and cultural boundaries into the African American community to learn as much as he can about that experience.

What is it that should make the black experience valuable and relevant to transracially adoptive families?

Although transracial adoptive children grow up in mostly white homes, their skin color will always define who they are and how they will be treated. We still live in a society where race or the color of one's skin is a factor in almost everything that happens in our society. It is important that a young person—in this case a young black person—who grows up outside of the African American culture and community recognizes that there is a perception on the part of others in the larger society about one's skin color. Therefore it is important from the point of view of black adoptees to understand the culture that society believes they are a part of so that they can better appreciate how people are responding to them. Another big piece is the importance of understanding the history of African Americans in this country from slavery to what we are beginning to define as the postracial era.

I think this postracial era that folks talk about is a dream yet unrealized. Also, for transracial adoptive families, their children continue to be judged, treated badly in cases, simply because of the color of their skin. Adoptees of color have also felt the harsh realities of being minimized and seen as invisible because in an unjust way their value does not measure up to their white counterparts'. Do you think that we have progressed into a postracial era? Have we moved forward as a people since the civil rights movement?

We are not there now. We are certainly closer and further along than we were thirty years ago, but we have yet a ways to go. The larger society is not comfortable with blacks in certain roles; although it is increasingly becoming better, it is not yet anywhere near where it needs to be to say that we are living in a postracial era. We are, I guess, what I would define as living "in between times"—between outright segregation and outright racism and this postracial era. In this in-between time some people are beginning to move over, and some people's views have changed significantly, but there still is a percentage of Americans out there who really don't believe that blacks and whites are equal, that blacks and whites should have the same opportunities. That is part of our challenge in this society today.

Even with having an African American president overseeing the national and international affairs of this country?

I think that having an African American president has pointed out the fact that we are not in a postracial era. Yes, there were a number of factors that made it possible for Barack Obama to become the first African American president—

What were those factors?

I think that it was a combination of how bad George Bush was, a combination of the candidate he was running against, but for the most part it had to do with the fact that Barack Obama is just an extraordinary man who was at the right place at the right time. The strategic use of technology by his campaign, and the fact that there were people looking forward to finding someone that they could follow, all factored into why Barack Obama was elected. I do think, by the way, that many of the young people who voted for Barack Obama were in fact, and are in fact, living in a "postracial mind-set" in terms of how they operate. But keep in mind that people are living longer. There is an older compilation of people whose grandparents owned slaves that are living today. There are those black people who remember segregation and are not yet all that comfortable with the idea of integration because they have not grown up with that *versus* a generation today who has grown up with white children going to the same swimming pool with black and brown children and going to the same classroom. I think it is a whole different situation for those blacks, generally speaking, over forty years of age, compared to blacks who are under the age of forty.

So would you say, then, that it is worthwhile for black and biracial adoptees of today to focus on the African American experience and culture, even though arguably a sizable percentage of their generation is now straddling the postracial line?

I think it is essential today! You cannot appreciate who others are if you cannot appreciate who you are. You cannot have a sense of what this country is all about unless you can appreciate your heritage and your ethnic background. So I do think that it is very, very critical that African Americans who have been adopted into transracial situations have a sense of their background and history, how their ancestors came to this country, and make a connection there too. I think that it makes them more valuable in participating in what is to be a postracial era.

For transracial adoptees like myself, to connect with our ethnic communities can be challenging and intimidating, depending on where we grew up. How can we as young adult adoptees navigate within the black community more effectively?

I strongly recommend that every transracial adoptee get a DNA test through the African heritage groups. There are a lot of them around that can basically connect that person to their ancestry background. That step is terribly important in my view to begin to talk about where does your ancestry come from and begin to read up on that.

That is brilliant. I still need to do that. So we will need to talk about that in more detail soon.

Also I would urge transracial adoptees who are religious to join an African American church or attend an African American church as early as possible. Even if they don't join one, or even if they may be adopted by a Jewish family, for example, still it is important to go and visit an African American church and get a feel for what is happening there and begin to develop some relationships within that congregation. I would urge them also to begin to look at black fraternities and sororities as they go off to college and consider joining one of them, as well as begin to look at some of the social clubs available at the college or university. Other basic steps that transracial adoptees can take are to become intentional in becoming friends with black folk. A good way to take that a step further is to spend time in the home of a black family—visit them overnight or for a weekend. I think those things will begin to get them activated in learning what it means to be black in America and what it means to be black in an urban setting.

CYRIL C. PINDER
Mentor and Former National Football League Player
INTERVIEWED BY TELEPHONE, JANUARY 14, 2012

Football connoisseurs will know that you were drafted by the NFL in 1968 and played for the Philadelphia Eagles, Chicago Bears, and Dallas Cowboys during your career. However, let's bring the playbook back to Hollywood, Florida, where you grew up.

My mom and dad were both from the Bahamas. They did not believe in football. They didn't want me to get hurt. My mom was concerned about that. In fact I only played two years of high school football. I was playing basketball, baseball, running track. At school it seemed like every day some instructor would get on the intercom system—this is when we had prayer in school—and he would say (after prayer), "Cyril Pinder, would you please join the football team?" They even got my little girlfriend to come in to ask me to play football. She said that she didn't want to date me anymore because I was afraid to get hurt playing football. I said that I wasn't afraid to get hurt. To prove that she was wrong, I went in and got some equipment, and the coach put me in as receiver. So I went and played wide receiver and caught eighty balls and ran twenty end-arounds for touchdowns.

The whole state of Florida went berserk. Who is this guy? Where did he come from? At that time, when I was playing football in high school, you took your equipment home with you. And that was what I was doing. On one day I saw my mom and dad as I was walking home from school. They were at the corner waiting for me to come home. And my dad said to me, "Oh, you're playing football now? What is that you got there?" I said, "That's my football helmet and shoulder pads."

He said in his Bahamian accent, "Ooh, you're a *big* man now." I said, "No, I just want to play football."

And also my counselor at high school said that because I was rated number 2 in my class, I was going to be eligible to go to college. He wanted to know if my mom and dad could send me. I asked my dad if he could send me to college. He said, "College?" My dad was a carpenter and wanted me to work right alongside of him. I said, "I don't think so."

So did you end up continuing to play football in high school?

Yes. I went on to play football but I intended not to. I went back to give the coach my equipment. The coach said, "Pinder, we are getting ready to give you the ball!" I told him that I did not want the ball; I didn't want to play anymore. He told me that I needed to play and that I was one of the best football athletes in the state of Florida. So I went on and played. I scored thirty-something touchdowns with thirty-five hundred yards rushing—as opposed to Tucker Frederickson, the number 1 running back, with twelve hundred yards. But he was the white guy coming out from South Broward High School at the same time I was coming out of Crispus Attucks High School in Hollywood, Florida. *And to this day*, even though my record was better, my record is called "the colored record."

That says a lot, unfortunately, about how far we have *not* come in race relations in this society.

I haven't forgotten that. But I realize as I have gotten older that those people are who they are, and that is why they are where they are. I am who I am.

So I went to the University of Illinois because I was not allowed to attend the University of Miami; they wouldn't open the doors to me at Florida State or University of Florida, or Alabama.

Why?

Because I was black. I didn't understand that initially. I didn't understand when these institutions told me that I was not good enough, but yet I had SAT scores that were astronomical. In addition, [in] the one video they showed of me playing football I scored six touchdowns in the first quarter. I didn't understand why I was being undervalued.

What was it like for you, as a young man living in Hollywood, Florida, migrating to the North in the mid-1960s to the University of Illinois for your college education?

My parents are from the Bahamas, and that is where the black folks run the show: in the Bahamas. It was different, though, where we lived in Florida. To give you an example, I never knew why mother wanted me to come home at 6 P.M. (before it got too dark) when I went to practices. It turns out that there were white folk driving around in pickup trucks around where we lived [and] killing black boys. This was in 1962 and 1963. Parts of Florida were tough! When I was growing up, black folks were not able to live in parts of Florida where there were white folks. If you were black and went on the premises near North Miami Beach, you had to have a card to say why you were there: You were there to pick up mangos or were taking away them big ole nice red snappers that were flopping on white folks' lawn et cetera. That's what you did.

Today my wife, Barbara, and I own a condo in Florida on North Miami Beach. I brought Barbara back to the Fontainebleau in Miami, which is an upscale resort, and the Diplomat Hotel. Back in the day . . . we had a place called the Sir John Hotel in Miami. It was the only place where black entertainment could go and stay. White folk would not let us stay at the Fontainebleau; they would not let us stay at the Diplomat. See, I remember all of this stuff.

When I moved from Florida to Illinois, I had a complete paradigm shift. I had never seen white folks in my world before. I had never seen snow before. When I was at Illinois, they took me into this little room in Memorial Stadium. They said, "Cyril Pinder, you have the potential to be the best running back." I didn't know who the hell Red Grange or Buddy Young [Illinois players who went on to the NFL] were because I was from Hollywood, Florida. I just never knew.

I was told there in that room the one thing they did not like was for the colored athletes [to be] interchanging with "white trash." That is what they called the white girls. And don't you know, the first girl I dated was Susan L.? She was a Jewish girl who had no qualms about us dating. We had a platonic relationship. Her dad came from Winnetka, Illinois. Anyway, he took us out to dinner one night and told her, "Cyril is doing very well, and you are going to have to stop seeing him because you will screw up his career." The next thing I know, her father transferred her to Northwestern University, and I never saw her again.

The next thing I knew, I was getting drafted by the Philadelphia Eagles. Initially I was not ready to play pro football, but Barbara, who I was dating at the time and who is my wife of forty-two years, was very smart. She said, Look, why don't you play pro football for a year and after that see if you want to be married to me? I went and I played pro and burned the candle at both ends. Sure enough, I wanted to get married. Barbara said that she wanted to still have me as a husband so we got married in 1971. The rest is history.

What did you do after your pro football career?

I was an investment banker on LaSalle Street in Chicago for the first ten years of my career after pro football and then went on to work for the media networks. I was doing very well. When I could, I was also helping Ed McCaskey [former owner of the Chicago Bears]. McCaskey called me his chocolate son. I remember at that time I was having a conflict with trying to do my job at WLS-TV, Chicago, and helping "Big Ed" out with the Bears. So he told me that when I retired, he wanted me to talk with the Bears. I promised him that. Surely enough, years later McCaskey's sons were running the team. Nobody knew that Big Ed was going to die when he did, but he died. As promised, I did connect with the Bears. But the Bears were so tight with the dollar, we never got a chance to talk about [collaborating] on anything. I think to this day, the Bears thought that maybe I was going to take somebody's job and I wasn't. I was just trying to help develop the franchise. In one of our conversations they told me that their season ticket holders were at 95 percent. I agreed with them but told them that the ticket holders were the *same* people; and now there is a broader network of people that can be tapped into, i.e., the blacks, the Hispanics, and the Asians; we can afford these tickets now. Unfortunately I don't think they really understood what I was saying. My talks didn't go over well with them.

Speaking about one's perception, how were you able to navigate in the business world, working primarily with white folks, when you clearly lived in a different world?

I strive to be professional. I hear what some people say about me, which is, "Cyril is so different than everybody else we know." I know what they are saying.

What are they saying?

They are saying that Cyril is different than the average black guy.

Why in your opinion do they say they that?

They say that because I know how to talk with white people and interact with them. I know how to dress for success. I know how to deal in a white man's world.

How did you learn this skill?

I learned it from going to the University of Illinois, from being around white people, just like you did.

I was living in Chicago during the spring of 1991, and I was able to secure an internship at WLS-TV, where you happened to be working at the time.

It was after I talked with you that I realized that you were a product of an interracial adoption.

What was it that you wanted me to get about who I was, particularly being raised in a white family?

I always wanted you to remember that while you sounded white, you were definitely a black girl. I wanted to drive that home. I wanted you to feel that. I wanted you to know that. I didn't think that you really realized [that,] as you would get older, a lot of this black disposition, a lot of this black attitude, was going to come out of you. And then those around you, particularly your family, friends, and coworkers, were going to know that you were not a little white Valley Girl. And you, more than anybody, was going to realize that. Hence, we have had a relationship for years and years. I have put in thirty years at ABC and since have retired. So here we are.

What is your definition of what it means to be black?

Being black to me—I'm sure a lot of people did not feel the way I felt about it, but growing up in Hollywood, Florida, I heard that southern drawl, and it would make the hair on my neck crawl. I just couldn't forget it. Here is a story for you. I was inducted into the Florida Athletic Hall of Fame. Somebody called my office at WLS-TV, and he could not pronounce my name. He called me *S-e-e-l*. That's when I was brought back into the day. He said to me in a southern drawl, "You know, we don't let colored folks into this hall of fame, but you are such an exception. You ran like you had feathers up your ass." Right then, I told him, here is the deal: you can send me what you want, but I'm not coming down there for this. Then Barbara insisted that I go.

I'm glad you went, despite how derogatory and rude this man sounded.

I knew it was a serious event because I saw my dad at the ceremony in a suit. But being black down there in Florida, being black at the University of Illinois, was very traumatic. And then, when I was a pro football player, particularly with the Chicago Bears, being black was traumatic at times too. The team back then in the early 1970s was completely separated, completely divided. It was the whites over here, the blacks over there. I remember saying to myself, "No wonder the team can't win any games." I have never forgotten that image. The coach told me one time . . . and I just realized what he meant. He said, "I like my boys coming from historically black colleges." I asked him what he meant by that. He said, "I like them from Grambling, Jackson State, and Morehouse." I noticed that the brothers from those schools were not making eye contact, just like those guys I remember growing up in Florida; they never made eye contact with the white folks because they were intimidated. The coach said to me, "You know what? You are so unusual. We have black guys looking for advancement on their salaries. You have never asked for a salary increase." I told him that it was because I didn't plan on playing professional football forever and that I was a college graduate, not someone who went to college just to stay eligible but truly a college *graduate*. From that day on he never really liked me. Of the ten years I played pro football, the two years I spent playing for the Dallas Cowboys were the best. Coach Tom Landry understood me. The team took a liking to me too. Now, Tom Landry couldn't pronounce my name either. [*Laugh*] He was a southern boy too. He had to say *S-u-a-r-i-l*. That's when I wished I had another name, like Joe or Willie or Jim.

How do you move in dark skin and thrive?

All you can do is be as smart as you are. Go get your college degree. Pursue your career, like you did. You just need to know that at some point some are going to like you and some are not going to like you, simply because of the color of your skin. It's tough. In my opinion there is a difference between blacks and whites. My goddaughter Stevie, who is at University of Illinois, said to me that "the athletes won't look at anybody who has a dark complexion like me." She is brilliant, but there are some people who won't take the time to get to know her. I spend my time telling her, "Get your degree. Do your job and do what you are supposed to do." And I hope and pray to God that Stevie doesn't feel like she needs to have a white guy to justify who she is; because if she does that, then she is in for a rude awakening.

Wow. It can be such a lonely journey at times, navigating in black skin. You, though, seem to get along with people regardless of their skin color.

It appears that way to you. But basically I spend a lot of time by myself. I spend a lot of time at home reading and doing the things that I want to do. A friend of mine, who I went to school with, is a big CEO of a major company. He told me, "You know, Cyril, I wished I had played pro football." He played on a team with me at Illinois. I said to him, "I tell you what. You give me your million-dollar salary; you can take my knees, my ankles, my toes, my shoulders—and the money, the $75,000 I made a year at my highest peak during my pro football career." He looked at me and said that he never thought of it that way.

So your point is that—

My point is, the pro career only consists of a minute length of time of your life, only a minute period. Me, personally, I would take the entire life cycle compared to that of being a good athlete to instead being a good student and doing what you're supposed to do to get along in society. The added burden as a black person is that you are never, ever going to go through society doing well without worrying about the reality that some place, somewhere, and—excuse my language—somebody's going to call you, as a person of color, a nigger. All I want you to do, Rhonda, is not show any surprise when somebody calls you that, because it is going to happen.

Oh, that has already happened, more than a handful of times. At that point in the early 1990s, when I was working as an intern at WLS-TV, where I met you, I was struggling with my hair. And I was

struggling with how I assimilate into the black community, at the TV station and outside of the TV station.

The biggest problem that you had through my eyes was that you were going to get it at both sides of the knife: The black community was not going to accept you because you sounded so white, and the white community was not going to completely accept you because you were too black. So you had a double whammy going. You didn't deserve that.

I want to go back to your career in TV sales. How did you get into the industry?

I got into the TV field through Ed McCaskey, who knew Joe Ahern, who was the general manager-president of WLS. I remember I told Ed that I liked what I was doing as an investment banker and that I was doing very well, making money. Ed told me that it was not up for a debate and that he wanted me over there at WLS. When I got there, I told Joe Ahern that I wasn't going to waste his time or my time: simply let the record show that I came over to the station to meet with him.

Then Joe Ahern spoke with Ed and told him that I would not give him the time of day. Long story short, Ed sent me back to WLS for the interview with Joe. I told him then that I did not know anything about media. Joe told me that I was a peddler and I could sell. I had no idea what a rating book was, but I took the job selling commercial airtime anyway and ended up doing it for a very long time. Then, when I moved to the ABC network, I was selling airtime nationally. So, for example, when I sold airtime to a company, you saw it in Alabama, you saw it in Florida, you saw it all over the country, wherever there was an ABC station.

I remember you went over to NBC too.

Yes. I went to NBC because the guy that was the boss over there told me that he was sick and tired of competing against me and losing deals. He told me, "We would love to have you come over here." I indicated to him first of all I was not going to come over there if he wanted me to replace another black guy, because that is not who I am. He assured me that it was not what they were going to do. Second, I told him that it was going to be very expensive to hire me. He said, "Fine. Just tell me your number." I then told him my number and he signed me up. I came there and did well. It's funny, that the same boss who I talked with eventually left NBC and went over to ABC at the network. Now he is one of the big men at that network. He is doing very well. I sent him an e-mail recently congratulating him. He freaked out.

Why?

When I left NBC and then ABC, I didn't tell anybody good-bye. In both cases I just left and went my own way.

So you don't believe in good-byes?

Sometimes, no. I have had time to reflect upon this. In my last position working with the network, my perception of my value turned out to be different than the company's perception of my worth. Before I was let go, I believed that because I was committed and faithfully doing my job for so many years, that I deserved the right to have a heads-up and more open communication about the transition.

I'm a firm believer that the job lost you; you didn't lose the job.

I realized that white folks are going to be white folks, and black folks are going to be black folks. I had gotten to the point in my career that I had become a little bit lackadaisical, and I let my guard down, and I shouldn't have. I was told essentially that I was making too much money. True, in that I was making a lot of money. I understand that. But I was worth it. I was definitely worth it because I was doing my job. I believe that I deserved to be treated better. All they had to do was to talk with me and give me a couple of days to talk it over with Barbara. I would have gone back to them and would have given my spot back. The guy that had to do what he had to do was a guy that went to Illinois with me and told me back in the day, "CP, we'll walk out of here holding hands; hand in hand." Well, it didn't happen that way.

As a black man with your character and experience, what lessons did you learn from this?

I thought that I had the right to be there. That is because I had gone in thinking that I was who I was and also, because of my accomplishments and hard work, I would flourish on that basis alone. I forgot. That did not matter. The bottom line: You are always going to be black, and they are always going to be white.

I know that these types of abrupt transitions also happen to white people. I also would agree that this reality disproportionately oc-

curs in communities of color. My question is, What helped you to rebound from this challenging situation with the least amount of bruises?

Mental strength: I always felt that I was as smart as white folk were. I just felt that I could do the job that they were asked to do as well as them. I am also confident that I have earned *everything* that I was paid in my career so far and will continue to do so.

Where do you get that self-confidence?

I probably learned self-confidence from my mom and my dad. I always knew that I was as good as anybody else.

How did you keep your self-confidence despite some of the hurdles you had to overcome in mainstream society?

Because I was thriving in their world. I just knew that if I had to take a test, or compete for something, that I was going to do as well as they were going to do. Also I had a name that I could be proud of—Cyril Pinder.

Why is it important to have mental strength [for] navigating in mainstream society, especially as a professional black man?

Mainstream society can wear a black man down. There are people who will try to make you feel inferior. I remember one time, when I was working with one of the TV networks, I was calling on a large law firm. This agency was a large account that I was dealing with for many, many years. Anyway, I went in to talk with the contact person of the account, who happened to be a white lady. I introduced myself to her and indicated that I was with the network. I had already sent over the specs, as we called it. Still, she just couldn't deal with me. My colleague from the network could not understand her negative reaction to me, either. It turns out, long story made short, I approached the contact person at this agency and asked her what the problem was. She said to me that there was a black man that raped her cousin. I made it clear to her that I was not that black man. She said, "It doesn't matter, Cyril. I am having a hard time getting past that." I chose not to call on that agency anymore.

How do you feel as a black man having to deal with the obstacles like the one you just talked about and many others you endure, day in and day out, simply because of the color of your skin?

As far as the obstacles, I feel betrayed by the white folks, because it is many of them who run these institutions/companies. But on the flip side, I do feel good when I get a white guy who genuinely likes *me*. Case in point, generally I don't talk about sports around folks because they would like me because I was a former Chicago Bear. I choose not to make that information a part of the equation. One time a guy came up to me and said, "Cyril, somebody told me that you played for the Chicago Bears." I explained to him that that was not what I do now. He thought that I should let people know that. I wasn't going to, a matter of fact. If you want to accept me for being a pro football player, to me, that is a different thing than to really know me.

When I met you, I didn't know that you played pro football, but I was not a sports fanatic, either.

That was good. You accepted me as a black man who does good work.

It is just like when I recently taught a media class at Kennedy-King College in Chicago. The students respected me; they appreciated learning from me. Sure, they talked about football, only because somebody told them that I played, but when they found out that I didn't want to talk about it, they were okay with that.

So the key is to get to know you for who you are and not simply for what you have done, like play pro football.

Correct, because I am not in that now; I don't do that now. I am a media consultant. I teach media. That is what I do now. I am not playing for the Chicago Bears anymore.

Well, I admire you very much. You have the ability to cross-cultural, racial, and economic lines. You connect with people. Yet I understand that there are some hard feelings that you may have because of how you have been unfairly and unjustly treated at times.

Yes. There are some very hard feelings. I am only sharing my thoughts with you and your audience because I know the purpose of this discussion with you. The average run-of-the-mill person is not going to know my feelings because I am not going to talk to them about my private thoughts. I want white parents who choose to adopt black kids to completely grasp that their kids are going to grow up; these kids are going to take on their own unique personalities and interests and move in society in dark and brown skin. And as parents you need to know how to deal with that reality.

Did you personally know other black/biracial adoptees raised in a white family? If so, what were their experiences, if you can recall?

Yes, I had quite a few acquaintances that were black and adopted by white families. One girl committed suicide. My understanding was that she found out that she was adopted and her biological daddy was a black man. The sad part about it was that her adoptive mom apparently didn't want her to know who she was and where she came from. And the girl committed suicide. It's not worth that.

For white adoptive parents who are reading this interview and are trying to discover strategies to help their children of color do well in life, what can you say to them?

All I can say is that for those white parents who choose to adopt a black child or child of color, they should of course give the child the best that they can give him/her, including a great education, *and* not let that kid be disillusioned in thinking that he/she is white.

And this is the truth here: I don't care if you have only a drop of black blood in you, you are black. You are black. You are never going to be anything else but black. These parents need to understand that their black boy or girl is going to grow up to be a black man or black woman. Think about it: You cannot make somebody grow up to be a white person. It's not going to work.

When somebody white tries to adopt a black kid, I am okay with it, but always let these kids know where their heritage is, where they come from. Don't ever try to change where they came from or their history.

Good point. However, for those adoptive families who realistically do not live near their children's ethnic community, what can they do for their children of color?

These parents need to be smart enough to take their children around black people. In my opinion they must do that because, bad, good, or indifferent, these children need to know where they came from. It's like you. I used to tell you every day, "Look in the mirror, Rhonda. You are not white. You are black."

So how do I and other transracial adoptees deal with that reality?

There is nothing you can do to change the perceptions of others. Transracial adoptive parents can, and should, give their children the best education, the best of everything that they can provide to them, *and* the transracial adoptees in my opinion need to work hard (hopefully with their parents' support) to never forget that they are black.

I still struggled growing up (and at times still today) with not feeling beautiful compared to the white standard of beauty.

Well, the white standard is the white standard. You, on the other hand, have to accept that and know that "Hey, I'm never going to be white." I told you about my goddaughter Stevie. She was going to school with all of the white folks. Stevie's parents, I would say, are very bright and so is Stevie. Judy, Stevie's mother, graduated from Mt. Holyoke; and Stevie's father, Steve, graduated from Stanford with an MBA. But when Stevie, who now is a young adult, was younger, she was swimming with one of her friends and couldn't understand why all her friend had to do was flop her hair. I heard Stevie say to Judy, "Mom, why doesn't my hair work like that?!" I instead answered Stevie's question. I told her it was because of the climate, where she's from. I continued, "You are from the sun." I went through the whole thing with Stevie. I further explained to Stevie that "these girls are not going to handle the sun like you can; and you can't handle the water in the same way that they can because they are Nordic." Stevie finally got it. Stevie understood that she was black. Stevie was also a gymnast, and then she developed into a big, buxom, good-looking young black woman. So she couldn't do what the little white girls were doing for long because her body was shaped differently compared to her white girlfriends' who had a smaller, much thinner frame. Stevie understood that she was different and accepted it.

I have to be honest: I think that it is a challenge for many transracially adoptive families who want to develop relationships with members in their child's ethnic community. . . . They understand that it is important for their child and their family but simply don't know how to go about it.

That is your job. That is what you're supposed to do.

Who?

You, Rhonda. You are supposed to coach these parents and encourage them when they are making good steps towards making those connections into the black community. You need to help these parents to ensure that their children understand that they are black or biracial and know where they came from.

These transracially adopted kids are going to grow up. That is the reality that I hope their parents realize. The worst thing that can happen is to have a kid that is confused. You don't want that to prove out. If these children have an ounce of black blood in them, then they are considered black in the eyes of society.

For example, Tiger Woods concerns me. (I recognize that he is not adopted.) When his daddy was alive, he could see that he was from a black man. That was his daddy. But when his daddy died, I think that affected his identity negatively. And then he was playing golf, which in my opinion is a white man's sport.

Why do you say that?

I say that because you need to have money to play the sport of golf, just like you need to have money to play hockey. We black folk, generally speaking, prefer football and basketball because all you need is a ball and a peach basket to throw into and a ball to catch and run to develop your skill.

Possibly, but you play golf frequently and you're very good at it—and black.

Yes. I know that is where a lot of business is done, on the golf course. I found that out, that that is where a lot of the white guys go to talk business. And I also realized that if you don't play well, nobody wants to play with you. So you need to play well.

Because you chose to mentor me, I have benefited from many of the principles you live by. How can other adoptees establish relationships with mentors in the African American community who can also teach these individuals principles, life lessons, like you have for me?

Mentoring you was not tough for me because you are smart and wanted to learn more. I decide who I want to be associated with, and I saw promise in you so I have stayed in your life. Other adoptees need to do what you learned to do and become open to good folks in the black community to be a part of their lives.

I think now, more than even when you were growing up but certainly more than when I was growing up, that there are a lot of black people in the community that are willing to help adoptive families and adoptees.

Where do adoptive families and adoptees find these amazing people?

We are at historically black colleges like Grambling State University in Louisiana; Spelman College and Morehouse College in Atlanta, Georgia; Howard University in Washington, D.C.; and Florida A&M (or FAMU) in Tallahassee. These are some of the institutions [to which] a significant number of black families are choosing to send their children.

Another avenue to connect with smart black people is participating in the Link organization. Essentially the Link represents philanthropic work where its members send the message that there is more to life than bouncing a basketball and throwing a football.

Here is a story: I went to a function the other night, and there was a group of black folks that all graduated from college. These young people have all grown up to be good citizens like you. There was also at this event people like my friend Ed B., who is a white guy who has adopted a black kid. What was neat was that Ed's son brought his biological mother to this event with them. Ed B. always reminded his son that he was a part of his family and a part of his legacy but also had a biological connection to his mother; this is where he came from. It is great to see. Ed's kid has done very well in school. He married a white girl because that is all he knows.

So you have seen that transracial adoptees can grow up smart and centered.

Correct.

And a contributing factor is—?

A contributing factor is for the parents to let their kids, especially adopted kids, know where they came from.

Can these parents do this without exposing them to their child's racial and ethnic background?

How are they going to do that? It is the responsibility of the parents to expose their family to black folks, and if they choose not to do that, I believe that they will have problems, especially with their black/biracial child.

Very good point. That is pretty tough if you are a white family living in Wheaton, Illinois, or any other predominately white community.

Rhonda, we are everywhere. All you have to do is look around and you will see black folks around you. Now with Internet it is easier to connect with folk than it used to be.

How do you, how do I, or any adoptee break down the reality of being black in a white world?

For me it is not a breaking down. It is just a normal reality. For you or other black adoptees that go home to their white parents/family members, it may be tougher to break down. But for me, I am not going to have a problem because I am older. I am looking at life and seeing the impact it has had on me. I am just trying to share that with you and your audience.

So this racism stuff can really embitter somebody.

This racism stuff is bitter.

Even for someone like you, who has a good career and continues to achieve financial stature?

Yes. Racism never goes away. Racism is always going to be there. I used to tell Tony, a family friend who is a successful black professional young man, that there are some people who are not used to seeing a good-looking black man, smart, that is in his position. He at first did not know what I meant. I told him that he would see. I knew that he had to see how people perceived him for himself.

So we have tens of thousands of kids in foster care; the majority of them are minority children. I know that there are considerable people in the black community that "adopt" informally through kinship care. Still, there is much work to be done to ensure that all of these children have a place to feel safe and grow in a healthy way. What is your view on what I just said?

I agree with that to some degree. The black community includes people like me and Barbara. We have certain kids that we are supportive of long term. The fact is that it is not going to be everybody; it's not going to work that way. If you try to save everybody, it will drive you crazy. It's caring for one person at a time.

You told me one time that I needed to learn how to play on Astroturf and I needed to learn how to play on grass. What did you mean by that?

It means that you run differently on Astroturf than you run on grass. If I had to play all of my games on Astroturf, I wouldn't have made it. Guys are falling on you and that ground does not give; it is concrete underneath there. It hurts. It hurts. The same philosophy applies to you and other transracial adoptees. You need to know how to work both areas. You need to know how to deal in the white world, and you need to know how to deal in the black world.

Thank you.

PART II

Civil Rights Era (1955–72)

AS ISABEL WILKERSON DETAILS so elegantly and eloquently in *The Warmth of Other Suns*, Jim Crow laws in the South gave rise to the Great Migration:

> Over the course of six decades, some six million black southerners left the land of their forefathers and fanned out across the country for an uncertain existence in nearly every other corner of America. . . . A good portion of all black Americans alive picked up and left the tobacco farms of Virginia, the rice plantations of South Carolina, cotton fields in east Texas and Mississippi, and the villages and backwoods of the remaining southern states. . . . [The Great Migration] would force the South to search its soul and finally to lay aside a feudal caste system. It grew out of the unmet promises made after the Civil War and, through the sheer weight of it, helped push the country toward the civil rights revolutions of the 1960s.
>
> (2010, P. 9)

However, even after the Jim Crow laws were dismantled following the U.S. Supreme Court decision in *Brown v. Board of Education* (1954), many blacks remained frustrated by the slow pace of change toward racial equality and social justice. Then, fifteen months after the *Brown* decision was handed down, tragedy riveted black America in August 1955. Fourteen-year-old Emmett Till was visiting relatives in Mississippi when he supposedly flirted with a twenty-one-year-old white woman. When the woman's husband found out, he, a relative, and another man set out to find the young boy. The men kidnapped

Emmett Till, brutalized him, and then murdered him, shocking the nation (Chandler, 2012).

Several months later Rosa Parks, a seamstress and secretary of the Montgomery, Alabama, chapter of the NAACP, was arrested after refusing to give up her seat on a city bus to a white man. Parks's arrest in December 1955 triggered a boycott of Montgomery buses by blacks, who comprised almost 70 percent of the system's ridership. The boycott, organized by a local minister, Martin Luther King Jr., and his colleague Ralph Abernathy, continued for 381 days, significantly reducing the revenue of the city's bus company. Ninety-nine percent of the city's black residents rode in carpools, took taxis, or walked. The boycott, the first major salvo of the modern civil rights movement, ended more than a year later, on the effective date of the U.S. Supreme Court's ruling that segregated busing is unconstitutional (Independence Hall, 2008–14; Ingram, 1956).

Subsequent efforts to force Americans to finally reckon with the racial, political, and socioeconomic injustices inflicted on African Americans for far too long included the dispatch of federal troops to Little Rock, Arkansas, to escort nine African American students to high school in 1957; lunch counter sit-ins (1960); the Freedom Rides (1961); the enrollment at the University of Mississippi of James Meredith, the first African American student to matriculate there (1962); and the spring 1963 attack on nonviolent protesters, including children, by police wielding fire hoses, night sticks, and police dogs in Birmingham, Alabama (Leadership Conference, 2001).

On August 28, 1963, came the March on Washington for Jobs and Freedom organized by six major civil rights organizations. It brought to the capital 250,000 men, women, and children of all races and ages in a peaceful demonstration. The march, which is credited with helping to secure passage of the Civil Rights Act of 1964, culminated in a rally at the Lincoln Memorial, where Martin Luther King gave his famous "I have a dream" speech:

> In a sense we have come to our nation's capital to cash a check. When the architects of our republic wrote the magnificent words of the Constitution and the Declaration of Independence, they were signing a promissory note

to which every American was to fall heir. This note was a promise that all men would be guaranteed the unalienable rights of life, liberty, and the pursuit of happiness.

It is obvious today that America has defaulted on this promissory note insofar as her citizens of color are concerned. Instead of honoring this sacred obligation, America has given the Negro people a bad check; a check which has come back marked "insufficient funds." But we refuse to believe that the bank of justice is bankrupt. We refuse to believe that there are insufficient funds in the great vaults of opportunity of this nation. So we have come to cash this check—a check that will give us upon demand the riches of freedom and the security of justice. We have also come to this hallowed spot to remind America of the fierce urgency of *now*. This is no time to engage in the luxury of cooling off or to take the tranquilizing drug of gradualism. *Now* is the time to make real the promises of Democracy. *Now* is the time to rise from the dark and desolate valley of segregation to the sunlit path of racial justice. *Now* is the time to open the doors of opportunity to all of God's children. *Now* is the time to lift our nation from the quicksands of racial injustice to the solid rock of brotherhood.

(KING, 1992, PP. 616–17)

Indeed as King underscored on that August day, the values of social justice, equality, respect for one another, and integration must be extended to all citizens, regardless of their skin color and background.

The changes brought about by the Civil Rights Act of 1964 and the Voting Rights Act of 1965 were immediate and dramatic, especially in the South:

The share of black employees at South Carolina textile companies jumped from less than 5 percent in 1963 to more than 20 percent in 1970 and to more than a third by 1980. Similar patterns were observed in all the Southern textile states. According to oral histories, blacks in textile areas referred to integration as "The Change," and associated it with the reversal of black regional migration in the 1960s and '70s.

Although the industry later declined in response to global competition, desegregation of textiles was the single-largest contributor to the sharp

increase in relative black incomes from 1965 to 1975, an exclusively
Southern regional phenomenon. . . . Not only did black living standards
improve, but mill workers with limited schooling were often able to send
their children to college, taking advantage of expanding educational and
employment opportunities elsewhere in the region.
(WRIGHT, 2013)

One consequence of integration was formal regulation of the placement of black children for adoption (Reid-Merritt, 2010). Previously
the black community had been shut out of the formal system and simply saw to it that parentless black children were informally fostered
and adopted by their extended families and communities, a practice
that sustained the youngsters through their childhoods and adolescent
years and nurtured them as adults. Black social workers became concerned that a child welfare system designed to meet the needs of white
children was not equipped culturally to meet the needs of black children from inner-city neighborhoods. An increasing number of white
couples became interested in adopting black children as the number
of available white infants decreased, a result of the availability of the
birth-control pill (1960) and other improved means of contraception,
and the legalization of abortion in 1972 (Reid-Merritt, 2010). From the
mid-1960s to the early 1970s approximately fifteen thousand black children were adopted by white parents (Davis, 1991). In many cases these
were white parents like mine, who had embraced the philosophy of
the civil rights movement and wanted to grow their family through
adoption; they eagerly agreed to raise black and biracial children as
their own.

One of the few times the transracial adoptive community collec-
tively heard from the black community was in 1972, when the National Association of Black Social Workers (NABSW) went on record
to voice its strong opposition to transracial adoption, particularly the
adoption of black and biracial children by white parents. The NABSW
was alarmed by the increasing number of black children who had been
removed from their communities and were waiting to be adopted. The
NABSW was especially concerned about the blatant forms of racism
that existed in American society and in the U.S. child care system and

questioned the ability of white parents to rear racially and culturally secure black children (Reid-Merritt, 2010).

After the NABSW's statement in 1972, the number of black and bi-racial children adopted domestically by white parents dropped off significantly (Reid-Merritt, 2010; Herman, 2012). International adoptions by white Americans surged throughout the 1970s, 1980s, and 1990s (Herman, 2012). Although the NABSW still stands firm on its 1972 position, the organization's voice has softened, acceding to transracial adoptive policies that grant whites easy access to black children in the foster care system (Reid-Merritt, 2010). Thus with minimal connection to the black community and no robust guidance from adoption agencies, white transracial adoptive parents were left to raise black children with insufficient knowledge of basic hair and skin care needs and with a dismal education about, and appreciation of, their child's ethnic community of origin and the varied experiences of that community or communities. When adoptees of color ventured out on their own, they were ill equipped to navigate the racial and emotional land mines lying just below the surface of American society.

MEMBERS OF THE BLACK community whom I interviewed for this section come out of the civil rights era. All extend themselves to provide readers with suggestions about how to connect with the black community. Through their experiences, expertise, hard times, perseverance, and self-reflection they offer basic tools that can strengthen families, especially transracial adoptive families, and provide information that will allow adoptees of color to move in society with added confidence, purpose, knowledge, and self-love.

Back in 1903 W. E. B. Du Bois argued in *The Souls of Black Folk* that the key issue troubling twentieth-century America was the problem of race. He fought relentlessly against Jim Crow laws and discrimination in education and employment. I was honored to have the opportunity to speak to Arthur E. McFarlane II, Du Bois's great grandson. I wondered whether Du Bois and all that he stood for had left a generational imprint on his descendants. What also makes McFarlane special is his comfort level with transracial adoptive families. He has made it a point to live a racially integrated life, including developing relationships with white parents who are raising children of color. (I first met him in 2000 at a culture camp in Colorado for white parents raising black children.) Transracial adoptive families are likely to find his words of support heartening.

Lora Kay's personal and professional lives are inspiring. Her words remind me of when, as a little girl, I felt that I was not good enough, pretty enough, or even smart enough to compete in this world. Today Kay (Lora Kay is a pseudonym) speaks to black girls who are bombarded by negative images of themselves, especially in the media, and gives them hope. Her work, educating at-risk youth in the Washington, D.C., metropolitan area, underscores her unwavering commitment to investing in the next generation of young people. Having this conversation with Kay was fascinating, as she is a mentor to my white nonadopted brother, Chris. I was interested in knowing how that relationship developed across racial and cultural lines.

Chester Jackson, like the other interviewees in this section, is a child of the 1950s. He grew up in New York City and speaks from an insider's perspective as he is an adoptive father himself and works as an adoption professional who places older children from the foster care system. He speaks honestly and compassionately to prospective adoptive parents about what it means to adopt and how to prepare themselves to take on this beautiful and complex commitment.

Henry Allen grew up in the Chicago area in the throes of the civil rights era. As a child he was fascinated by both Albert Einstein, whose brilliant thinking Allen credits with "changing the physical world," and Martin Luther King Jr., who Allen believes embodied the ability to think critically about ways to stimulate holistic social change. As a young person estranged from his own family, Allen lived with a white missionary family in Illinois for several years, an experience that gives him insight into the experience of black children adopted into white families. Further, both as a professor who has taught transracial adoptees in his classrooms and as someone who (with his wife) has interacted with transracial adoptive families in his community, Henry Allen is quite vocal about what he has perceived. I specifically sought to interview Allen because of his life experiences and his professional expertise in issues of race and culture. Here he discusses the influences of race and culture on human interactions and why it is essential for transracial adoptive families to examine their own behaviors and understand these constructs within their family units.

ARTHUR E. MCFARLANE II
Great Grandson of W. E. B. Du Bois and Advocate for the Preservation of Cultural Heritage
INTERVIEWED BY TELEPHONE, JANUARY 2, 2012

I am very pleased that we were able to connect and do this interview. As the great grandson of W. E. B. Du Bois—he was someone whose works I had the pleasure of reading about in literature and in the history books, but to you W. E. B. Du Bois was your great grandpa, mentor, and friend. Before we discuss the influence he had on you personally, I am interested in knowing a bit about your immediate background.

I was born in Greenwich Village in New York City at the end of the 1950s. My parents were married in New York, and I grew up for the first four years of my life in New York City—in the Bronx and in Harlem. My parents divorced. My mother remarried and I came out to Denver, Colorado, with her and my stepfather, and I lived in Denver until the time I was eleven years old. Then at the age of eleven, I went back to New York City to live with my dad. This was in 1969. A few years later, when I was seventeen years of age, my dad died. I stayed in New York City until I graduated from high school. Right after high school I moved to Upstate New York, where I attended the State University of New York at Brockport. I graduated from Brockport in 1980 with a major in psychology and a minor in African and African American studies. I then went back to Colorado and went to graduate school to gain further educational background in the field of social and clinical psychology at the University of Colorado at Boulder. Today I work for the Colorado Department of Public Health and Environment, where I have been for twenty-five years [in a number of positions, including serving on a program evaluation team that determines whether certain state-run preventative health programs—addressing, for example, cancer, dental health, women's wellness—are effective].

What were some of the values you were taught as a child by your family?

I certainly would say that from my mom and her side of the family I was taught the value of education and the importance of going to school and developing an ongoing intellectual curiosity. From my dad I definitely gained much more of a sense of working with people, being compassionate and empathetic and figuring out three questions: What do people need, what direction do people need to go, and how do you help others?

Growing up, who were some of your role models?

One of my role models was, for sure, my father. He was an amazing man. His side of the family actually has a pretty amazing story, just like on my mom's side. The W. E. B. Du Bois influence comes from my mom's side of the family. W. E. B. Du Bois is my mother's grandfather. But it was my father's grandfather who came to New York from Jamaica. My great grandfather on my dad's side bought up homes and land and was able to create a good business that was passed down through the family. So when I returned to New York as a youth, I was working with my dad to do upkeep on the brownstones that we owned on 137th Street. My dad was also a police officer, so he worked odd hours, but I was able to see that he had a great approach with people and a great personality. So, yes, my dad was definitely my hero and one of the people I looked up to. Also I had a teacher in junior high school who mentored me, who took an interest in me and took me under his wing. He and I have stayed in touch to this day. I still talk with him regularly and get Christmas cards from him. So I think that I have had amazing people along the way, like my parents, my grandparents, and great grandparents and a bunch of really good friends and teachers in my life.

As a youth and African American growing up in Harlem, did you experience racism?

Let me go back. I went to an elementary school here in Denver, Colorado, that was racially mixed. We were one of the few black families around. There were a couple of Latino families. Most of the kids I went to school with were white. Still, I excelled. I was a great student academically. I was in band. I was in choir. I was acting. I was doing a lot of different things. For me, in elementary school, race was not an issue because I was doing pretty much what I wanted. I was getting good grades and everything through my eyes then was fine.

When I went to junior high school in New York City, it was all black. In fact the school was made up of all blacks and all boys. My class was the last year of all boys in the intermediate school called Frederick Douglass Intermediate School 10. Obviously there I did not have a race problem. We had some white teachers. But there again I was one of the better students academically. My teachers were actually very much on my side and complimentary to me. I grew up as a leader and never had any particular race issues.

Did you feel more validated attending an all-black boys' junior high school compared to the more racially diverse elementary school in Denver?

I wouldn't necessarily say that I felt more validated as much as I felt like I could see more people like me. In my elementary school I only had one black teacher, and then, like I said, there were only a couple of black families. So I didn't see a lot of people like me in elementary school. As a contrast, when I got to junior high school the principal was black. The assistant principal was black. A handful of the teachers were black. I had the opportunity in New York to see more people like me in positions of leadership. The assistant principal in junior high school was a disciplinarian. He was like another dad to me. The teachers there had high expectations for all of the students, even those that had disciplin[e] problems. The teachers who were black and white wanted for all of us to be exceptional achievers in math, in science, in the arts, and in literature.

Was there a time in your schooling that you sensed that you were perceived as different, where you were measured not by your accomplishments but by the color of your skin?

Yes. That definitely happened to me when I got into high school. I was one of a handful of kids who went to the highly selective Stuyvesant High School. New York City has what it calls specialized schools, and there were five of them when I went to school. Now I believe there are nine. These schools focused primarily on math, science, and engineering and also music, art, and the performing arts. At Stuyvesant you had to take an exam to be considered for acceptance. Only the top achievers could get in. And once we got in, it was a huge challenge academically for all of us. I remember that there was much more of a sense of being smart than there was of being white or black.

Interesting. The great equalizer was education.

Still, what I saw in high school was racial segregation. We self-segregated. The black kids hung out with the black kids; the white Jewish kids hung out with the white Jewish kids; and the Latino kids hung out with the Latino kids. I remember a group of us black kids got together and played card games during our breaks. It was there that I learned how to play the card game whist, also called bid whist, which is similar to spades. I think we enjoyed this time together because we wanted to feel more at ease and not have to always be under that microscope. So I think we self-segregated for those reasons.

The other big thing that was really critical in terms of race awareness for me was that these kids at Stuyvesant came from all over the city. You took an exam to get into the school; once you got in, it didn't matter what borough you lived in. The experience I got from attending Stuyvesant was very educational, not just academically but personally. As students many of us became friends. We were actually traveling all over the city to hang out with each other, whether our friends were black, white, or Latino. And so I was going to Brooklyn; I was going to Queens; I was going to Greenwich Village. I remember going to some of these white kids' homes, and this one woman in particular, who was the mother of one of my friends, was a member of a highly prominent and wealthy Jewish family. As I walked in my friend's massive home, I saw the black doorman. But what was just as surreal was that I was walking into my friend's family-owned building with their name prominently engraved on the side of the building. Another friend of mine, his father was a world-renowned geologist, an oil guy, and he owned a building on 76th Street. Another one's mom was a well-known child psychologist, and that family owned a whole-floor apartment on 72nd and Broadway and had a black maid. And yet another one of my friends, his family owned a home out in the Hamptons, and they invited all of us to their home one summer. There I saw black and Hispanic people mowing their lawn. The list goes on. Taking in all of those images was a big deal and made an impression on me.

What did you take away from those images?

I wasn't necessarily treated poorly because of being black or who I was. But there were clearly some differences there. You didn't see a bunch of black faces outside of Stuyvesant when you went to these people's homes unless they were the faces of the people who were serving them.

I was starting to get awareness in high school, from a lot of different perspectives, about race and growing up in Harlem. I was living in the middle of Harlem, but I wasn't a poor kid. My dad owned the building that I lived in. I had my own bedroom. In fact my Harlem friends all came over to my house because I had music, I had space, and we could all lounge around. So I had this very different side of the racial dichotomy going on, where among black people I was the topnotch person. I was on the top of the hill, if you will. And among white people I was just kind of last. And so certainly in some ways that was for me a good lesson in some of these disparities between people. I became more aware as I listened to people and watched black people and white people. I think what it gave me was a real opportunity to be that bridge because I could relate to both sides of the equation.

It wasn't until I got to college that I really felt racial prejudices towards me. And even then it wasn't from the people of the college; it was from those in the town where I was living. Where I went to school was in a very small town called Brockport, New York, upstate between Buffalo and Rochester. The town was small. There I could relate to the businesspeople in the community; they were friendly to me. But I could remember instances, like walking in town and being called "nigger" by some school kids in a bus going by. I heard them yelling, "Look at the nigger walking down the street!" It was a different contrast from walking down the streets in New York City where I grew up. Also, when I went to graduate school in Boulder, Colorado, I experienced a more hidden racism that wasn't the in-your-face kind, like on the streets of Brockport, New York. In graduate school I really wanted to do some work around social power. My research committee at the university had issues with the methodology that I wanted to apply to my research work, mainly because it didn't fit in to the conservative approach the institution or department I was under wanted to take. I think having a black person engineer these ideas, and being the great grandson of W. E. B. Du Bois, caused my work to be perceived to be even more threatening for the institution.

What messages did you learn from your family—particularly from your great grandfather W. E. B. Du Bois?

When I look at the messages that I got from my parents, particularly from my mom's side, a major theme was that *you are the great grandson of W. E. B. Du Bois*. Over time I came to a clear understanding of what it meant to be his great grandson, how important his legacy was, and what sorts of expectations people had of me because of my great grandfather's legacy. Starting with my great grandfather, when I was three months old he told me [as I learned in his last autobiography] that he expected me to take up the mantel that he had worn for ninety years at that point, to really be a person who is changing the world. [In his remarks at Paul Robeson's sixtieth birthday party, my great grandfather] gave me some specific advice around finding a job that the world needs to have done and that I enjoy doing. Those sorts of pieces made it really clear that he had expectations that I was going to be someone who was going to make a positive difference. I understood and internalized those same expectations from my mom and from others on her side of the family as well.

In terms of my dad's side of the family, I got the sense from my father that he wanted me to be a good person: to be a person of my word, to be a problem solver, someone who is standing in front and standing tall. I think those were the big messages I got. Because I grew up in Harlem with my dad, there weren't a lot of white people around. I didn't experience a lot of racism. And I didn't go home and talk to my dad about much of that stuff. Now having said that, when I came up with a white girlfriend from high school—Dad raised an eyebrow. He didn't say anything or convey that, by me dating her, it was a bad thing, but she only visited with me at my house one time. She took a taxicab to Harlem, and then trying to get her a taxicab to get her home was tough. All of the rest of the time I would go to her place down on 74th

Street. And so there were subtle things like that which I didn't take all that seriously at the time. But as time went on, I saw some of those nuances more clearly. One night when I was leaving her home, her dad was sitting in the living room reading. He asked me to step in for a word. He said to me in a very serious manner: "I know that Rachel loves you and that you love her. We really like you, but this isn't going to go anywhere. You are not going to marry my daughter. My daughter is going to marry a nice Jewish boy, and that is all there is to it. Just so we are clear." It didn't have anything to do with me being black; it had to do with the fact that I wasn't Jewish.

So from your adolescent years you learned to detect the subtleties of religious or racial differences. One of the trends that we have seen in the transracial adoptive community in the past two decades, as you may know, is a growing understanding of the need for white adoptive parents to learn more about their child's racial, ethnic, and cultural heritage(s). You are a strong contributor to the Heritage Camps for Adoptive Families, Inc., in Denver, Colorado, particularly the African Caribbean camp. How did you get involved with the heritage camps, and why is it important to you?

One of the leaders of the African Caribbean Heritage Camp found my name somewhere and contacted me. I was told by her that they were specifically trying to get black community members in the Denver metro area to participate more in the camp because they wanted the kids to see black leadership. I tend to say yes when people ask me to do something I think is important for the community. One of the years I attended, I talked about public health, particularly the health disparities among persons of color. I have also served as a facilitator on panel discussions and group sessions around these topics.

I was very interested in understanding this whole transracial adoption notion. How do children of one racial and ethnic group live with parents who are from another racial and ethnic background? When there are issues impacting transracial adoptive families, I ask: Is what's really going on here about race or about society's perception of families like these? Or is what's really going on here about parent-child relationships? As I spent more and more time with the heritage camps, particularly with the African Caribbean camp, I was able to interact with and listen to transracial adoptive families. I found that the answers to my questions are made up of a very complicated mixture impacting these children and their parents. I think heritage camp is important for transracial adoptive families because it allows these families to get together and exhale. It gives them the opportunity to connect with other families that look like them and who may be struggling with similar issues, without being judged. For them it is a home away from home. And what has happened to me over the years is that I feel at home there too. When I am with the heritage camp community of people, I feel like I can be me. It is a wonderful feeling.

After getting face-to-face time with transracial adoptive families, what do you think is the value, for these families in particular, of learning about the African American culture?

I think that what ends up happening for white people in general, and let me say I don't think that it is done maliciously, but they are ignorant about African American history and the experiences of black people. They just don't know it. They were not taught it, so consequently those that adopt black children don't necessarily recognize that they should teach their kids about it. What becomes the real intellectual exercise for me is to make sure that the parents and the kids get the information with the hope that it will generate some good discussion about what black history is about. So that people will want to learn more about W. E. B. Du Bois and the many other African American contributors to society within their own community and globally.

Walk me through what you might say to these families.

I don't say anything different to them than I would say to any other group that asks me to speak. I talk about W. E. B. Du Bois's life; I talk about his writings, his accomplishments, and the controversy that has surrounded him. I try to make the history come alive for my listeners. I want people who have not explored black history to really delve into learning about what black folks really are like and what they have accomplished. For instance to *know* that it was a black person that invented the three-way automatic stoplight and the modern-day shoe-making process and many other inventions, as well as to *know* that black people have always owned land, is very empowering. And in fact to also *know* that black people were not just slaves but that there were cultures in the North where blacks owned property even before the end of slavery is huge. To *know* and *understand* that black folk have fought for this country in the American Revolution and in any and every war since—all of these are pieces of information that one has to search for in our society unfortunately and are not traditionally taught in the classroom. And so when I talk about black history in the framework of my great grandfather, I want people to take from that a sense of curiosity, a sense of wanting to learn more about the black experience and culture. For transracial adoptive parents I want them especially to take the next step and share the rich knowledge of the African American experience with their black child.

I want black youth, whether they have black parents or white parents, to embrace the idea that they can be who they are meant to be *as proud black people*. As you know, for black kids who are being raised in a white privileged home, it is really important that they grasp the fact that they are not white; *they are black*. It is true that these kids get some advantages by being raised in a white family and environment, and they should take advantage as best that they can; however, these kids need to understand clearly that when they walk out the door, people around them don't see a white kid, they see a black kid.

I am always reminded by my mentors to always remember that I am black. What does that mean, exactly, for black adopted children who have a sense of privilege from being raised in white homes?

What that means is that these kids are going to be treated differently despite being raised in white families. *We have to come to grips with our racist society.* And we have to come to grips with the fact that when these black individuals, including black adoptees, are seen as someone black, that is different than being seen as someone white. You can have two individuals together, one black and one white, with equal talent, equal gifts, same grades, and same clothes. For the black person in this American culture, he/she is still a black person, and many times that is perceived negatively.

So in this country the color of one's skin dictates someone's perceived value?

Yes. Social scientific experiments have been conducted for forty to fifty years on this stuff. Let's look at the housing situation. If you take a black family and you give them the same name and the same income and the same jobs as a white family, and you send the black family out into the real estate market to find a home, the black family gets treated differently most [of the time], if not every time. Even though on paper a mortgage banker may think a potential buyer is a good bet, is someone who is going to pay his/her bill, all of a sudden once they show up and they are black, things change. We've shown those realities experimentally.

I know. I will tell you that when I have purchased property or handled business transactions, I have done as much as I could over the phone to seal the deal before I showed up in person, just so that I can minimize the hassle you are talking about. To me, being raised in a white family, this reality based solely on the color of one's skin is very shocking to me. I know who I am and that I am someone who strives to be a person of integrity. It is therefore an insult to my person when people make assumptions that I am "less than" because of the color of my skin and that I don't deserve or can't afford to purchase a home, a car, what have you, even though the paperwork says I can. It is so frustrating to deal with this reality. How do you tell parents how to prepare their children for this nightmare?

The sad thing is what you are talking about happens regularly. The million-dollar question is, How do you teach a child that this is going to be what happens and that this is the direction that things are going to go? At some levels it is a challenge to have to explain the "whys" to your children.

Where do you start?

I think that you have to start at the basic level, the same level that black parents have to start at with their black kids. "This is the way the world is, child." If I was a parent that is trying to explain a given reality, I would be pulling out the poetry. I would be pulling out all of the resources that I had available that could explain in a safe way to my child what is going on in our society and how those issues are being discussed. The unfortunate thing, I think parents tend to put off those tough questions because they are not sure if their child is ready to talk about it, or some parents don't think certain acts are going to happen to them or their child, or they may even think that the reality will change by the time their kids grow up. And so parents put off those hard conversations to have with their children. My advice to parents is, Don't put any of it off. Have these conversations as early as you can with your child.

My friends have adopted a son transracially. He is four. Recently he was playing around with some crayons and toys. Well, he decided that he wanted to be a superhero. And of course in his mind superheroes are white. Joey was in his room playing with crayons. He literally took a crayon and tried to color his skin white so that he could be a super-hero. At four years old he is making these kinds of choices. His mother was like, "Wow! It is time for us already to have a conversation with our son about race and the fact that there are also black superheroes."

It is a hard conversation to have, but it must be done. I am sure that there are others who may have a different view as to when and what they tell their child about these difficult conversation pieces.

Yes. There are some parents who do not want to be too eager to start these hard conversations with their child at an early age, whether it is because they don't want their kids to be limited or to feel that they are always going to be persecuted, or the world is going to treat their child badly and even thinking that everyone in the world that is white is a bad person. Obviously growing up with white parents, you as a black kid are going to know that not every white person is a bad person. In time you need to know that there are white people—*and* black people out there—who may treat you badly. Also there are clearly black people out there that don't think that white parents should adopt black kids, and you may run into some of those people in the grocery store, just like you could run into someone white who does not approve of another white person raising a black child. I think that you need to deal with both sides of that equation. I think the way to do that is let-ting kids know what the reality is when it comes to, in this case, race in America. It is important to let these kids know that this is something that needs to change and that you hope that they will be part of the group who is part of the change.

It is very fascinating to me. Back in the 1970s there were trans-racial adoptive parents (and others) who truly believed that because, in part, of W. E. B. Du Bois's work in addressing the color line

problem of the twentieth century and, of course, the Reverend Dr. Martin Luther King Jr. and many other civil rights advocates towards a world that was racially integrated, race relations would have improved significantly. Thirty years later, we still have the problem of the twentieth century with us, and the dream as articulated by the Reverend Dr. Martin Luther King Jr. is not yet realized. I don't think that this country will be in a postracial era anytime soon, but what needs to happen for us to move closer to that goal?

I still think that the work that my great grandfather was trying to do all of those years ago, starting back at the time when he was in graduate school at Harvard, was to educate white people and black people about what black people are like. For me in this time frame, in this society, a big part of that is simply telling your story, whether you are black, white, Asian, Native American, et cetera. Sharing those stories, I think, puts us in a position where we see exactly who we are — how similar our needs are. I think storytelling is the answer because it breaks down those barriers. Now is there a need to have laws? Yes. We need to have laws and policies in place because we can't legislate how people feel; we can legislate what people do. So in expecting better behavior and in legislating better behavior, we can make some useful changes. However, I think that what those changes do is give access to telling the story, access to quality services, access to making sure you are perceived, or at least treated, in some equal fashion. And then you get the opportunity to exchange your story and the possibility to break through stereotypes and revisit any ingrained prejudices or racism one might have and question the legitimacy of it.

Okay, now I am thinking of white families who have adopted a black/biracial child and are living in predominately white communities. I am not saying that is bad, but it does present added difficulty in trying to achieve what you are talking about, folk from many different racial and ethnic backgrounds sharing their story. Some of our families have a difficult time going into the black community. How do you deal with that?

That is what needs to happen. Those families need to go into the black community. Go to a play at a black theater company in the city.

Go to a musical that is based on African American history or African American struggles. As difficult as that can be, really getting that kind of music and pathos is important. An August Wilson play is very different than Shakespeare.

Getting the exposure to writers like Nikki Giovanni, Alice Walker, and Langston Hughes is as important as getting exposure to William Faulkner, Mark Twain, or Ian Fleming. It is that broad exposure, that cultural knowledge, that is so important for everyone, regardless of their racial background.

What are five books that are in your personal library that you would recommend for white adoptive families to read?

I would recommend folks read: *The Souls of Black Folk* [by W. E. B. Du Bois]; *The New Jim Crow: Mass Incarceration in the Age of Colorblindness* [by Michelle Alexander]; *The Power Elite* [by C. Wright Mills with contributor Alan Wolfe]; *Medical Apartheid: The Dark History of Medical Experimentation on Black Americans from Colonial Times to the Present* [by Harriet A. Washington]; *The Color of Wealth: The Story Behind the U.S. Racial Wealth Divide* [by Meizhu Lui, Barbara Robles, and Betsy Leondar-Wright].

Great selections! As we near the end of our discussion, I would be remiss if I didn't not ask you: How did W. E. B. Du Bois influence your life?

As a young child my first real memory of my great grandfather was when he died in 1963. My mother had moved the family to Denver, Colorado, from New York, and I recall the household being in a great deal of turmoil. Obviously he had a great influence on my life before that moment and a profound impact since then.

Du Bois is my example of what one person can do to change the world.

Through his books—*Suppression of the African Slave Trade, Philadelphia Negro, The Souls of Black Folk, Black Reconstruction in America, The World and Africa,* and many others—he showed us many sides of what it means to be African and African American while laying a firm foundation for future scholars and research. Through his autobiographies he showed us glimpses of his view of the world and pictures of his life. Through the organizations he helped start, the Niagara Movement, the Pan-African Congresses, the National Association for the Advancement of Colored People, and the Peace Information Center, he built ways for his vision of a more just and peaceful world to achieve fruition. Through his time teaching in the small schools around Fisk University, at Wilberforce University, and at Atlanta University, he made clear his belief that higher education for African Americans was essential. Through the many articles he published, he laid out clear positions on issues of the day and as the editor of the *Crisis* gave many African American writers and poets a place from which to launch their careers.

The last area that Grandpa influenced my life is in his critical approach to the history that was going on around him. It has taught me to listen well to people discussing issues, in an effort to capture both sides. It has taught me to connect the dots between the pieces of information I gather and reflect that larger picture back to the world. Finally, his life showed me the connection between people, no matter how far apart in distance or time, illuminating just how the differences in race and wealth can, but should not, divide us.

Last, what would you like your legacy to be?

My strength revolves around bringing people together from diverse backgrounds. I would hope that people remember me as being a bridge to people from many different backgrounds and finding commonalities through all of the emotions diverse souls bring to the table.

LORA KAY (PSEUDONYM)

Principal of a Charter School in Washington, D.C.

INTERVIEWED BY TELEPHONE, MAY 14, 2012

Dr. Kay, there is so much that I want to talk with you about because you are a black woman, mother, and educator. I also think that all families, especially transracial adoptive families, can learn a lot from your life's experience and see through your eyes a rich aspect of the African American community. Recently I had the oppor-

tunity to visit the charter school you oversee in Washington, D.C. Let's begin our discussion there.

The mission of the charter school I serve is to create learning communities in lower-income urban areas where all students, particularly those who have not succeeded in traditional schools, can reach their potential. At our charter school students develop the academic, social, and employment skills they need to build rewarding lives and promote positive change.

We provide high-quality academic programming and comprehensive socioemotional services alongside an unwavering commitment to meeting all of our students where they are academically, socially, and emotionally.

Over 70 percent of our scholars enroll in college (two-year and four-year), a rate of college-going that well exceeds the national and D.C. average for African American students who are first-generation college-goers. Notably we are seeing an increase in the percent of our alumni who persist in college. Approximately 70 percent of [our] students who enroll in college remain the first year.

In what capacity do you serve in this organization?

As principal I lead the academic program and strive to ensure strong school management, highly trained school staff, and strong student outcomes.

At the charter school you work closely with students who are primarily African American and originate from low-income communities. My question to you is, How do you engage the untapped intellect of these children?

Resiliency is one of our guiding principles. We believe that we must program appropriately to ensure that our students persevere—so we push them and we pull them into success. We use our wraparound services to support our students—and this may mean visiting the home, picking up students, providing meals, offering paid-internship opportunities, et cetera.

Likewise, we never give up! We believe that hope is alive, trust cements every relationship, change takes time, parents/families are our partners, and effort counts. Our students know that they can count on us. They know that pencils have erasers; we all grow up, not back; and the uncertain becomes certain because of a great love for the work.

One of the reasons I am honored to interview you is that you are also an inspirational mentor to my white nonadopted brother, Chris, who appeared in *In Their Siblings' Voices*, which I coauthored with Rita J. Simon. How did the two of you meet, and what was it that inspired you to cross racial and cultural arenas to invest many years in him?

Chris first came to me as a teaching candidate at Kettering Middle School [a public school] in Mitchellville, Maryland, which is in Fulton County. I knew right away that he was the type of person that I wanted teaching our students, who were primarily African American. Chris loved to talk, teach, and engage students in real-world situations. When I retired, I recruited Chris to come to my charter school.

Chris has helped me expand my own definition of diversity to include one's humility and caring. Diversity is more than race and ethnicity, religion, or background—it's style, talent, and critical thinking as well. Chris has taught me to respect others' points of view, to wait patiently and be still, and to honor relationships. In Chris I see the spiritual me. And I'm still a work in progress.

How can we as black/biracial transracially adopted women and men of color find our compass? How do we become more centered on all of who we are? And does Afrocentric education have relevance in our lives today as a tool to guide us—if so, why?

My words of advice are to travel, travel, and travel—visit faraway places, experience different people, fall in love with a way of life of another—and create a photographic journal of what is observed. Capture the wind, smell the rain, and touch the sun. Then reflect on the experience—what you feel, and the way you feel, and who you are becoming. Find your compass through living and experiencing—and feeling the good, bad, and ugly things in your travels. Be alone, and then get lost in the crowd in order to find out who and what you are. You will find your center and your passion for something that is greater than yourself. I would think that Afrocentric education is relevant to *all* people. Everyone must learn what it means to be Afro centered.

Everyone must learn what Afrocentricity looks like and feels like. But everyone does not have to embrace it.

What does Afrocentricity mean to you?

In Fulton County, Maryland, my educator colleagues and I went through an Afrocentric time in the early 1990s. We invited many renowned speakers in the field to come to our school and conduct symposiums and special trainings around the issues of Afrocentricity.[1] From everything that we learned during that time, it became mandatory in our county to understand Afrocentricity and the black child. Essentially, Afrocentricity looks at what it means to be black, what it means to embrace the way black people talk, look, and act. For a while we had people come to the meetings who dressed in Afrocentric attire. They focused more on Africa in their discussions. You could see that richness was pervasive in Fulton County, and this Afrocentric phenomenon was new. It was something that a lot of people wanted to learn more about and get more into.

How long did this Afrocentric period last, if you recall?

I would say that it lasted for about four or five years or even longer. Everybody was doing it: wearing African clothes, planning trips to Africa, and embracing that way of living. Many educators wanted to embrace the Afrocentric way of learning and thinking within the curriculum. There were so many good, good books out around this topic and many great speakers. It was a whole paradigm shift for our county.

After that period the Afrocentric trend passed. There was still some feeling that we have to understand culture, but at the same time it waned. Our county was one of the most educated communities in the country. There were lots of people getting master's degrees, doctorate degrees, probably more so than in anywhere else. There were a lot of people, African American politicians, upper-class African American parents—so the movement kind of lost its momentum. It is like if you think about mixing paint and you put white or put another color into black, what you get is a little watered down. But I think the Afrocentric movement is good. I think that everybody should know it. I am looking at my bookshelf and all of the books that I bought back then. Some of these books were required reading in our county. Such as one by Marguerite A. Wright called *I'm Chocolate, You're Vanilla*.

Yes, in fact *I'm Chocolate, You're Vanilla* is currently on the recommended reading lists of key adoption bloggers and adoption agencies. I know there are a lot of white parents who have adopted, or are in the process of adopting, African American children in particular who are familiar with the book, many who have read it. I think very highly of Dr. Wright and her work.

Great! I am looking at another book by Bruce A. Jacobs, *Race Manners: Navigating the Minefield between Black and White Americans.* There is another one called *Children of Color: Psychological Interventions with Culturally Diverse Youth,* edited by Jewelle Taylor Gibbs. Several of these have been recently revised.

If you could pick five books from your personal bookshelf that you would recommend for parents who want to appreciate the richness of the vast black experience, as well as the historically racial and socioeconomic challenges that blacks have faced, what would they be?

The Dreamkeepers: Successful Teachers of African American Children, by Glory Ladson-Billings (1994); *Raising Black Children: Two Leading Psychologists Confront the Educational, Social and Emotional Problems Facing Black Children,* by James P. Comer, M.D., and Alvin F. Poussaint, M.D.; a classic called *Talley's Corner: A Study of Negro Streetcorner Men,* by Eliott Liebow and Charles C. Lemert; *Walking in Circles: The Black Struggle for School Reform,* by Barbara A. Sizemore; and *Paul Laurence Dunbar High School of Little Rock, Arkansas: Take from Our Lips a Song, Dunbar, to Thee,* by my mentor Faustine C. Jones-Wilson and Emma Glasco Davis. The list goes on.

Do you think that while Afrocentrism has waned a bit in your county, it is still relevant today?

I think that Afrocentrism is very, very important and relevant today. When I went on a trip to Germany, I was supposed to go over there to train educators on how to start a mentoring program. Initially I didn't know anything about Heidelberg, Germany, where I was going. I had to embrace that culture and learn all that I could before I went. Then I could fit in during the weeks that I lived there. When you are immersed in a new and different culture like that, you have to learn something. And then you pull out the best pieces that fit your perspective. So I am just thinking the same applies with Afrocentrism. You have to know, especially if you are teaching or raising minority children (whether they are children of color or children who are bilingual), how to appreciate and understand the richness another person brings to a certain situation. But you don't have to embrace everything.

For some families who have adopted children of color, it can be uncomfortable to segue into a community of color, specifically the black community, especially if they [the families] don't have a reference point. What tangible things can these families do to make this transition easier or less threatening to them?

First of all, people have to be comfortable with who they are and their circumstance. Then I would say that they should move slowly but yet intentionally into social settings in these communities. Sociologist James Comer says start with the social. Get to know people, get to know their style, and then you can push into education—the teaching, the learning, and the history of the way people live. When I say "social" I mean church activities can be social, whether people are Christian or Jewish, et cetera. The goal is to push into social situations where you are going to be easily accepted. Outings and picnics are also good social settings to participate in to help break the ice, so to speak. Then a person can move to the education or historical background of another person and get to the root of what that person is feeling.

You attended Howard University in Washington, D.C., which is a historically black college. Did you choose to attend a [historically black college] as a way to embrace your racial and ethnic identity?

I did not attend Howard University because it was a historically black college. I attended Howard because I lived in the District of Columbia and could not afford another school. I gained much from Howard University. I gained my self-respect! Howard validated my worth in a major way. I learned that it was okay to have hair that was different, hips that were wide, and it was okay to wear size 9½ shoes. Howard made me read, explore, question, and create.

How did you make the transition from Howard University to University of Maryland, where you completed your graduate work?

I received my bachelor's and master's degrees from Howard University. One of my professors there, who later became a very, very good mentor of mine, who has written outstanding books in black literature, told me that if I stayed at Howard, I was playing it safe and comfortable and that if I was going to work on a Ph.D., then I would need to reach out and go to a different university.

I was accepted to the University of Maryland and began my Ph.D. program in 1989. It took me about eight years to earn my doctorate. When I first started taking classes there, I was in class with *all* Caucasian women. (Back in the day at the University of Maryland, there were not a lot of people who looked like you if you were black.) And I remember one day I was sitting there, and I was wearing a red "go-go" hat, which is tall cap that was worn in the 1970s. The professor asked a question about race, and I almost slid in my chair because I was listening to some of the white students describe black folk based on stereotypical images they saw on TV. In class some of the white students would stare at me and whisper to each other about me. Back then many black students at the University of Maryland dressed in bright colors, which was considered risqué compared to the white students, who wore more conservative clothing. I already felt out of place and different. After class that day I went home and cried and cried and wanted to drop out of the program because of how uncomfortable I felt. Perhaps that is why it took me so many years to get through my program, because so many times I had thought about dropping out. However, during my program I met a Caucasian woman who became an advocate for me. She was an outstanding professor. I also found myself reading more of Dr. Martin Luther King Jr.'s speeches. And right away he became my favorite speechwriter because so much of what he said, he followed up with critical action. That was such a life-changing piece for me. In fact Dr. King's words and actions became a driving force that helped me get through my doctorate work.

I remember [that] after finishing my doctorate I was promoted to principal. I called my mentor saying, "You know I am having a hard time making the transition into the principalship because the writing of a principal is so technical; it is not therapeutic, and it is not emancipatory." But the writing that I did all of those years, trying to share myself hermeneutically as a black educator working with black girls, which was my topic of study, was so rich. So much came out of that experience.

With all of your many accomplishments and ups and downs over the years, who is Lora Kay today?

I am very comfortable in saying that I am an African American woman who has been a single parent for about twenty years and who has struggled like most. I used to think that the struggle was a minority situation. But it is not. Women struggle all the time across race spectrums. So I am an African American woman who struggled educationally and economically. I struggled with my own physical demeanor because I am tall. My features are definitely African. In addition I would say that I am very, very family focused, family oriented. I think that is because I was a home economist first. One of the things that I will say is that I am a person who has made many mistakes but has grown from those mistakes and am very happy about that. I have been married twice. Now I am in a place in my life where I am not interested in marrying because I feel like I have so many other things that I want to do.

In addition I continue to do community service. I am working at the charter school in Washington, D.C., and devoted to my family. My grandmother raised me. It was very special. It was a rich situation where you got to know why people were hungry, why people had to work, why people had to travel—where we could go, where we couldn't go in the city, why education was important—and you got the push and the support. My family, we weren't poor but we weren't middle class. There have constantly been times where I have gained over the years an appreciation for life, for family, for education, for work, and for people of all racial and ethnic backgrounds.

You were instrumental in developing a program that helped instill in young black girls a sense of self-worth. Could you talk about that program? I think black and biracial transracial adoptee adolescents especially can benefit from the lessons taught through this program. So many of us struggle with embracing our bodies and our hair.

When I was serving as the principal at Kettering Middle School, your brother, Chris, and I would talk all the time about the students and their potential. I remember Chris saying, "This student should be in the talented and gifted program, but she doesn't want to be because the talented and gifted program has mostly white students in it." So I started a club and had a group of these girls come and meet with me one hour a day. I was going to take them out of home economics or whatever class they were in, and we were going to talk and have sessions in my office. There were about twelve girls in the group. They would pull up chairs around my conference table, or sometimes they would be sitting on my floor. So at the end of the year I said to them that we were going to have this activity for my "dozen roses," [as] I used to call them. "You are like roses," I told them. "You are beautiful. You are blooming." Some of the things we did in these sessions [she called the program the Rose Court] was we talked about racism and ethnicity. We talked about everything. We talked about homework and why it is important to go to college, these kinds of things. Now how empowering is that when you are having that kind of conversation with the principal of the school?

Well, the next year you would not believe: parents were calling me and asking me, "What is this Rose Court you did? Can I get my child in the program?" I said, "Ma'am, it was just a small focus group. It was not anything big." Do you know, that next year I ended up with about eighty-nine girls? So I asked the kids if they were willing to meet after school. They said, "Oh, yes!" The parents were very supportive. They gave their kids permission to stay after school and then when it was over have them ride the school's activity bus home. The following year the numbers grew even more. At that point I needed to use a microphone to talk with them. I needed more help. We ended up with parents, mothers, and women becoming a huge part of it. We structured the program and broke into small groups of about ten to fifteen girls; we had at least five or six moms in the cafeteria running this event. Mind you, this was at the end of the school day at 3:30 P.M. Parents would take off work to help out with this program. We talked about sexual activity and what that means. We had nurses coming to our events. We focused on good nutrition and wellness. Bullying was a huge topic. We were dealing with bullying years ago. For thirteen years we did this!

I took the program seriously. I took attendance and monitored closely how many of the activities each student attended—and they were required to attend the majority of them. They had to participate in four of the five activities that year or close to ten activities, depending on how many we had that year. One activity, for example, was a field trip to Hampton University in Virginia; another one was a field trip to Spelman College in Atlanta, Georgia. [Both are historically black colleges.]

If you completed everything and wrote a detailed journal—and keep in mind that I was making this stuff up as I was going along—if you did that, then at the end of the year you would be eligible to participate in the cotillion. And people were saying, "What is a cotillion?" That's why I say, know your roots. I would explain to them that a cotillion was a formal dance and acknowledgment from the Old South.[2] So I brought out old articles about black girls at a cotillion. I showed them pictures of black girls wearing the formal attire, white gowns. When I did the cotillion for our girls at Kettering Middle School, they had to be escorted in by a male role model. It could be a father or a male teacher. We had the cotillion at a nice, large place. There was a procession when you came in. There were five hundred to a thousand people in attendance, and we served a sit-down dinner for the guests and the participants. When the girls came in, the best thing is, I was describing them and not focusing on, Oh, she has on a pretty nice white gown, et cetera. I was focusing on: "This is Rhonda. She is a 4.0 student. She loves music and art. She is planning to go to Roosevelt High School. She is going to major in—." Those are the kinds of things that I focused on. Parents and family members were blushing and taking pictures and videotaping.

This program became so popular and relevant to the students and parents that I even had a superintendent call me and say, "Are you doing the same thing for the boys? We don't want to get into any trouble here." And I said, "Oh, yes, we are—we have a little boys' group here too." I had to actually send him documentation. That is what your brother, Chris, worked with; the group called themselves the Gentlemen's Association.

There were about five or six black male teachers that worked with him and a couple of Caucasian teachers.

I really think to improve the self-esteem of specifically black females, they have to be connected to something positive. If you don't have Girl Scouts, there needs to be a teen club, a club that is all about them. We even had white girls trying to get into the club at Kettering Middle School. That kind of got touchy. My area superintendent called me and asked me, "What are you going to do with some of these parents who want their white students to get into the club?" I told her, "Well, then, they can come in too." As I conveyed to my superintendent, the conversation was not going to change. It's about girls hitting that ceiling, feeling good about themselves, no matter what their race, ethnicity, or religion. It's about knowing who they are, feeling good about them[selves], having some social activity, and learning about each other. Some of the retreats and workshops we had were amazing.

It was a very positive experience for me too. I was recently contacted through e-mail by one of my "roses." She is in her forties and has three children. She asked me, "Do you remember me? I am one of your old roses, and I want to start this program in my church." I had another girl from Fairfax County in Virginia who is a teacher over there and asked also, "Do you remember me? I want to start the Rose Court program at my school." So I would send a lot of links to them and others who were interested in learning more on how we developed and organized the program, including . . . the literature we used, et cetera, as a way to help them establish their program.

Also I did have biracial girls in the Rose Court, and it really helped them. I had one girl, for example, who looked Caucasian, but her father was dark skinned and from Africa, and her mom was Caucasian. Pretty much no one knew before the cotillion. Then her father escorted her in. And of course I knew because I had parent conferences with her parents. The next year, as an eighth-grader, this young girl was a new person. She was very proud of the fact that her father was African. Before she kept it quiet, on the "down low," pretty much. Participating in the cotillion was a big step for her. But we had other cross-racial cases like that, where girls blended and learned a lot from each other.

Thank you for sharing that. I think all families, including our transracial adoptive families, can learn from something like the

Rose Court program you spearheaded. What advice can you give to today's generation of parents who are raising black children or children of color on how to prepare them to thrive educationally and maintain good self-worth?

Parenting is a growth experience. I doubt if any parent is perfect— but hopefully all parents can grow to be courageous caregivers who care about themselves, their children, and the world. Parents should model honesty, introspection, self-love, global thinking, literacy, and lifelong learning.

Finally, what do you see as the role of educators in addressing the needs of children in the twenty-first century?

The educator's role is to model diversity, teach children to love themselves and respect others, expose children to the world while promoting appreciation for humankind, ensure technological experiences, promote critical thinking, and to close the gaps (i.e., achievement, access, equity).

I so enjoyed spending time with you! Thank you!

CHESTER JACKSON
Professional Adoption Worker and Adoptive Father
INTERVIEWED BY TELEPHONE, JANUARY 14, 2013

Chester, it is wonderful to talk with you. I want to jump in and ask you how you chose adoption as a means to build your family.

On some level I think that adoption chose me. To give you some background, I was born here in New York City. When I was about five days old, I went home with a woman who was not my birth mother. I didn't discover that little piece of information until I was about thirty-two years old. That would play a big part in the whole adoption journey for me.

As an adoptee I am curious how you worked that out in your own heart and mind.

It was an incredible revelation to me and quite a relief. I knew that in my family there was something wrong or something that was not quite a fit for me. In my family we did not discuss adoption information.

But I knew that there was something different about me as early as I had memory. As I got older and started asking questions that kids ask, like, "How come I don't look like this person or that person?" I found out information. For instance I had an older brother and he would tell me stories. One of his favorite stories that he liked to tell is that Mom found me in the trash. So when I approached her about it, I never got an answer that said what I was saying was ridiculous or not true. Instead I always got this skirted answer that was never quite satisfying.

Let me fast-forward. I am going through my life doing what I am doing. One of the things that I discovered early on is that my role in life was to make my mother's life *happy*. My brother on the other hand was very good at being bad, and I was very good at being good. So that was my role. I didn't do anything in my mind that I thought would bring shame or embarrassment to her. So I went through this whole childhood of mine as a "good kid," but in reality I was simply a robot. I did what I was told to do. I didn't think. I didn't make any choices or decisions. Anything that had the possibility of being wrong I simply didn't do. If it was the wrong choice or the wrong thing to say or the wrong direction to go, I didn't do [it]. I waited for my mother to tell me what I needed to know or do.

So I am going through life kind of stilted and feeling a little weird because I am living in my own bubble. As life would happen, I got hurt in junior high school. That took me off the scene for a while. I broke my hip and I was hospitalized through a series of unfortunate events for a number of years. That was important because it isolated me from my peer group and from all of the things that would be a part of a normal kind of adolescence.

I get into high school finally, and I'm going through high school, and I decided to go to John Jay College of Criminal Justice in New York because I wanted to be a lawyer. I don't remember ever *wanting* to become a lawyer; I was just told that is what I wanted to do. So that is what I "wanted" to do. At John Jay I had my adolescence. I had my period of rebellion. I like to tell people that I basically lost my mind. And I did. But I met some people there that were key people in my life and continue to be my friends today. One of my friends during that time was Pat O'Brien, who is the executive director now of You Gotta Believe, the agency I work for. After graduation we went about our lives and kept in touch periodically. Somewhere around 1990, Pat called me and said, "Chester, I have this job that I think would be great for you." He told me that he worked at this adoption agency, and if I came on board, I would get to interact with a wide range of people and get to mentor kids. I didn't know anything about adoption agencies and didn't have any interest in that. But, again, I was just kind of floating along on a breeze so I thought that this was as good a thing as any. So I went for the interview. After my interview I knew that I did not get the job. I went back and told Pat that there was no way that I was going to be hired. He told me not to worry about it. It turned out that Pat convinced the person who interviewed me that I was the right person for the job. So I got the job.

If you can picture it, I am now working at this adoption agency that places older kids. Back in those days "older" kids were eight years of age. This was all new to me in terms of kids, social work, et cetera. My function then was to go out and meet the kids and do interviews and videos with them. Then I would go back to the agency, and I would introduce the information that we had to the prospective adoptive families. Basically I was the broker, essentially the go-between between the kids and the families. I had some success with that partly because I'm an amenable kind of guy. I did that for six years. As I got more and more involved in the agency and as the kids got older, something miraculous happened. . . .

Somewhere between 1991 and 1992 my wife and I were going on a trip to Canada. In those days you didn't need a passport. You just needed your birth certificate, driver's license, or your voter's registration card to get in and out of Canada. I knew that I had my birth certificate, which I planned to use. Two days before the trip, when I decided to pull out my birth certificate, I couldn't find it. Finally, I told my wife that I would go to the Bureau of Vital Statistics and get a copy, and then we would get on a plane the next day and life would be good.

So I go down to the Bureau of Vital Statistics. I will never forget. I get to the window after waiting a long time in line. I told the lady at the window that I needed a copy of my birth certificate and that my name was Chester Jackson. She did her thing on the computer and then asked me where I was born. I told her. Suddenly she got this strange look on her face. And then she informed me that I was not in the system. I asked her, "What do you mean I'm not in the system?" She pulled me closer to the glass and said, "Go over to the phone booth. Call your mother and ask her what name is on your birth certificate." Where a lot of people would have had a tantrum right there, me being a robot said, "Oh, okay." So I went over to the phone and called my mother up. And I said to her, "I'm down here by the statistics and they can't find me. So they told me to ask you what name is on my birth certificate." I am waiting for her to say the usual—"What are you talking about? That is ridiculous." And what I got instead was a long pause. I'm thinking that this should not be a complicated question. This will give you a sense of my mother, who I loved dearly of course. She then said to me, "Tell her to look under 'D. Mitchell.'" Now it was my turn to pause, and I asked her who D. Mitchell was. And she said, "Oh, it doesn't matter because she is dead now." So I go back to the window. I gave the lady the name D. Mitchell. She punched in the name in her computer and there it was. I didn't have any identification, so she couldn't give me a copy of the birth certificate. But she did give me this new revelation.

To give you a sense of where my mind was at that time, even with this new revelation and me working at an adoption agency, I did not connect the dots that I was adopted. I went back home and told my wife about what happened. I told her that it was ridiculous, and something didn't seem right but that they told me that I could use my voter registration card instead, so I was going to use that. We go off to Canada. My wife is giddy with excitement and tells me, "I bet you were adopted!"

I couldn't fathom that I was adopted. Why wouldn't my mother tell me long before I was thirty-plus years of age?

After my wife and I came back, I sat down with my mother. I can still see her lounging on the bed, smoking a cigarette. She asked me about our trip. We talked. Then she took a long drag on her cigarette and handed me an envelope. I open it up and it was my original birth certificate. The first thing I noticed as I looked at it was that my mom's name was not anywhere on it. It was a shock for me. Now in that moment it was everything I could do not to sing with joy. Because in that moment I realized that *this is it! This is what has been wrong with this picture my entire life. All of this time I was thinking it was me, and it was them.*

Even in my elation, and it was like a load was lifted off my back, I looked at my mom and in her eyes there was such pain, such anguish, and such fear that I immediately went into my thought pattern that this is my mom and nothing hurts her. I then explained to her that my birth certificate was only a piece of paper. It didn't matter et cetera. I began to push my own feelings down. I did however feel an incredible amount of relief.

Over the following months my mom and I did touch on the issue here and there because she never really liked to have conversations of this sort. But somewhere down the line we had a direct discussion about my adoption. I asked my mom if it would have been easier to deal with if we got this out in the open earlier. She said to me basically that she was afraid to tell me that I was adopted. She didn't think that I would love her and that she feared somebody would come and take me away. I remember clearly [that] she then said to me in her most serious mommy tone, "I wished that I would have gone to my grave before you found this out." That was probably the most devastating piece in the whole situation.

How did those words impact your person, psychologically speaking?

When my mom said that to me, it was not so much devastating to the man standing before her as it was to the little boy, the little toddler in me, who was asking the greatest person in the world for help, and they are saying that they wish that they could die without giving you *any* help. That is what I felt. And in that moment I realized that, even though there are all these platitudes that folks say—and I am sure there is some truth to them—the bottom line for me as that kid was that this was not about me. This was about a grown person making a decision about my life without regard to what effect that would have on me. That turned my emotions into anger. I never gave a hint or shared with my mother, who is now deceased, that part of my emotions. "Pissed off" doesn't even describe it. I can't even explain to you how angry that made me.

It is interesting in the adoption world the word *relinquishment* is often used to describe when a child has been taken from his or her biological parent and placed in another home. To me the severing of one's connection with their biological mother and father does not feel like relinquishment. It feels like *abandonment*. I don't know how you dress up that feeling to make it seem more palatable. The feeling of abandonment continues to affect me in my adult life. Anytime I go through transitions, the little girl in me cries out, "Am I going to be okay?" It comes from the feeling of knowing what you touched on, that adults made decisions on my behalf as a child without necessarily considering the effect those decisions would have on me or even asking me what I thought, how I felt, and how those actions would change my trajectory lifelong. In reference to your experience in trying to get your birth certificate, still today I do not have access to my original birth certificate. It's crazy.

Yes. I understand. There was a time for me that big changes, anything that sounded like criticism, I most definitely could not handle. I remember my mother and some of my relatives would tell me that I was "too sensitive," because I would feel things and be hurt by things that weren't necessarily meant to be hurtful in their opinion.

For the first probably four years I was at Downey Side for Youth, the adoption agency I worked at before where I am now, things went pretty well in the beginning. Then, as I got more involved with the kids and got to know them as people and what their journeys were like, it got harder for me to be detached. It got harder for me not to personalize how prospective families responded to these kids. At that point I was not doing parent training, but I was in the room when parent training was conducted, and I met with prospective parents participating in the training. I remember particularly being very intolerant of the folks that came forward for children that we *didn't* have. These folks were asking for babies. This was an older child agency. I just didn't have any tolerance for that question. I stated to them with much irritation, "Please, go someplace that does that!" My thinking was that is about you. That is not about what the need is. The need is, there are all of these children of this age, and here they are, and you are telling me about some child that may or may not exist. I was almost a mess when it came to dealing with that kind of issue. That was where I was in that period. Unfortunately my attitude and how I expressed it . . . got me in trouble at different times along my career. The good news is that I have come a long way since then. Thank God for that.

At another place in my career I was a recruiter. My job was to convince people to adopt, to make it possible. Not at all did I feel that. I didn't want to convince people. I wanted to tell people that if I could talk you out of it, then you need to go away. So there I was, this angry middle-aged man. I had a real hard time separating my professional life from my personal feelings. It made it difficult for me to relate to families and to have an intelligent conversation around the subject of adoption without getting visibly emotional. This was the person that I was at that point.

During that same time my wife and I were talking about adoption because neither one of us came from large families or families that had a lot of kids. But we didn't have the need to have a little baby. In fact, if we could avoid that, that was certainly our plan. We decided that while I was working at the agency I would pay serious attention to the adoption piece, which I did. Like a lot of people, though, I thought that an "older kid" was six years old or seven or eight.

So I'm doing my job at the agency, meeting and interviewing kids. This is in the early 1990s. And I met this young man named Robert who was sixteen years old. Everybody at the agency loved him, including me. The minute I met him, he reminded me of me and all of the things that drive me crazy about me. I wasn't thinking about that at the time, but reflecting back on it, he was like me in foster care, even though I had never been in foster care. I could see so much of myself in him that I was immediately drawn to him. At the time none of that thought process was happening on a conscious level. This kid was a great kid and wanted to be adopted. He was sixteen years old, six feet tall, and three hundred pounds. He was this huge teddy bear. I was determined to find this kid a home. Sadly we had a really hard time connecting him with potential parents because they were intimidated by him.

One day after many frustrations I went home and said, "Honey, look who I found." I told my wife what a wonderful kid he was and shared his story with her. The long and short of it was that we decided to move forward with Robert. We set up a visit where he lived in a group home. It turned out that the week that we were going out to visit Robert, my wife found out that she was pregnant. Yet we went to the group home and sat with Robert outside and chatted. One of the last things I told him was that my wife was pregnant. We asked him how he felt about that and assured him that if he was okay with it, we would be okay with it as well. After talking with Robert we decided—which again was a wonderful lesson for me in later years—that we were going to visit with him and have him come to our house every weekend and every break until the baby was born. It was a long, long time. I tell families now not to do it the way we did. It does not help anything. It is not real life. You are not going to learn anything about your child until they move in.

As it turned out, as my wife got more and more pregnant, she wanted us out of the house. So Robert and I had a great time spending time together. I would pick him up; we would go to the movies. We would go to the car show. We would go to the park. Time passed and time passed, and then our biological son, Brandon, was born. At that same time Robert moved in. It so happened that Robert has a sister named Ebony, who was fourteen years old. She was living in a foster care home in the Bronx. Since she was Robert's sister, it was natural that my wife and I would visit with her and have her over to our house. However, for Ebony adoption was not on her radar. She actually said in later years that she fully expected the whole adoption situation with Robert to dissolve because that was what his pattern was for a long time: people would love him from the beginning, and then his behaviors got out of hand and it all ended badly. So she wasn't going to sign on for that. But as it turns out Ebony eventually did move in with us. So we went from zero kids to two teenagers and a baby in a span of a year.

What did you tell them about what adoption meant to you and for them?

Because I worked at an agency where everybody built their families through adoption, adoption made sense to me. My wife and I did not look at adoption as a bad thing or a secretive, shameful act. Adoption was simply how these two children came into our home and into our lives. That is really what my underlying message to all of the prospective families and people out there is: that adoption is just the way that children come into our lives. It's like their hair color and eye color and how tall they were when they came into the home—that is just how they are. There is no power in that. It always drove me mad when people would want to whisper the word *adoption* and say it like it should be something shameful like, "I don't think they can handle it." That is the adults' issue, not the kids'. The kids are going to handle it the way we handle it. If we dissolve into tears every time they mention their birth family or anything that reminds them that they were not born of them, then of course these kids are going to have some reaction to that. Adoption is just how it is. It is a circumstance. That is how children came into our lives. And we are glad we could do it.

So were you able to listen to your children talk about their life with their biological family members?

Yes, absolutely. One of the advantages of adopting older kids—now I am sounding like I am trying to sell you on older kids—is that we don't have to fill in those blanks for them. In our case our children have aunts and uncles and cousins living in the Bronx that were a part of their lives. I remember when Ebony first moved in especially—Robert was the kid that I wanted. Ebony was the child that I needed. Robert, like I said, was the clone of me. I wouldn't have learned anything from parenting him. He did what I told him to do, and when I was upset he calmed right down. There was no challenge there. So he was the kid that I definitely wanted. I loved him "from jump." But Ebony was the child that I needed. She was the one that was going to turn me into a parent and make me do the stuff that parents need to do in order to be parents.

Seeing that I am not a parent, please help me. What is it that "parents need to do"?

I think that parents need to understand that our responsibility, once we decide that this is the child that we are claiming, that we are responsible for, is to do everything in our power to make their life better. Not just their life and their circumstance but their *internal* life, i.e., their spiritual and emotional life, as they walk in this world. Because we are saying, "I 'gotch' you. I am going to take care of you." And taking care of "me" is more than keeping me fed and clothed and having a roof over my head. Taking care of me is when I say, "I hurt here, and I don't know why." Taking care of me means you being strong enough to say, "Let me help you try to find out why." As opposed to being so afraid that we have to pretend that the biggest thing in both of our lives never happened.

One of the beautiful things about adopting older kids is that you don't have to have that pretense I just talked about. That is what drives me so crazy about folks that are adamant about needing to adopt babies. Of course babies need homes. I understand that. However, so often it is the parents' way of pretending that this, adoption, didn't happen. That we are starting from scratch. That is detrimental not only to the child but to you as the parent. Because whatever you feel about the fact that you didn't give birth to this child, you are going to transmit that to the child through every pore in your body. You know, from the things that you cry about to the way that you touch him to the things that you say. Now the only thing that you are not going to transmit to this child is that it is your issue, not theirs. Kids are going to absorb it. And that's 100 percent about the messages that we as parents give to our kids. I think that we as parents have to provide an environment where our kids can be safe 100 percent—and that's physically safe, emotionally safe, safe to explore questions that they may have about their circumstances. If these kids cannot explore these things in their own homes, then where are they going to get that?

In later years I have come to appreciate the power and the depth of infertility. When I first started in this business, my thoughts were, to those who were struggling with infertility and wanting to adopt a child, "Get over it and move on." I see this issue differently now. Largely because my birth children have brought to me a different kind of joy, I have a good deal of more empathy for folks who are dealing with fertility issues. My advice now to parents, years later, is "Please deal with this, the pain of it. This is not going to go away. You need to sort it out, or when this actual child comes, he or she is going to be the total antithesis of this imaginary child you have in your mind."

How does a parent sort these feelings out?

They are, in my opinion, going to need to separate their stuff from their kids' stuff because these kids are going to need their parents 100 percent. It's a tough nut to sell. We get folks at our agency sometimes who are deep into the miseries of infertility. And until they get to a place where they can accept that they are going to become a parent through adoption, and parenting is ultimately their goal, it will be extremely difficult for them as they parent. Their misplaced emotions will have an impact on their child. Once you get folks to the place I'm talking about, then how they become a parent becomes less and less relevant. Then it becomes more about the young person, the child actually in front of you. And that is when the parent is in a place where they can do some good for the young person and themselves. The bottom line is if you, as the parent, aren't taking care of yourself, if you are emotionally a wreck, that does not help your kid to become healthy, wealthy, and wise.

How should parents go about advocating for their kids, particularly their adolescents? I ask that because when I was a teenager, I was molested by an adult that was respected in the community. My parents were shocked emotionally and struggled to know how to help me. For me I felt shame. But I also felt that my family did not advocate for me. How do parents learn how to give that hurt child what she needs?

The first piece of it, I think, is that we as child and family professionals need to be realistic about what we can train people to do. The reality is, even if you spend every day for six hours over a two-year period with a family, you are only going to see what they show you. And as adults we can have so many layers of control, so many things piled on top of it so we don't feel, we don't think about, we don't experience, we don't touch on the places where it hurts. That's why I think that, in terms of parent preparation, the very best thing that professionals can do is to help parents touch those places within themselves. I am not necessarily talking about it in a therapeutic kind of way but in a way where we convey to the parent that this is what you are going to have to deal with, because that child, whether the child is a teenager or an infant, is going to put you, the parent, in touch with all of your darkest fears and pains. In our agency when it involves a teenager, we tell parents, "Look, if you are looking for a honeymoon when you bring your child home, forget it. Forget a honeymoon—you don't want a honeymoon anyway. You want to know exactly the areas where this young person needs your help." And every single behavior is going to be a flag saying, "Can you help me here?" If they lie, if they steal, if they are promiscuous—every single behavior is going to be an indicator that this is an area where they need your help. Can you handle it as a parent?

One of the things we ask folk as they come through our processes is, "Why are you here?" And you know what people say? "I am here because I love children. I am here because I have a calling. I am here because my childhood was so great that I want to share. Or I am here because my childhood was so bad, and I don't want any other child to have to go through that." There are all of these platitudes, all of these politically correct things people say. And it is not . . . that there isn't some kernel of truth in what they are saying. But the reality is that is not what brings people out. Because if that was the case, our agency would have these beautiful shows like the Dave Thomas production, *Home for the Holidays*. We would have classrooms full of thirty thousand people, because most people have those sentiments. That is not what motivates people to take time out of their lives, to open up their lives to strangers and all of the things they know are going to come down. What motivates folks to do that is deeply individual. As an example, my daughter Ebony is one of the most incredible advocates that I have ever seen, especially for her own children. A part of that is because as a teenager the world was an unsafe place for her.

Ebony was constantly ready to defend—not so much physically because she is not a fighter in that way. But I mean on things where I would feel hurt; she would feel anger and respond to that. If you can imagine, Ebony was fourteen years old when she moved in with these people who did not know anything about parenting, had kids, and were stressed! My craziness was [that] I thought my job as a child was to be perfect. So anytime my kids did anything that resembled imperfection, that was like flipping me the bird. It just inspired such rage in me. It wasn't about the behavior at all. It was about "this is what you think of me?" The bottom line in all of this is that it made for a very difficult decade *for me*. Ebony was who she was. For a decade we went back and forth. However, those things that drove me crazy as her father, I later understood that these were the things that would make Ebony an independent and successful woman. It just doesn't work when you are fourteen years old and have a parent that doesn't understand [that] standing up for yourself is good. You want her to be an advocate. You want her to be able to stand up to adults. We, as her parents, just needed to shave the edges off and get her to a place where she didn't have to tell her boss to drop dead. That is essentially what we did for her, shave off the edges. She is still who she is. The blessing in this is that there were definitely values and lessons that Ebony learned from my wife. We were amazed that Ebony took in any of it. There was no indication in the years that she lived with us that she was getting any of what we were teaching her.

I am speaking from the perspective of being an African American woman who was raised in a white home. I am also speaking for other transracial adoptees raised in white homes and living in predominately white communities. How do African American transracial adoptees deal with hair and skin issues, abandonment issues, shame, trying to be perfect, not fitting in, et cetera? How do they learn to balance all of these complex issues intelligently and effectively?

It is very difficult. I think more universal than that, we as adoptive parents have to first deal with the fact that this child was not born to me. It is not good or bad. It is just different. The reality is that we have to embrace that. What that means is that they were not born to me; they had a life before me. And anything that was a part of their lives is a part of my life. Just like when you get married, you marry your husband or your wife. You have a mother-in-law, a sister-in-law, this, that, and the other. It is all a part of you. That is why this idea that "this never happened" is so detrimental. We can't deal with anything if we can't deal with the biggest thing in our life. The biggest thing in our life is that this child was not born to me. Sometimes we hear the question "Should we be placing black children into white homes?" My personal opinion is that, if the choice is between a family and no family, then they need a family because no *system* is going to do anything that resembles good for any kid. I'd rather see a kid struggle like you are struggling, Rhonda, than to spend ten years in somebody's foster care system. *That is truly hell. That is truly hell.*

Some of the stories that you hear from these ten-year-olds, fifteen-year-olds, and twenty-year-olds are unbelievable things that happened to them *after* they got into foster care. We, the professionals, take them out of their birth families to protect them and put them in danger, day after day after day. What happens when you are in foster care for any length of time is that you lose your citizenship; you lose a piece of your humanity. You become like furniture. You become like property. People move you around as if you are not human. Yes, we definitely need to be helping folks to understand that, if you are going to adopt transracially or internationally, you need to embrace where these children come from. There are things that the adoptive parent is not going to be equipped to deal with. That is the bottom line. I remember at the Downy Side Agency, again this was some time ago, in one of the classes that we required folks who wanted to adopt transracially to take, we asked the question "Would you marry a person from another race?" And you sit around a room of folks, and it is amazing, in a controlled environment like that, you can see how difficult [it is] just *thinking* about it and *imagining* what would that be like, to be married to someone of another race. It is fascinating to see how people struggle with that question. And then you say to them that I am going to bring a child to you and you're going to be this child's parent. If you are going to adopt transracially, or you already have, you have to get comfortable with the fact that your child comes from wherever they come from. And if that doesn't have anything to do with you, then you need to find a way to make that bridge for them because they are going to need that information. Sometimes potential and adoptive parents will say that they are willing to talk about race and adoption and that they have no issues with where their child comes from. But the fact that there is no representation of their child's background in these parents' lives speaks volumes to these kids. It is a huge thing. Even the best people with the greatest hearts are going to have trouble in this area of transracial adoption. This is the world that we live in.

Especially as you are raising kids, kids are looking to you for everything as their parent. And then of course they reach that point where you don't know anything. One thing that they know for sure is that "I am not you!" Everything gets intensified. I think that it is so important, especially if we adopt children as infants, that we have to get comfortable with everything that makes up this child. And whether it is their hair or where they are from, we have to acknowledge the fact that these things need to be addressed. There is no pretending that it didn't happen because everybody around you is not on the same page as you are as the adopted child.

It is like informal adoption, particularly as it relates to me. My adoptive mother (the woman that raised me) was my biological mother's best friend. It sounds like a country western song. The rest of the story is that my adoptive mother's husband might actually be my biological father. This was an open secret that of course everybody in the family knew except for me. My brother—who is five years older than me and another informally adopted kid, totally unrelated to me and totally unrelated to them—one day comes home, and my mother says to him, "This is your brother." The story that my mother found me in the trash made a lot of sense to him. For a five-year-old, that is as good an explanation as any. I also had an aunt who was a domestic worker at that time and would bring home random stuff, like a chair, a coat, a rug, et cetera. You can see how my mother's story made sense to my brother.

What I wished would have happened, instead of my adoptive mother saying to family members that she found me in the trash, was that she would have taken the opportunity to instead broach my adoption story truthfully. I wanted to say to her, "Mom, if you take the shame out of adoption by being able to say the word without bursting out into tears or turning it into something big and dramatic, then it would have been normalized for me." But I couldn't say that to her because I didn't think that she could handle it, even years later.

How would you have wanted your mom to explain adoption you?

She could have explained it in an age-appropriate way that would have made sense for me. If I asked her at seven, she could have responded to that question one way; and if I asked her at age nine, she could have said it another way; and if I asked her at twelve, she could have said it another way. I wasn't looking for the cold hard facts. I would have been able to put the pieces together. And as we both got older and matured, I am sure that we would have learned how to then have an intelligent conversation about adoption. Like I said earlier, generally speaking, one can only talk about this issue when the adoptive parent is *comfortable* with the fact that while they didn't give birth to a given child, or conceive him, that does not make the adoptive parent any less of a mother or a father. The child belongs to the adoptive parent(s). And the way that the child came to the parent(s) was through adoption, formal or informal. So in my case, since my biological mother couldn't take care of me, my adoptive mother chose to adopt me, which is a wonderful loving act.

I am just going to put this next question out there. Do black people adopt formally?

My wife and I adopted two of our kids formally, although my wife is not African American; she is [of] Swiss [heritage]. Also, from an agency perspective, the answer is yes. Many of the folks that come through our agency are, first of all, people of color. Second of all they are people that have a connection to the youngster that they are interested in adopting. So at our agency we do have a fair share of social workers, therapists, teachers, and bosses—people who knew a kid was in a tough situation and opened their home to them. The reason we push adoption per se as a legal procedure is because it is clean. It is clean in the sense that "I adopted you so you are my child." It is easy for all of us as grownups to relate to that. There are some situations where we advocate that, for this particular kid, formal adoption is not the way to go. An example is my son Bobby; he is the one that my wife and I have legal guardianship of. To give you some background, sometime after moving to Pennsylvania, we moved here to Pittsburgh—our son Brandon was in second grade, and our daughter Geneva was little. We lived in the suburbs in a predominately white community. Back when we first moved here, there was a family that we connected with who had a son named Bobby. Bobby was in the same grade as our son Brandon. We knew that the mother of this family had adopted Bobby, who also happened to be biracial. So Bobby was on my radar. As the years went on, Bobby's mother became ill. We learned about it.

In small communities everybody learns about everything. So my wife said to me that we needed to let Bobby's mother know that if she did not have a plan for Bobby, then we would plan for him. At that point I had understood that the first adoption my wife and I did was about me. It was something that I needed to do, and she went along with it 100 percent. I wasn't going to put her in a position again to ask her to make this kind of commitment, even though I was thinking all along that we needed to do this. So, thank God, she understood that and was on the same page as I was. We went to Bobby's mom and shared with her that we were adoptive parents as well and that we understood her situation and that if she did not have a plan for Bobby, that we would certainly be willing to take care of him.

As it turned out Bobby's mother did have a plan for him, which was a very good plan at the time. Bobby's babysitter, who had been his babysitter since he was eighteen months old, was going to take care of him. She essentially ran a day care business. Bobby's mother, who was a nurse, would drop him off at six in the morning and would come back at seven in the evening to pick him up. So Bobby would spend hours and hours with these folks, and they said, "Hey, we will take care of him." So I said to them that was a great plan. They had known him all of his life—literally. We had done everything that we needed to. We were off the hook. As Bobby's mother became sicker and sicker, she came to us one day and said to us that the family said that they could not take care of Bobby. So my wife and I said, "Well, of course, we will raise Bobby."

In the beginning of our discussion I said that adoption chose me. This has not only been the biggest thing in my life, this has been the meaning of my life. I have so many lessons that came to me through this experience. The loss that I feel is because I know it is a loss, but it is not like I would have chosen anything different. One of the stories that I love to tell is, at this point we went back to Brandon and Geneva, who were little, and told them about Bobby's situation and said to them that "Mommy and I are thinking about bringing Bobby into our home, and what do you think about it?" Brandon, who was Bobby's friend, wanted him to come in to our home. Geneva had a little look on her face. I said to her, "Honey, I just want it to be the right thing to take Bobby in." She said to me, "Daddy, how could it not be the right thing?"

That is beautiful.

It still makes me tear up. There is no greater lesson in life than sometimes you have to do things because it is the right thing to do. Who knows if it is the smart thing? It is just the right thing. And this is something that my wife and I can do because we have lived that situation. We can do this. So we went back to Bobby's mother and said certainly. She passed away that summer. And Bobby moved in with us. He was thirteen at the time, and now he is twenty-two years old. He just left, Rhonda, while we were talking, to go off to church. The point of all of this is to say that Bobby's mother didn't want an adoption. Now, she had adopted him, but part of her adopting him was that she wanted her name to continue. She didn't want him adopted again. Now she didn't tell us that in those words, but it was clear that us formally adopting Bobby was not her intention nor was it his intention. And we have had many conversations with Bobby over the years about this, and he doesn't want to be officially adopted but knows that we are his family. I say this to say that when we as adults claim children, the only thing that matters is our decision and theirs. When you are dealing with older kids, they have a decision on whether or not to move into your home. No kid is going to move into your home kicking and screaming. When they don't want to be in your home, then they are out of your home. We in our agency have to help parents understand that.

If you are having any doubts about whether you are a legitimate or authentic parent, then that is your stuff; that is not the kids' message to you. The kid might say to you, "You are not my real parent or you're not my real mommy." And, really, all that means is, "You didn't give birth to me!" And your answer to that needs to be, "I know. But I am still the one that is telling you that you need to be home by 10 P.M. et cetera." The point of it all is that we have to understand that kids are going to do what kids do. A part of that is using any weapon they can to test us as parents, to see where we are weak and where we are strong. And if you are, in this case, a foster kid who has been traumatized, it becomes life and death for the child to understand what does this adult do when they are at their weakest point? How do I get them there? How do I keep them there so that I can find out how safe I am in this environment? And that sometimes goes on for years.

That is intense. I think that mind-set from the perspective of someone like a foster care child who has been traumatized can go on into adulthood.

Absolutely!

I can speak for me. I think that piece that you talk about is something that I had to discover within me. I think that in my life it was "Let's achieve. Let's achieve. Let's achieve. Suck it up. Don't feel it." I empathized with others, but I didn't stop long enough to realize that the child in me had fear in her. I had felt abandoned over the years, even though I understood my life to be blessed. But at the same time [with] any major transition in my life, I tend to question my worth. Am I lovable? Am I a good child, a good person? Am I going to be okay?

Yes. One of the things that I like to help people get a handle on is, as children, as we try and figure out our place in the world and what works for us, some kids decide that achievement works. And so they do incredible things. They strive and they achieve. And we as parents love them and give them kudos. And then some kids go the very opposite way. It is the same energy. It is the same energy in their hearts that is driving them. The only thing that is different is the path that is in front of them. Some people pick and are chosen to achieve, and some people pick to buy into the other way.

What are the values that you and your wife teach your children?

Here is the thing about my wife. Now we have been married since 1988, and we knew each other a long time before that. One of the things that drew me to her is that she was—and still is—perhaps one of the most decent human beings I have ever met anywhere. I mean fundamentally. She loves people. She loves life. She is one of those people where she asks you how you are doing and she wants to hear it. She is just one of those incredible people where the world is a very wonderful place for her. When we first met each other, I was at a stage in my life that I call my "People Suck Days." I was in this funk. Individual people were okay, but as a collective group, people just sucked. I felt that there was no goodness in this universe. So when I met this person who actually honest to God believed to the core that life was good, I just could not stay away from her. I think that to some degree her mind-set is what has sustained us over all of these years. When it came to adoption, my wife knew that was what I needed to do, and she knew because it is her nature to care for me. She understands what I need. And I think on some level she knew that I needed to adopt even before I knew that I needed to do it. When she said yes and signed her name on the dotted line, she was all in. "All in" in adoption means that mothers bear the brunt of all of the angst, all of the anger of the child. Guys are almost always the good guys. Moms get it with both barrels. And my wife did not shy away from that. And we had some rocky patches because we are all human beings, and we have limits and things that we don't think we can take. But the most loving thing that my wife has done for me (even though she would not say it this way) is going along with me on this journey. I say to folks that if you have a partner that is willing to go on an adoption journey with you and be your partner in this, that is an amazing thing. That is a huge asset, and something that needs to be encouraged and protected. If you are someone who wants to adopt but does not have a partner, then certainly you need to find people in your life that are going to be there and are supportive of the *best* you.

I say this because adoption takes a lot of work. Parenting takes a lot of work. I don't think people come forward to abandon kids or to hurt kids. Rather I believe that people come forward and then their pain gets in the way. The pain seems so big that the only way to get rid of the pain is to get rid of what "caused" the pain, and that becomes the child. And unfortunately some of the people who love us are going to say things that are not openly supportive but what they think is the answer, like "If you were happy and cheerful before the child came, then obviously this kid is the problem." In a very loving way they say, "Look, you have done everything you could. Look at what you have gone through. Look at what you have invested. Look, nothing is helping. What is going to happen in ten years?" These are not bad people. These are people who love you, the parent. But they are giving you advice that is not supportive of you because that is not who you want to be. The pain is telling you yes, get this kid the heck out of here. But the reality is that this is not who you signed on to be. And if you are encouraged to let this happen, you are not going to be the same. Is it going to be the end of you? No, but a little piece of you is going to die. And that is not what you came forward to do. It is not surprising that some people may discourage you, because in their own way they love you. However, they didn't go to the adoption classes like you did. They don't know the kid like you do. All they know is your pain. They see you in pain. They want to see you get out of pain. That's why you need to find people who can say, "Yes, I know what you mean, but this too will pass."

What resources did you use as a family, or [do] you recommend as a professional, for adoptive families who are going through particularly patchy times?

Thank God for our family. I worked at a place where every day was like being with a support group. So many of us were, one, adoptive parents. Second, we have so many people on staff who are former kids of foster care. My daughter even worked for us for a period of time. We have people who are adopted. So when you came into our agency, you had all of this support, and it kind of unburdened you.

What is the piece that is missing in the adoption practice, in your opinion?

The piece that is missing in adoption is the understanding that adoption is forever. It has to be forever or it cannot work. Parenting is the fact that you have no choice. Your kid is your kid is your kid. And no matter what they are doing, they are never going to stop being your kid. The problem with adoption is that we, being the professionals, the system, let parents off the hook. It lets people think that you can do this halfway, that you can be a pseudoparent, that you can be a mentor, et cetera. What we call that is "commitment lite." If you are not committed, then you don't have to think of solutions. You don't have to do a thousand things. You can do five things and say, "I have done everything that I could do!" The reality is . . . you are saying . . . that "I have done everything that I am going to do, and it is over." Nobody would give you the grief they are going to give you if you were talking about your birth child.

So why are we still struggling in society to understand that adoption is legitimate and viable? Why do we make such a differentiation between forming a family biologically versus through adoption?

I don't know if it is the chicken or the egg. I don't know if we treat adoption as a second-class way of forming a family because it is not genetic, it is not biological. I don't know what came first. The one thing that I know for sure is that we are working at cross-purposes [in] trying to encourage *everyone* to adopt, because everyone doesn't want to adopt. Everyone doesn't need to adopt. Everyone doesn't want to be a parent. I think that we as a system need to focus more energy into *finding* those folks for whom this is a legitimate way of going. And of course there is the ugly side, where there are billions and billions of dollars tied into maintaining kids, keeping kids, and thinking of new and fancier ways [of] keeping kids in [foster] care longer. We can't deny that that is a piece of it as well. I definitely think that the very best thing [about] the foster care system, or at least those of us professionals dealing with helping people decide whether or not adoption is for them, is helping people get honest with themselves. It doesn't matter who the kid is or what you do, if in your heart of hearts, as a potential adoptive parent, this is not for you.

How do adults, particularly those of color, get through the adoption process, which as you know can be quite intimidating and invasive?

I am sure that a lot of folks don't want to recognize it, but whenever you talk to most adoption agencies about people of color, or even the people who have the tendency to do the best with the kids that are in the system, right now what they will tell you is we cannot find families of color willing to adopt. And the reason that they cannot find these families is because we set up a system that is designed to exclude people. It is designed to weed out people before we even get them in the door. What I tell people who are thinking about getting into this process is that there are a couple of realities that you have to deal with: One, you are not going to single-handedly change the system; two, you have to accept that this is the way it works. And one of the things that you have to figure out up front is, What agency are you going work with? If you call as a person off the street wanting information and they, the agency, treat you like trash, know it is not going to get any better when you have one of their kids. Simply put, you make a phone call. You like the way you are treated, then you take it to the next step. If the agency doesn't get back to you, or they treat you like a bother, or there is nobody who is available to talk with you about the adoption process because it is not their job, there is a message in all of that. That is what it is. If you look at the folks who have historically been the social workers who are doing the assessing, there is no wonder why you don't see many families of color adopting formally. The secret to any adoptions, especially teen adoptions, is you find somebody within an agency that has a connection to the kid who thinks that they are more than just a statistic. That is when your teachers come in, your social workers, your bosses, and your family members. The problem with the system is, "We have taken Johnny from that family so there is nobody in there that could be good enough to do this." It is not that the families are not there; it is that the system doesn't want them.

In New York City we are what is called a recruitment agency. We don't have children in our care that are not in families. So we don't have foster homes or residential treatment centers or group homes. When you make your money based on having kids in your care but not in a family, it is counterproductive to be thinking about putting them in families. The other piece is we come to the foster care system as consultants, and we say, "Hey, look, we can find a family for this kid." And what we want to do is look at the kid's record and determine who they know and who their family members are. The pushback that we get from the system is, "So right now you are telling us that we have had this kid in our care for ten years, and you are going to be able to do something that we haven't been able to do?" Rhonda, the truth of the matter is that the foster care system hasn't been looking for this kid to enter into a permanent home. Once you come into foster care, the clock stops for the child. The only clock the system is looking at is when you turn eighteen or twenty-one so that they can get rid of you. Nobody is looking to get you into a permanent home. . . . I know that institutions like to get us on the kick that if there are all these families out there, why don't they come forward? The reality is that we as a system don't want families to come forward.

That is a sad commentary on the state of the foster care system in America.

Here is a classic example of what I am talking about. I am working at an agency, and I am taking a kid from another agency that has worked with me for three years at that point. This is Ebony. Ebony gets pregnant as a teenager. Back in those days there wasn't quite the rush to finalization, so technically, even though she was living with us, she was still in foster care. There were cases where older kids moved into foster care, and it wasn't until two or three years down the road before there was any kind of finalization. So Ebony was not legally finalized, but she was pregnant and living with us. So I called up a social worker, someone who I had known for years and had placed other kids with. I say to this social worker that Ebony was pregnant. What do you think was the first thing that came out of her mouth? Now this is not an evil conniving person. This was a caring person who I had known for years at that point. And she had known Ebony and Robert even longer. The very first thing out of her mouth was, "Oh, my God, where is she going to live?" The *assumption* was that I was going to put her out. Now understand: these were not happy times. So the thought of putting her out was not the furthest thing from my mind. But what this social worker's statement did for me was that it infuriated me. I understood that if that were my biological child, nobody would say something like that. The lesson in that is that this was a woman who understood at the time what my talk was. This wasn't her thinking, "Chester is going to put her out." This is the reflex of the job. The girl gets pregnant, then she is out. Her behavior is "too extreme." I wouldn't even have had to say, "Come get her." All I would have had to do is agree with this social worker. That is the *danger* of foster care.

Wow! I was in foster care for two years. You would think that I was there even longer with the mind-set that I developed because of that experience. I had this internal mind-set that told me that, growing up, I had to make sure my legs were "sewn tight" so that I would not get pregnant and thrown out of my adoptive home. I knew that I needed to make sure that I completed elementary school, high school, and college because I had, again in my mind, "What would people think of me without these credentials? I am already black, and a foster care alumna, which to me, growing up, equated to a throwaway child. I am still working through the dark side of the foster care reality as an adult. And it was only two years in one placement for me.

But look at those two years. Those are the years when you are absorbing everything. Talk about magical thinking. These people are giants in your life and in your world. So, yeah, I am not surprised at all what you have and are dealing with because of your foster care placement.

And then you go into another home through adoption, whether it is inracial or transracial. The food is different, and the sounds and rhythm are different. All of these clear changes and transitions are difficult. It's interesting: even today, when I hear an adult yelling, it physically does something to me emotionally. If I am going to a mall and I hear, "Boy, get over here!" I literally can get ill. Where does that come from?

That comes from being traumatized. That is where that comes from. You don't get untraumatized. You just learn to live around it. If you can imagine, children can be so challenging, just the everyday precociousness, doing what they do. Imagine you have a young child living with you that doesn't mean anything to you. Forget about loving them; you don't even like them. This idea, "When I get rid of you, I will get another one." What kind of message is that? And this can come from well-meaning people who are tired, frustrated, and not always supported. Forget about the abuse and the crazy people. I am just talking about everyday folks.

As we close our discussion, tell me: What does the name of the agency you work for, You Gotta Believe, mean?

The reason we named the agency You Gotta Believe is because the one thing that we all decided when we were founding the group was the only thing that mattered was your belief system. You have to believe that these kids are adoptable. You have to believe that you can parent them and that they can have a bright future. Unfortunately there are oodles and oodles of people in this profession who don't believe.

What is the legacy that you want to leave for your children?

Ultimately I want my kids to understand that I always tried to be a decent person and that I valued civility. I really believe that there is no reason why we can't go through this life helping each other. There is no reason why there has to be hatred and animosity between one another. I want my kids to know that I cared about people, and I want them to care about people too. I want them to be good people by contributing more to this society than they take away. In other words I want them to leave the world a better place instead of hell on Earth. And one can do that in many ways and in big ways. In that is the blessing.

HENRY ALLEN
Professor of Sociology
INTERVIEWED BY TELEPHONE, JANUARY 2, 2012

Thank you for your willingness to be interviewed about transracial adoption. First I want to acknowledge your extensive work in sociology. This includes the many hats you wear as a renowned scholar and international author and lecturer whose focus includes ethnicity and diversity in American higher education, and criminology. What are you working on professionally right now?

There are two long-term projects which are the culmination, I hope, of my career. One, I am doing a book called *The Mathematics of Academic Systems*. This book essentially is a mathematical analysis of all of the systems of higher education on Earth, starting with the four major ones: the United States, the United Kingdom, Israel, and Canada. Some people are not into technical, scientific stuff. So the second book would be on academic systems, global science, and *society*. Just like United Nations looks at the impact of various phenomena on actual human lives, the goal there is to take all of these mathematical models, all of this sophisticated data analysis, and ask the questions, What does it [the data] *mean* for a particular society at this particular time? What does it mean for it politically? What does it mean in terms of family? What does it mean for it economically? What does it mean in terms of religion?

What has inspired you to take the incredible path you have to make an indelible impact in higher education and on society?

My childhood hero was Albert Einstein. The reason I was fascinated by Albert Einstein was, here is a small little guy, whose *thinking* changed the world. To me thinking has always been core. I played athletics, but I was really never hot in it. Music was okay. I enjoyed those kinds of things, but it seems to me the core of understanding the future of society and where we could be is with *thinking*. Just like Einstein's thinking changed the way we think about the physical world, I feel as though it has been a lifelong compulsion of mine to use thinking to change the way we *think* about the social world—the social world being much more complex. You've got both formal and informal dimensions. You've got folk to deal with and folk that don't act right. We have a lot of chaos and catastrophe and other things that we deal with that are not the same thing as what natural scientists or biological scientists deal with but are infinitely more complex. So to bring the best thinking to this area is something that I have been inspired to do.

I was blessed through the years to have not just Einstein as sort of my core guy, but I grew up in the age of Martin Luther King Jr., who was trying to encourage social change. I always felt that one of the weaknesses of Martin's movement is that he didn't deal with the *mentality*. Some of these people—he believed in nonviolent resistance and social change—but a bubba is a bubba is a bubba. And it seems to me, unless you change Bubba's mentality and mind-set, you're not going to have *long-term* progressive change. So, again, it accentuates the way people think. When I think about the way people think, I just don't think about education, which is the transmission of knowledge. I think about what I call an academic system, which is the *production* of new knowledge. And hopefully knowledge that is much more rigorous than the current cultural knowledge that people may be using; which may be a repository of what they learned in the past, old ideas that they celebrate that have no real significance or impact on the reality that we live with today. I was also inspired by good teachers along the way. My parents pushed me. But, really, the driving force was my fascination with Einstein, and then trying to become the social scientific Einstein has been my goal.

Let's focus on transracial adoption, particularly white adoptive parents who have or are adopting children of color. Transracial adoption is a very complex system.

Before I became a professor, in the last year of high school I had trouble with my parents, and I ended up kicked out of my house. So for three or four years of my life I had to live with a white missionary family [in Illinois]. I was a part of their family, and I would travel with them to their relatives and went to all of these predominately white places. At least I was smart enough, as I was going through college, to be able to ask questions about why these folks were unable to see aspects of African American experience and life. They were well-meaning people. They had compassion, but I don't think they ever really understood the kind of situation that African Americans experienced. For example, this family went to white schools. They had very few blacks that they had contact with. Even though they had compassion, like I said, they did not have expertise.

What is it about race and culture that remains controversial globally for human beings, particularly when it involves crossing the racial and cultural divide?

Let me use an analogy, first, that may help. We've all seen—I am sure your audience has seen the explosion of an atomic bomb or a hydrogen bomb. You got that big mushroom cloud that comes up. And those are the visible things. In other words, when the elements split, it releases all of the energy; it forms that cloud as an expression of unleashing that energy. Well, what some people may not know is that it is the *invisible* radiation that comes from the blast that is even more deadly than the blast itself. And so when I think about race relations, we got it wrong four hundred years ago or we got it wrong when we started this whole colonialist, racist bent in culture, and it spread across the world. The reason why we have such difficulty is that most people don't know *how* we got it wrong. They feel that something is wrong and they want to do right, but this is not necessarily founded on truth and accuracy. It's not founded on a real *intellectual repentance* over the dumb ideas of the past. So I see a lot of people [black, white, Hispanic], you name it, are fumbling over ideas of the past that they are not quite sure of. They are very confused about these ideas unless they have the sort of rigorous expertise, and it took me decades to read hundreds of books, thousands of articles, to come up with that. As the Bible says, "Once you know the truth, the truth sets you free." The key is to realize that these ideas are *socially constructed* by human beings and just like radiation continues from a blast, they continue to affect people unless you have the proper equipment to resist that radiation. And it seems to me that you need the proper *intellectual* equipment to resist the radiation. If you go back in time, these ideas were sown into institutions, they were passed through socialization to children; they are now part of pop culture and part of humor. You see them being recycled in redundant ways all across the society. So to expect one individual or small groups of individuals to resist all of that is almost asking for the magic of a Disney movie.

So then would you say that race matters?

There are two ways of looking at race. Race as an *objective* concept does not matter. But because people have used that concept *subjectively* for power, prestige, wealth, to exploit others, the consequences of that *do* matter. And what we are dealing with is that, while some people are aware of the objective definition or issues related to race, most people are not. But everybody is affected by the consequences one way or the other. They are affected directly or overwhelmingly. If you are highly educated and have money, you can be affected tangentially. But everybody is going to be affected by it. It is the fallout from the blast of the past.

So for adoptees of color raised in white homes, what can they do to get it right or how can they *recondition* their minds to accept themselves for all of who they are, and then how do they develop a high self-esteem, given that we still have a society that continues to devalue people of color?

Let's look at it on two levels. On the one hand, I am going to give you a simple little model, and then I am going to talk about social networks for the second part. This [first] model is *structure*, which has to do with the way things are patterned. *Processes* are the way things are created. And then the *outcomes* are the results of the structures' and the processes' interacting with one another. If you look at the typical white parent that adopts a transracial kid, you have to give them credit for love and compassion. Plus they do it out of what is called — forgive me, I hope I am not insulting your audience — liberal guilt. But at least they are doing *something*. It is better to have some love, some compassion, something positive coming into a child's life rather than for them to grow up isolated, alienated in an institution that really does not care about them. Kudos for the compassion.

But compassion without *expertise* and *experience* is dangerous. A lot of white parents, yes, they have compassion, but they lack expertise and experience. They lack expertise because they themselves have "goofed-up" ideas about race. They may be doing it [transracial adoption] because the kids are cute. Or they are doing it because they feel a sense of social obligation. Those are all nice kinds of things, but their decisions should be based on a real *rigorous* understanding of history, biology, genetics, and sociology. And most parents don't have that going for them when they adopt children from a different ethnic group.

Let's connect item 2 with item 1. We talked about structure, process, and outcomes (item 1), but the second thing (item 2) I talked about was *social networks*. Because a lot of parents, particularly white parents adopting minority kids or African American kids, don't have social networks across a *range* of African American peoples . . . when these [white] parents get a kid, since they don't have that set of networks, there is a tremendous void in the social experiences that a lot of transracial adoptees have *because* of the lack of expertise and lack of experience of their adoptive parents. Now you can take the same scenario with a white adoptive parent or whatever, if the parent has compassion, but they *do* have expertise and they *do* have experience, then you have a very different possible outcome for those kids. So to me one of the problems that you have with transracial adoption is that—just like we have drivers' education and hope that drivers' education will make a better driver—before you have an adoption of a kid from another ethnic group, it seems to me that you should know *something* about the history, you should have some social network connections—across the *broad* range of experiences—as it relates to the ethnicity or the background of the kid or child that you are adopting. If you don't have that, then in my opinion your compassion is not good enough. If you really have compassion, you will get the kind of expertise and the kind of experiences that qualify you to be a good parent to that kid.

So if I, let's say, as a white adoptive parent, have the expertise and experience to raise my black child, how do those credentials

translate step by step to my child's developing and maintaining a healthy sense of pride and self-esteem in herself?

For one, your child will be a reflection of your own social experiences. If you are smart, you will examine yourself before you have the child and say, "Am I from a segregated context? Am I going to bring this black kid into an all-white neighborhood interacting with white folk? Am I going to have messed-up or misguided views about race, racial subordination? Am I going to bring the kid formally and informally into an environment like that?" If you are a smart parent, you would say *no*! If you are a smart parent. If you are a compassionate parent but not smart, you'll do it. And that's what happens: a lot of these kids become suicidal and they have problems, because the parents don't think about their own self-assessment *before* they adopt these kids.

So what questions should potential transracial adoptive parents ask?

Number 1, ask yourself, What kind of networks do I have? Do the people that I associate with at church, at work, in my community, in my extended family reflect a diverse range of people, some of whom represent the ethnicity of the kid that I am adopting? Those are the liaisons that are necessary for the kid to have role models, to bond with, and take care of their hair—

I was waiting for the hair topic to come up.

My wife, Juliet, for example, she regularly does the hair of young girls who are transracially adopted. The parents have no clue how to deal with their kids' hair so they bring them over to our home. Juliet has to show compassion and braid their hair and all of that stuff. Now we have done that every place that we've lived. I get upset with her doing that. But I understand her compassion because she wants to help these kids. She sees these kids go to school with kinky hair that is not maintained, all messed up. And of course that is going to affect the kid's self-image. They are around young kids, and they are going to tease you if your hair is all messed up. You're compared to kids who come from a different ethnic group, and they have a different standard of beauty, and you don't have that—that's a torturous situation to put a young kid in, in grade school or in high school. What are their hair care needs? What kind of clothing should they wear? How is that related to history? How do we go to events, theater, historical events, or social events that reflect the ethnicity of the kid? If you are not willing to do that, then in my opinion your little compassion can be a dangerous thing, just like a little education can be a dangerous thing. I think in most cases you have many mess-ups because you have people who are very compassionate but *naive*.

Let me go back to something you just said. Why does it frustrate you that your wife cares for the hair care needs in particular of the transracially adopted kids living in your community?

It frustrates me because I realize how much more nurture these kids need than to just have their hair done. The fact that their hair is all messed up and nobody helped them to deal with that, to me, is a sign of neglect or ineptitude of the parents. Okay, why didn't you think about this before you adopted the kid? Why didn't you have a plan for how the kid is going to develop and how they are going to be nurtured? How are you going to meet their needs for self-esteem? How are you going to deal with those kinds of issues, because most parents don't think about that? And the reason why Juliet does this for these kids is because the parents come, they meet Juliet, they're in crisis, "Oh, what can I do?" Juliet is the black savior in the sea of whiteness, and then all of sudden they want to use her to help them with the needs that they have, that they're not sure what to do anything about. I get upset about it because my wife is *overburdened* with something that the parents should have taken care of *before* they adopted the kid.

As someone who is a person of faith and attends church, how do you think transracially adopted children should see themselves [even though] many of these adoptees . . . may be struggling to understand their racial identity and place in this world, especially given the shame society can place on children who have been relinquished?

One of the things that is missing, I think, in all of this church life is this idea of the sacredness of the image of God. More important than the ideas of race that we have placed in our society is the fact that God made you in his image. And that is not a mistake. Even if you were adopted, an orphan, or abandoned, or if you have a situation like me, where your parents kick you out, that does not mean that there is something wrong with you. Look at the story of Joseph in the Bible. I just finished reading it today. Joseph was sold to slavery in the Old Testament, and he rose to be pharaoh of Egypt. Look at Moses, who was an adopted kid in an Egyptian situation. So God has special purposes for adopted kids. It's not the experience; it's the way people tell you about the experience. And unfortunately what happens is that kids often internalize the experiences of people who don't know much or who are misguided, and they allow that to form their self-image.

Do you think that there is hope for other transracial adoptees?

Yes, with the right kind of mentoring and the right kind of sponsorship. But you know, I won't give the names, there were kids that were at Calvin College [in Grand Rapids, Michigan, where Allen formerly taught] that, instead of moving toward the light, toward a guy like me who could actually help them, they were afraid of me. They had internalized the stereotypes: He is black. He is inferior. He's black. He is too militant for me. He is black. He is going to reveal things about me that I don't want to face. And so they moved away. Unfortunately they are going to live a troubled, frustrated, schizophrenic life. I know that as a social scientist. You can only help people who want to be helped. Unfortunately there are some people who are trapped in very bad transracial adoptive situations that don't know how to get out but are afraid to go to people who can help them with this situation.

How do parents and adoptees find people like you?

The same way you find salvation. You gotta be humble. You got to reach out and say, "I need help; can you help me with this? I am wrestling with this issue. Is there something that you may know about this? Or somebody you can lead me to?" You have to have humility. Even as a transracial adoptee, you need to, first of all, cling to God and say, "God, I don't understand everything that has happened to me in this situation." And when you meet people with integrity who have particular expertise that might relate to your situation, you have to be willing to say so—I am not saying everybody who has expertise is necessarily a person of integrity, but for those that you find that do have integrity, you have to be able to go to them and say, "I am wondering about this."

One of the rhetorical schemes that people use, for example, is "I have this friend that has this problem—can you help me, help my friend?" And of course the counselor knows that the person knows that by talking about your friend, they are actually helping you too.

True! But is that discourse strategic and effective for the adoptee or the parent?

You as a transracial adoptee/parent may have to deal with backlash. There are some blacks that are insecure about their status, so insecure that they can't see the love or compassion from other ethnic groups. And they feel threatened by that. Obviously there is a lot of hell and oppression that a lot of blacks have gone through in this country and continue to go through it. And for some of them, if there is a white person or an Asian person adopting a kid, they feel like the kid is going to be lost to the race forever. In some cases that is possible. Even in the case of my own kids, who grew up in predominately white communities, that can apply—where you come from a different culture than the one you are raised in, and you can grow up and not have the same vision for helping African Americans as somebody who grew up in a more indigenous circumstance. I just think that compassion and love with expertise and experience is a key aspect to this whole problem. And whether you are black or white, the same rule applies. There are those commercials that I always see that talk about "happily ever after," where people are adulating through the tulips and kissing the little babies and all of that kind of stuff. But the babies grow up. They don't show *that* part in the commercials. The babies grow up, they may be self-destructive, they may be engaged in criminal activity, and they may even commit suicide. And people *don't* show that stuff. That actually happens when people don't have the kind of expertise and the kind of experience to nurture somebody to become all of what God wants them to become.

Looking at the day-to-day activities of blended families, for example, some white parents who take their family out to eat at a restaurant talk about getting stares from people because they have a black son or daughter. How can parents deal with this kind of uncomfortable situation?

For these parents I would recommend that they have black friends who are liaisons to help them with that situation. However, because we live in a messed-up society, there are going to be some stares. A classic example is look at [the late] Michael Jackson and his kids. Here you have Michael Jackson, the great African American singer, his kids looked almost like Anglo, white. When they went out, I am sure they got stares. "What?! This is incredible!" But it seems to me, obviously, Michael Jackson had love for his kids or he would not have sacrificed or made it possible to care for them. To me, love with expertise and experience and the right kind of nurturing networks is a positive thing.

But what about the pain that these children may go through?

Parents need to prepare their transracially adopted children for the pain. The pain is going to be there. People are going to misunderstand you. There are going to be some positive experiences. There are going to be some negative experiences. There are going to be some neutral experiences. That's life. A kid has to learn to deal with it. I wish it was all "Goody Two Shoes." I wish that we lived in a country like *Star Trek*. We don't!

Isn't there a step-by-step guide on how white parents can raise their transracially adopted kids, in particular, to become fabulous?

I will say this. As a sociologist, when we think about sociology, we think about the impact of groups. We think about culture. We think about status, where people rank in social networks, and we think about socialization. If you are going to be successful as a transracial adoptive parent, you have to have a strategy or a blueprint for helping your kid cope with those issues, some of what we just talked about. Parents must think about what kinds of groups are going to influence the way their kid grows up, their sense of identity. Everybody knows that young kids are influenced by peer pressure. Are the peers that these kids are going to interact with going to nurture their identity as an African American kid in a transracial situation? Are they going to be neutral about that? Are they going to tear down their African American identity? Are they going to neutralize their African American identity? Parents have to think about these questions. Secondly, we move from just the groups on to culture. What kind of culture are you, as parents, celebrating? If all they, transracially adopted kids, get is white European culture, don't be surprised—because the implication of that is that somehow, if you are not white European and high status, then you are inferior—and so don't be surprised if these kids come up with the attitudes that anything that is of African American vintage, compared to European, must be low on the totem pole or insignificant. In other words God must have made a mistake when he made you, because obviously you don't think like them [Caucasian people], you don't talk like them, you don't act like them, and you don't like their music—which is false, but at least kids think about that.

So you think about the whole issue of culture, you think about status, what kinds of social networks are in place for the transracially adopted kid. If all of the powerful people that you see are made up of all of the smart people of one ethnic group, and you never see or interact with somebody who is smart [in] the group that you are from if you are an African American kid, and you are always around whites, and the whites are always superior to the African Americans you interact with, you get the idea that only white folks are smart. Until you meet somebody, like you did when I was at Calvin College, to find out that, hey, some of us can kick all of these white folks in the rear end intellectually, without a doubt. Not that you want to do that, but the idea [is] that God gives his gifts to people depending on his purposes. And this idea, that there is a white supremacy intellectually, is a bunch of junk. White folk may have more experience, more ties, more institutional connections, but it doesn't mean that they are smarter, and it surely doesn't mean that they are better.

So you have to deal with this whole notion of social networks and status, and then lastly you have to deal with socialization and outcomes. Socialization is that whole process in which you absorbed all of this, your interactions with people, the sense of culture, and institutional issues. That is a lot for a parent that doesn't have a very good social scientific or sociological understanding. That's an awful lot for a parent to deal with. Unfortunately most parents don't have that understanding and pass on the kind of pathology that eventually you see in the transracially adopted kids. A lot of these kids will grow up confused, schizophrenic, mixed up; they don't know what's going on. It is a sad thing to see, but I have seen it over the last thirty years. It is sad to see what happens to some transracial adoptees that don't reach out and do not try to move toward this greater understanding.

How did you deal with the color of your skin as you navigated through the doors of higher education and the doors that you went through to achieve what you have to this point?

Quite simply, I thought I was bad from the time I was born.

Bad, **meaning smart and strong!**

It's like this. This is going to sound very harsh, so get ready. Any civilization that put people in slavery for two or three hundred years cannot be a smart civilization. So I came to the conclusion that the mere fact that this civilization was predicated on hundreds of years of slavery means that it cannot be intellectually superior to anything that I have done, because no real smart person would have engaged in that kind of activity. In other words it's tainted. The idiocy of the civilization is tainted by its barbarity. The scripture talks about two superior principles: Love God with all of your heart and with all your soul and with all your mind (Matt. 22:37). And the second is like it: Love your neighbor as yourself (Matt. 22:39). If you break any one of those commands, it doesn't show that you are intellectually superior. When you break those commands, it shows that you are intellectually inferior.

I say this in my class on criminology. It upsets a lot of my students. Rhonda, you know I teach at a predominately white campus. I say to my students that the things that happened during slavery and colonization and segregation: we put people in jail and throw away the key for people who act like that now. And yet that was sanctioned in this civilization, and it created the kind of social institutions and social interactions and patterns that we see today that everybody wants to forget. It's just like denying a rape or denying a violent crime. Part of the psychosis in the Western civilization is denial, which is a sign of guilt and a sign of its inferiority.

So when I went to school, I thought almost like Moses: you learn what the Egyptians say or, like Daniel, you learn what the Chaldeans say, but you never let it get to you. And I think that those biblical examples of being a Jew in pagan Babylon or being Moses in pagan Egypt or being Joseph in pagan Egypt, those are the examples that nurtured me. I always thought in God's strength I was always superior to that stuff.

Where do you see transracial adoption moving in the future? We have already experienced the impact of the civil rights movement as it relates to transracial adoptions in the form of creating a surge in white parents' adopting children of color, and the color-blind factor. What is the future for these families?

I see a multiple-tier model. On the popular level you are always going to have people who do things without thinking. I am sorry to say that. And you are going to have this in transracial adoptions. There are people who are going to have compassion and love but no expertise or experience. And you're going to have many of the same circumstances that you have seen across the last thirty years. On the other hand, you have some special forces. Some parents say, "You know, I want to go all of the way. I really would like to learn as much as I can, establish the networks I need, have the experiences." And we might have something like a professional development model, where they adopt a kid but, say, within a decade, they are under the mentorship or supervision of somebody who's accomplished in race relations or has accomplished expertise and can mentor them and guide them and expose them to networks. That's the sort of Mercedes or the high-tier end of the transracial adoption market. Unfortunately most people are going to tilt toward the low end, and people are going to align themselves along that continuum. Do you want the high-end experience or do you want the traditional experience? Unfortunately people will self-select themselves along that continuum as to where they fit in. I think that there is tremendous potential for transracial adoptions in this era. You have more images of people from different racial hues. But images without expertise are also dangerous. The structures are passed down from history. You can have a lot of people who have different looks, but the structures never change. The processes don't change. They continue to produce the same sort of outcomes that we see. Unfortunately I don't see a lot of leadership in the church. I don't see a lot of leadership in government. I don't see a lot of leadership, even in the academy, to do anything about those kinds of issues.

This discussion has been extremely eye opening.

Rhonda, I really support your work. Probably some of the things that I have said will upset people, but I am a sociologist. That is why you become a sociologist, to do things that upset people. You cannot have change unless sometimes people confront the reality. I really appreciate the opportunity to be a part of this project. I hope that something that I have said will be helpful to you and to your audience.

PART III

Post–Civil Rights Era (1973–Present)

PASSAGE OF THE VOTING RIGHTS ACT OF 1965 and inauguration of affirmative action programs (particularly on the federal level) opened up opportunities in education and employment long closed to members of minority groups, and legally enforced discrimination and discriminatory social customs began to disappear. The number of blacks elected to office also increased exponentially; prominent examples include W. Wilson Goode Sr., mayor of Philadelphia (1984–92); Harold Washington, mayor of Chicago (1983–87); David Dinkins, mayor of New York City (1990–93); and Douglas Wilder, governor of Virginia (1990–94). African Americans even began to dare to dream of a black president with the well-run presidential campaigns of the civil rights leader Jesse Jackson in 1984 and 1988. Other powerful black leaders in high positions included Colin Powell, secretary of state (2001–2005) and chair of the Joint Chiefs of Staff (1989–93); Condoleezza Rice, national security adviser to President George Bush; Michael Steele, chair of the Republican National Party in 2009; Cory Booker, U.S. senator from New Jersey and former mayor of Newark (2006–13); and Eric Holder, U.S. attorney general (2009–15). The talk show host, entrepreneur, and philanthropist Oprah Winfrey became a household name and one of the wealthiest people in the world. Now little black boys and little black girls can *see* themselves in these men and women who look like them and are achieving greatness on the national and international stage. Even with these advancements, however, the socioeconomic, political, and emotional scars of racial inequality and injustice continue to take a toll.

Today many African Americans still battle disproportionate poverty and incarceration rates, unemployment, and drug use. The NAACP reports that from 1980 to 2008, the number of people incarcerated in the United States quadrupled, from approximately 500,000 to 2.3 million people. African Americans account for only 13 percent of the population nationally but constitute nearly one million of the 2.3 million people incarcerated in the United States. Nationwide, African Americans account for 26 percent of juvenile arrests and 58 percent of youth admitted to state prisons (NAACP, 2009–14). Five whites use drugs for every African American who does, yet ten African Americans go to jail on a drug offense for every white who does. African Americans also serve virtually as much time in prison for a drug offense (58.7 months) as whites do for a violent offense (61.7 months) (NAACP, 2009–14).

Economically African Americans are losing ground. According to the Urban League, in a report issued in April 2014, the underemployment rate for African American workers was 20.5 percent, compared with 11.8 percent for white workers. (Underemployment is defined as high-skill workers who hold low-paying jobs or people working part time who desire full-time work.) The report also said African Americans are twice as likely as whites to be unemployed—the unemployment rate for blacks was 12 percent in February 2014, compared with 5.8 percent for whites (Holland, 2014).

Despite these well-documented disparities and structural injustices, many transracial adoptive families still insist on being color blind, although this also means overlooking their adopted child's racial and cultural differences and needs. This "race doesn't matter" attitude was further reinforced by passage of the 1994 Multiethnic Placement Act (MEPA) and the 1996 Interethnic Adoption Act (IEPA). The purpose of MEPA was to (1) decrease the length of time children waited to be adopted; (2) prevent discrimination on the basis of race, color, or national origin in the placement of children; and (3) identify and recruit foster and adoptive families who can meet the needs of the children.

IEPA was enacted to allow the federal government to assess financial penalties on a state if that state was found to be in violation of MEPA and had not enacted a corrective action plan within six months. For example, a state social worker who delays placement of a child for no other reason than to place that child in a same-race household has violated MEPA.

By attempting to prevent discrimination in placement practices both laws sought to decrease the length of time children, a disproportionate number of whom are minorities, wait in foster care for a permanent adoptive home (Smith & Hjelm, 2007). Out of fear of being penalized, and with great pressure to place increasing numbers of children of color in available homes, adoption agencies inevitably struggle to fully meet the racial and cultural needs of these children who enter white homes. Doing so would treat these children of color differently based on race and would therefore be in violation of the law (Smith, 2011). In fact "many adoption agencies have therefore stayed away from imposing courses, seminars, and lessons to prospective adoptive parents altogether" (Smith, 2011, p. 94).

In *Finding Families for African American Children*, Smith, McRoy, Freundlich, and Kroll (2008) question the effectiveness of both laws in placing black children in permanent families. Their study suggests that while there have been small increases in transracial adoptions of black children from foster care (rising from 17.2 percent in 1996 to 20.1 percent in 2003), the improvement has not meant that black children are adopted from foster care in proportion to their representation in the system. Livingston and colleagues (2008) further reveal that even though the time that all children remain in foster care has declined, African American children still stay in foster care an average of nine months longer than white children. More research should be conducted on the long-term outcomes for transracial adoptions as a result of both pieces of legislation.

I consider the jury to still be out on the MEPA-IEPA requirements and whether placing children in families without ensuring that their adoptive parents have multicultural skills is in the best long-term interests of these children. I contend that mainstream adoption agencies need more people of color in leadership positions to better serve transracial adoptive families and recruit potential adoptive parents to meet the needs of a racially diverse group of children in the system.

In an effort to move transracial adoptive families beyond their embrace of a color-blind mind-set, an increasing number of black and biracial adoptees have begun to tell their stories about growing up in white families and in mostly white worlds since the early 1970s. Their

powerful narratives discuss how they approached adulthood with fragile racial identities and few cultural tools to help them navigate in
mainstream society or handle racial slights, discriminatory actions,
and stereotypical assumptions (Hoard, 1998/2007; Simon & Roorda,
2000; Bertelsen, 2001; John, 2005). They were also often unable to
move comfortably in either white or black America. Nor could they
understand the multiple communication styles of black America or the
varying cultural lifestyles within that world. Many transracial adoptees
have revealed personal stories of shock, deep loneliness, low self-worth,
emotional trauma, a desire to belong, and a desperate need for healing and direction. Central to their pain were issues around race and
identity (Hoard, 1998/2007; Simon & Roorda, 2000; Bertelsen, 2001;
John, 2005).

What many black and biracial transracial adoptees were not prepared for was that the societal realities they faced were the same as
those facing other people of color. The information that white transracial adoptive parents needed to give their children did not exist in the
white world; these parents would have to interact with black America
in order to understand the problems most likely to trouble transracially
adopted children.

THE PEOPLE INTERVIEWED for this third section come out of the
post–civil rights era. They speak directly to white transracial adoptive
families, foster and adoption agencies, scholars, and mainstream society from a place of love and unapologetic honesty on issues of race,
discrimination, foster care, adoption, and family. In an effort to be
especially transparent to transracial adoptees, nonadopted siblings, and
adoptive parents, these interviewees do not hide their vulnerability or
sheer grit in telling their stories. Clearly their hope is that readers will
set aside color-blindness as a utopian but counterproductive notion
and replace it with a thirst for social justice, racial equality, inclusion,
humility, and self-reflection.

My interview with Vershawn A. Young powerfully demonstrates
that race still matters. Young grew up in the projects of Chicago in a
predominately black and low-income environment during the 1970s
and 1980s. Despite his academic achievements, he feels that America

continues to view him, like most black Americans, as unequal or—put another way—like an unwanted visitor in the country in which he was born. In our candid discussion Young shares his thoughts about race, culture, and class with vulnerability and academic rigor.

Michelle M. Hughes, a single mother, is a product of interracial marriage. She and her siblings grew up with a white mother and a black father in the Chicago suburbs. She credits her parents' own strong racial identities for giving her a strong sense of self as a biracial woman. I especially wanted to talk with Hughes because of her extensive work with transracial adoptive parents and adoptees of color. She has witnessed the progression of the transracial adoption movement in recent decades and has done good thinking on the multifaceted issues affecting transracial adoptive and multiracial families. Not only is she an adoption advocate and adoption attorney in her professional world, she is also the adoptive parent of a black boy.

Mahisha Dellinger's story is an example of how vision, hard work, perseverance, and being true to oneself can make dreams become a reality. She used her personal struggles in finding hair care products to establish her own line of quality products designed for multiethnic individuals with a spectrum of hair textures. What started off as a small endeavor has in a little more than a decade become a multimillion-dollar business that spans the globe. Before she became an entrepreneur, Dellinger experienced the fear, humiliation, and isolation caused by racial discrimination in the corporate workplace, the scars of which she still bears. Throughout the ups and downs of life, her biggest joys and satisfaction have come from being a loving wife to her husband, mother to her beautiful and smart children, and a member of a loving and supportive family.

Several years ago I read an article about the interracial marriage of Deneta Howland and Bryan Sells at Harvard University. Shortly thereafter I contacted Dr. Sells and asked her to lend her voice to this book. She represents the fourth generation of college-educated black women in her family. She was born at the end of the civil rights era and raised in a small town in Illinois. From a racially and economically diverse high school in College Park, Maryland, she pursued an education at Harvard University and then went on to medical school in Tennessee.

Today she is the founder and owner of a pediatric center in Atlanta. Both she and her husband, a civil rights attorney, continue to fight for social justice, equal opportunity and care, and access to resources for all people. For them, expanding their family by adopting a child from the U.S. foster care system is a viable possibility.

It was important for me to talk with someone who has an insider's view of the child welfare system, so I was delighted to be able to include an interview with Tabitha, chief of the child welfare bureau for the Washington, D.C., metropolitan area. Concerned about preserving the privacy of her family, Tabitha asked me to use only her first name. In my discussion with her I was eager to know what she thinks are the societal issues that send children into the system. Also I was interested to know how she has handled specific placement situations. I was moved by her compassion for children, knowledge of the child welfare system, and her holistic approach to addressing the needs of children in the system. Her heart, knowledge of black history, and passion for strengthening communities are evident in every facet of her life.

Many transracially adopted children deal with trauma associated with the loss and grief they experienced because of their primal separation from their birth mother and from their physical and emotional separation from their birth family and community. In our conversation Bryan Post addresses trauma in the adopted child that is manifested in negative emotions and behaviors—anger, frustration, depression, hyperactivity, and stealing—and shares his strategies for teaching parents to calm their child using a love-based approach. Post is a national trauma expert and therapist for adoptive families. He also is an adoptee himself; as a child he struggled with behavioral problems, which he discusses in his candid and compelling interview.

Shilease Hofmann grew up in the inner city of Toledo in the 1970s and 1980s. She is the mother of two black teenage boys and is married to Kevin D. Hofmann, a transracial adoptee and author of the memoir *Growing Up Black in White.* I was pleased to be able to speak with Hofmann and was especially interested in how she and her husband respond when their sons have suffered racial insults. Because Hofmann regularly interacts with white transracial adoptive parents, she has developed a familiarity with this group. As a result she does a good job of unpacking some of the salient issues that transracial adoptive families confront and offers suggestions about how best to address them strategically.

My interview with Chelsey Hines is one of the most emotional conversations I had in preparing this collection. My purpose in interviewing Hines was to get her perspective on her experiences in the foster care system. She was born in 1992 in Aurora, Colorado, and entered the foster care system at a young age because of parental drug abuse and other problems reported to the child welfare authorities by a relative. When she was nine years old, she was adopted by a white family. This interview is quite intimate, touching on issues of loss, vulnerability, survival, loneliness, inferiority, race, and invisibility. I hope this interview helps readers see the child welfare system through Hines's eyes.

Demetrius Walker, entrepreneur and cofounder of dN|BE Apparel (he says the acronym stands for "dangerousNEGRO Black Empowerment"), is the final voice in this collection. Walker grew up in New York during the crack era of the 1980s. He lived in the projects and saw some of the ugliest images of poverty, crime, hopelessness, and addiction. I wanted to interview him because he focuses on helping black youth to escape poverty and approaches issues that confront transracial adoptive families and adoptees of color with passion, vision, and thinking. He became involved with adoption heritage camps in 2007 after a transracial adoptive couple responsible for lining up speakers for a camp read about his work and invited him to participate. He has since formed special relationships with transracial adoptive families and regards them as members of his extended family.

VERSHAWN A. YOUNG
Author and Scholar
INTERVIEWED BY TELEPHONE, JULY 28, 2012

I want to read an excerpt of a poem you wrote called "shiny" from *Your Average Nigga: Performing Race, Literacy, and Masculinity*, the book you based on your dissertation.

as dark as i am and tryin' to pass
somebody needs to kick my black ass
for using proper english all the time
when the rest o' my family's spittin' rhyme
dressin' all preppy, talkin' all white,
somebody tell me this ain't right

my skin so black folks think maybe it's blue;
who am i foolin', Two Eyes? Cain't be you
I wash and scrub and cosmetically bleach
but this doggone pigment just won't leach
so tryin' to be white ain't working at all,
since the only attention I get is in the mall
when heads turn to see the nigga with the silver dollar tongue
wondering, who dat talking deep from the diaphragm and lung?
(YOUNG, 2007, P. 38)

What was going on within your own identity as a young black man to create such deep, painful, and complex work? Why would you want to be white?

I grew up spending most of my life actually wanting to be white. I think that a lot of black people want to be white. They may deny it, but I think that many of them do, especially when we think about the skin-lightening creams, when we think about the hair-straightening products, and we think about the market for the colored eye contact lenses, which were really big in the '80s and '90s among black people as well. There is a deep psychological desire in black culture that wants to be white. Now, I think that the reason why black people want to be white is not necessarily because, first and foremost, they think that white people are better looking or more beautiful, although I think that it becomes a performance of whiteness for black people to try to aid whiteness optically and aesthetically, but rather I think that we internalize from a very early age that white people are the privileged people in our culture and in our society. They do not come across on TV and in representations in the movies as having the same degree and intense problems that African Americans face. And they are not represent[ed as] being treated in the same way, in the same degraded, insensitive, highly skeptical manner as black people. They have a *range* of freedom that black people do not have. What I mean by a range of freedom [is] I believe and see and think that black people as a whole understand that white people are given the benefit of the doubt, whereas black people are viewed with deep skepticism. And so it is more of a psychological response. Most people think that because black people are allowed to go to the same schools as whites that we don't live in an era of segregation. Right now, that we have it made. That everything is okay. They say, "Look at the black reporter on TV. Or look at yourself as a black author."

Yes, we as black people have a measure of opportunities that we now can access, but we can't negate the hundreds of years that it took to even get to this moment and the deep imprint that it has made on us culturally. That is the first thing. The second thing is opportunities are nice, but then the psychological trauma that we have to deal with on a *daily* basis in order to keep those benefits is enormous. I argue, and some people may disagree with me, that we have to *act* like white people in order to keep those same opportunities that people say we now have just because we are citizens. We don't have them just because we are citizens. White people have them just because they're citizens. Black people are only allowed to take advantage of these opportunities *to the extent* that we are able to downplay our blackness and take up what is considered to be white culture.

Yes, and I think that when you say in the first stanza of your poem "as dark as i am and tryin' to pass / somebody needs to kick my black ass / for using proper english all the time / when the rest o' my family's spittin' rhyme / dressin' all preppy, talkin' all white, / somebody tell me this ain't right," it is as if there is an internal struggle or even a paradox between recognizing that you are black and reaching for that "whiteness" in order to feel like you are able to compete in a white world or setting and then being frustrated about making that huge concession to your person.

Yes! Yes! Yes! Exactly!

The paradoxes in the poem you wrote depict the challenges transracial adoptees face, I think, [in] living in different worlds

simultaneously but needing to be responsible for nurturing their own identity. How did you reconcile these paradoxes within yourself? And as it relates to your poem, why should someone "kick your black ass"?

[*Laugh*] You know what? It is because I was duped. I wanted to believe that if I did all of the things that were prescribed for me to do, which I did not see as being codified as white at the time, that I would be successful. So I keep trying to do those things—if you just get a college education; if you just get a master's degree; if you just get a Ph.D.; if you just don't talk back; if you just talk at a low "hush" at a restaurant; if you just don't wear baggy pants, et cetera. Those kinds of things: if I just didn't do the wrong things and did all the right things . . . I would have the American dream. The poem that I wrote is saying basically that is a myth for black people. Some black people don't get it until they have an experience like "Skip" Gates [the Harvard professor arrested by police after he forced open the jammed front door of his own home].

He is the chairperson in his department at Harvard. And then he gets stopped by the police at his front door. Some people don't get it until they have their "Skip Gates" moment. It is a shame that it takes them so long. But that was a "kick in his black ass." See what I am saying?

Yes.

He got kicked in the ass at that moment. The reason why you can say that he did is because he said, "You don't know who I am" to the police. And then he said he was going to make a documentary about black racial profiling. That is what the line in my poem means.

In 2007 *Your Average Nigga: Performing Race, Literacy, and Masculinity* was published. I remember thinking what an explosive title for a book. I thought the "N-word" had been buried, not to be resurrected. Why did you choose to use the word *nigga* in the title of your book, and what messages did you want your readers to retain from reading this book?

I chose the word because I knew that it would get some attention. And also it spoke in one word what the book was about. It was about both my identification and my disidentification with being a black man. But also it spoke volumes about what it means to be a black man in this society. And even though I am a black man with a Ph.D., to some people I am still just an average nigger, not just with the *a*. A nigger with an *a* is making it soft and palatable, even though it still isn't palatable. To me, I walk down the street and I am still eyed with suspicion, with a racialized lens.

Rhonda, you can't ever bury a word. We don't have control over language to that extent. Some people may think that we do. We do not. Language is not something that is easily domesticated or controlled, regardless of the fact that the NAACP had a ceremony in 2006 or so to bury the word *nigger*, which I think was utterly ridiculous. It seems like it was a cartoon—it was so ridiculous that you would have a mass ceremony of people giving eulogies and prayers and extending a funeral ritual for a word. But the book *Your Average Nigga* has still done well despite the fact that the word was attempted to be buried at a certain time and people have had a lot of negative things to say about my choice of using that title. The book is doing well because more people understand the message I am expressing, once they start reading it, than those who don't.

Now the subtitle, *Performing Race, Literacy, and Masculinity*, what does that cover?

It covers the range of enactments in speech, in dress, in the way we behave, the way that we interact with other people. Basically it is the range of enactments that black people have to go through to be successful in America. I call it the burden of racial performance that black people are *required*, not only by whites but by other blacks as well, *to prove through their behaviors, their speech, and their actions the kind of black person that they are*. Really, there are only two kinds you can be. In the words of comedian Chris Rock, you can either be a black person, which is a respectable, bourgeois, middle-class black person, or you can be a nigger. As Chris Rock says in his show, "I love black people, but I hate niggas."

So . . . when a black person walks into a room, always in the other person's mind is the question "What kind of black person is this in front of me?" They are looking for clues in your speech, in your demeanor, in your behavior, and in everything that you do—it is like they are hyperattentive to your ways of being in order to say, "Okay, this is a real black person. I can trust them. I'll let them work here. Or, nope: this is a nigger, look at the spelling of their name: Shaniqua or Daquandre." We get discriminated against based on our actions. So that is what the subtitle was trying to suggest in performing race. And in performing literacy, just what is the prescribed means for increasing our class status? A mind-set: "Okay, black people, you guys have no excuse. You can go to school and get an education like everybody else." I wanted to pay attention to the ways in which school perpetuated a structural racism through literacy, the way in which it sort of stigmatizes and oppresses blackness in a space where it claims it is opening up opportunities for black people. Of course, since I am a man, masculinity and how masculinity is performed is really important.

I can't imagine the added pressure a gay man must experience trying to perform blackness and masculinity in both a black and white world.

That is interesting that you mention that. The book that I am writing now is asking the question about whether or not our gay black brothers have a more difficult time. I am not so certain that they do, because one of the theories that I have been playing around with is that when you think about American culture, you recognize that we are still living in a patriarchal culture, where white men dominate. If you think about [it,] black men [are] required to be men on the basis of their gender or biological sex designation, but in this white patriarchal society they're not allowed to play the role of men in mainstream culture. In other words black men don't wield the same kind of power. They don't have the same kind of opportunities as white men do. So in that way they resemble women overall. This is not just me saying this. E. Franklin Frazier [the famous African American sociologist] made this comment. I am actually quoting him when he said black men resemble women in the personality that they have to play in order to be successful in America. And also sociologist Robert Park, back in 1929, said the same thing. He said the black man, or the Negro, was the lady of the races.

So in some ways I think that white culture—and this is not every white person but it is navigating in our cultures here in America—sort of has less fear of black gay men than it does of straight black men. And I think that the straight black man may have a more difficult time in other words because I think that part of the domesticating that goes on requires men to downplay their masculinity. So if they are more feminine, they are less threatening.

You moved from the projects of Chicago to the halls of education and had to navigate in both black and white worlds; you also moved in an economically disadvantaged world and an economically accessible one. You may not have been transracially adopted, but there is a correlation between your experience and that of many transracial adoptees. Tell me about your reality being raised in Chicago. How did you survive—and dream?

First of all, Rhonda, let me tell you that most, if not all—I don't know all—but most black people who are successful and who come from a background like mine probably more than likely had along the way a white surrogate parent. It's just the way our culture is. Most successful black people can point to one, two, or three close intimate relationships with a white mentor that helped them get to where they are. So all along in my childhood, my white teachers took an interest in me because I think I was different from my contemporaries, from my peers. My mother was educated, and she took school very seriously, but we lived in the projects. All of my siblings did well in school. I already had a different kind of way of speaking and behaving and thinking about the world compared to some of my peers. And so my all white teachers—I can only remember having two black teachers out of ten years of elementary school (including pre-K and K)—they took an interest in me, and some of them took a real personal interest in me, driving me in their cars to places, giving me personal advice, and allowing me to call them on the phone.

I have not thought about this before you asked your question, when you said that "although you have not been transracially adopted"—adoption is a formality. Of course I think the people that are transracially adopted have a deeper experience than the one that I am claiming to have now and that I've claimed that other blacks who are successful have. But we are in some ways adopted into a "play family" of whites. I would be interested to hear what white people think about this, but I will venture to say that in my experience many liberal whites who are interested in a successful African American feel that it is part of their responsibility to develop instant relationships with blacks and to shepherd them into the mainstream or provide access, to protect them, in a sense. I often see this, even in my own white friends and colleagues and so forth. While in part it is an excellent thing to have these kinds of relationships, the problem is, and there is a problem, they often continue to have a paternal relationship with black people as opposed to allowing black people to come of age. You know what I am saying? They, these black people, are always pets to a certain extent, and it becomes a problem. Even though the white people that I am referring to want to provide these opportunities, somewhere in the back of their mind and in their subconscious, they don't see them as equals. If you're always having the responsibility of shepherding somebody, that person will never be equal to you. And so I think that it is a double-edged sword. I think that it is a great thing, and I think that it has been wonderful in my experience, but I also think that it has consequences. I believe that is why I experienced so many problems with whites who I had intimate relationships with—by *intimate* I don't mean sexual, I mean close relationships with—because they saw themselves in a paternal role, even though they were my friends or whatever, and then, when I exhibited my equality with them by having the right to say and do the things that they were saying and doing, they became offended, I think because they did not see that as my role or they didn't expect me to exhibit the same kinds of characteristics and attitudes and dispositions as they had.

While I have not heard the term *pets* used before in referring to the paternal relationship whites have with black adults in a formal or informal adoption setting, I do see (and have experienced) patterns of paternalistic/unequal relationships between white adoptive parents/adoption professionals and adult adoptees of color. When I have experienced what you talk about as an adult within the adoption arena, it feels like I'm being patted on the head, and there is a usually a "caring tone" the person uses when they tell me essentially that they know what is best for me as an adoptee—and they barely know my name. The good news is that discussion on this issue is starting to take place in the transracial adoption community because it is a reality.

Having said all that, how were you perceived by the community you grew up with in the projects?

I think it varied. Some of them saw me as an oddity.

Was this community predominately black?

Yes. It was all black. I don't remember a white person or a Hispanic person in the two-mile radius of where I lived.

I was perceived as an oddity for a while. Rhonda, I never changed. I was always me. I knew that I wanted something out of life. I wanted to be successful. I just had dreams. I always strived to achieve greatness and success, and so once they saw that and saw the difference between me and them, and the fact that my success was coming at an early age of sixteen or seventeen, they began to have great respect for me, and it has not diminished to this day.

You earned your B.S., M.A., M.Ed., and Ph.D. degrees within an intense and compressed period of time. During this stage of higher education, how did your identity develop? Did you feel smart, valued as a person and as a black man, specifically? Was your own rhythm and experience reflected in the curriculum you were taught and in your college experience? If not, how did you compensate?

I felt like I was becoming the Vershawn that I had always been. In terms of my identity, I would not have felt complete or full if I did not have a Ph.D. I knew when I was in high school that I was going to get a Ph.D. There was no doubt about it. I felt like that was my trajectory, just like people go from childhood to adolescence to adulthood. That's just what we do when you get older. That's how we socialize people into our world: you are a teenager, you are an adult. To be the black man that I knew myself to be, I needed to get a Ph.D. And I have two master's degrees. You don't need two master's degrees to get a Ph.D. But I didn't feel restricted in my own mind in any way. I felt great! When I say that, I am not saying it in a superfluous way. No, I mean that like Alexander the Great. I felt like a great person. I felt accomplished. I felt like I could do things. I used to have flying dreams. That's how school made me feel, and by getting these degrees I felt like I was Superman. I have a very high self-concept and very high self-esteem. I am not overblown. I am not arrogant. I don't say no to myself. I let other people say no. I am not afraid to ask questions or try new things.

Where did you get that from?

It came from my childhood. I think that it came a lot from my mother, who allowed me a certain kind of space. Now don't get me wrong: my mother was complicated. She tried to restrict me, too, because she was afraid that as I moved into the white world that I would be harmed. Though she also knew that the only way for me to be successful was to provide me with educational opportunities, and she supported those. I grew up in a large family. I have eight siblings. Being number 8—I have a younger sister, and she is number 9—I had to fight for myself or get beat up, so to speak. I saw that, too, when you knew how to get things done, things went better for you. And then I just learned. Like I said, it meant so much to me, to my self-identity, to be educated as I am.

One of the most eye-opening and raw experiences I think for many black and biracial transracial adoptees, like myself, who have been raised with a color-blind mind-set, is that we eventually step out into a harsh and indifferent society without our white parents or siblings to validate us. That color-blind bubble that we grew up in [was] filled with a hefty dose of white privilege bursts. The unfortunate part is that for too many of us, we don't have a playbook on how to deal with walking on a street, sitting in a restaurant, serving on a board, or being stopped by a police officer while black or brown. What are the rules that you abide by? What are the rules for, particularly black males, being stopped by the police? Given that you are quite educated, are you now exempt from some of these rules?

I think that my education, my middle-class identity, my sense of culture and understanding—all of that works for me to insulate me sometimes, not all of the times, from the routine surveillance and oppression that other black men face. Because I am somewhat domesticated in my blackness by me being a professor—and other characteristics, like growing up with five sisters and Mom all the way to my curiosity in reading books—I come across as different from the black men that are most threatening. And I also know how to capitalize on that when I go into, for instance, restaurants. I ask questions insightfully and those I am talking to hear it in my speech. They see my mannerisms, and they hear a kind of college talk. And so it does insulate me in some ways. I realize that my bourgeois sensibilities and performance protect me.

However, I dislike the fact [that] some people think that all black men should be me, and [that] if they were, they wouldn't be in as much trouble as they are in. That is ridiculous. Black people—women and men and children—should be allowed to be as varied as any other group of people. To put them all together into one role or one model is outrageous. I can't stand it when other black middle-class or upper-class people like Bill Cosby come out criticizing underclass black people for doing this or that. Nobody comes out and criticizes whites on the basis of race for shooting up people in Columbine. They don't say, "Oh, that is a white person and they need to get it together!" No!! In other words every human on the face of the earth is imperfect. Every racial group has people who commit crimes and do all sorts of things. And black people should not be scrutinized to such an extreme degree for behaviors that every racial group exhibits. So, no, I don't think that they should all be like me. I think that racism should just stop!

Recently you published another book, *From Bourgeois to Booji: Black Middle-Class Performances* (2011), which looks at the progress of the black middle class . . . from the post–Jim Crow era to the present. What is the premise?

Let me define the difference between *bourgeois* and *booji*. *Bourgeois* describes our common perception of middle-class people. It is the French term that basically means middle class. Now there are degrees of "middle classness," but I am not going to go into that. In general *bourgeois* means the middle-class sensibilities, attitudes, ways of living, and ways of thinking. *Booji*, on the other hand, is a black term that sort of means *acting* like you are middle class. Sometimes the word is used in a positive sense. For example: That person is very booji. But sometimes the word is used as an epithet to say that that person is acting like something that they are not, like they are acting white, so to speak. Or the word *booji* is used when the person is acting too snobbish, like they are looking down on people who are just like them.

The idea behind my book is—in E. Franklin Frazier's study the *Black Bourgeoisie: The Rise of a New Middle Class in the United States,* there was a group that was not really discussed. In this [1957] study Frazier said that people who benefited from civil rights opportunities and from the civil rights bill that were underclass but because of affirmative action et cetera they were able to raise their class status—this was *not* the group he was studying.

And so my book actually is a book that looks at that particular group of people. Who are black people, who like myself were raised economically poor but took advantage of affirmative action opportunities and increased their class status? What is their perception [of] America, class identity, gender, affirmative action, et cetera?

Because I think that the middle class should not just be studied by sociologists or in sociological categories, it is really a book that looks at the black middle class from an arts and humanity perspective . . . how poets think about black middle-class people, playwrights, and visual artists. There are also essays on womanhood and manhood.

In your opinion, especially given your education and life experiences, how can white parents who adopt transracially help their children of color competently navigate in different worlds without eliminating the core of who they are?

White people who adopt transracially need to do some autoethnographic work. I think that of course they need to look at how they can benefit their kids that they have adopted, but I think that they also need to think about themselves. What does it mean to be a white person in this society, and what does it mean to be a white person raising black kids? I think that they would do themselves a great benefit by being open to the ugliness as well as the beauty and cultural and interracial interactions in relation to transracial adoption. They cannot ignore their white privilege and the ways that they will pass on some of that white privilege to their kids and some of their white privilege that won't be passed on. It is difficult. Parenting is difficult no matter what race you are or what race your kids are, but it is even more difficult, I think, transracially. I am not saying that it shouldn't be done—it's just more difficult. Also I don't think that white parents adopting kids of color should try to define what white is or try to define what black is for their kids. They should give their kids a *range* of opportunities to mix with different types of people in different types of groups with some freedoms.

My wife has two kids that are biracial, white and black. And I witnessed with them—and they are teenagers, one is thirteen and one is sixteen—a *tremendous* racial struggle, their difficulty with trying to define themselves as white or black. My wife is black, but they would say to me that I am so dark. I could have let that stuff get to me at first, but I had to nip it in the bud.

How exactly did you nip the situation in the bud?

I told them yes, that I was dark and they were light-skinned, and why did that matter? I couldn't really get into a theoretical conversation with them at the time. But I did not want these categorical racial distinctions based on skin color being brought up in my house. I am the step-parent, but I was the person who was being pushed to the edge because I am dark.

Through my actions I hope I am showing my stepkids that it is not okay to make superficial distinctions about people. This is still sort of transracial, when I think about my experience. I try to have my stepkids around all types of different people: around my colleagues at the university level but also around people from the 'hood, around people who are white and people who are black. Also it is important for them to be in company where black and white people are *together* and not just separate, so they don't think that they have to be this way with one group and that way with another group. These kinds of diverse interactions are tremendously important to me for my stepkids to have.

Dr. Young, thank you immensely for your time. I know that your schedule is full to the brim, and you have to head out to an appointment. Your words today have opened my mind further on the issues of race, identity, and adoption. It is much appreciated.

MICHELLE M. HUGHES
Adoption Attorney and Adoptive Mother
INTERVIEWED BY TELEPHONE, JANUARY 21, 2013

Michelle, it is a pleasure to speak with you about children, families, adoption, and race. Given that you are a biracial woman, adoptive mother, daughter, adoption attorney, and a transracial adoption

expert, I think your perspective will be fascinating. First, my condolences go to you on the loss of your father. What are two key values he taught you that you apply to your life today?

One of the things that I asked my father was "What is your philosophy of life?" He said, "Live it." I think that internally I have always taken that away and have always believed in living my life and gaining new experiences. In fact I often say that I am more interested in spending my money on experiences than on things. That was definitely one of the values that I took away from him. Frankly being frugal is another value that I took away from both my father and mother. The other thing that I would say, especially because of his passing being so recent, [w]hat has definitely left an imprint on me is the whole concept about fighting for what you believe in and that everybody should be entitled to respect as a human being, regardless of race.

Some of the things that have come out during my dad's passing shed light onto who my dad was and his desire for a racially integrated society. For example, one of the stories that I recently heard was about my dad's time as a World War II veteran. He was stationed in Tennessee in the South in the 1940s. He was part of a movement that pushed for racial integration on that base with regards to the library. And as his friend said, "Your dad lived to tell about it." And so as different stories came out in different parts of his life, I realized that he had always been pushing for racial integration. It wasn't just personal. It was public. Another story is that he would walk into grocery stores and fast-food places, and if there were not enough blacks or no blacks, he would find the manager and tell them, "You need to hire some black people." To know that my father actually voiced that concern, I think is probably part of the legacy of why I have such an outspoken personality and sometimes tell people what I think, which is not always in my best interest, but I do it anyway.

Tell me about your childhood: What was it like to be biracial and to grow up with parents from different racial and ethnic backgrounds? And can you expand upon how the 1967 *Loving v. Virginia* decision shaped your reality and that of your parents?

I think that the 1967 *Loving v. Virginia* decision impacted me more as an adult as I understood what my parents had done.[1] My parents were married before the decision. So when they were married, inter-racial marriage was actually *illegal* in fourteen states. And as a child I remember hearing stories. For example my father is from the Jim Crow South Texas, to be specific. So we would fly to Texas. Now remember in the 1960s and 1970s flying was really expensive. But we would fly to Texas because there was no way that we were going to drive through Arkansas and Mississippi to get to Houston. It would be dangerous. So the fact that my parents were interracially married during a time when it was not popular, and in some states dangerous, it did impact our family, but I don't think that I fully understood the meaning of the case and how it affected me or them on a larger scale as a young child. From what I understand, there were some family members that disowned my mother because she was going to marry a black man. My white grandfather refused to come to the wedding because my mother was getting interracially married. However, his wife, my white grand-mother, whose parents refused to come to her wedding because she married a Catholic and she was Lutheran, made sure she was at her daughter's wedding regardless. Fast-forward several years later: I have memories of fishing with my white grandfather. I do believe people can become more racially enlightened, especially in interpersonal re-lationships, if they choose to. Neither people or cultural norms need to stay stagnant, as evidenced by the *Loving* decision and my grandfather.

I think that my parents' marriage in many ways affected my identity because my parents *were* married. One of the reasons why I think my identity as a biracial woman is so strong is because both of my parents were always present in my day-to-day life. Both of my parents' racial identities were always present. One of my friends recently said that my parents were the only interracial couple that he knew who did not lose their racial identity when they got married. So my father, despite being married to a white woman, was still a black man from [the] Jim Crow South, and my mother, despite being married to a black man, is still the white farm girl from the North. Each one of their racial identities really impacted me because it is not only that I am a part of both of those racial identities, but it is also the integration of those identities. For me I always saw white and black getting along. I'm not saying my parents did not have their struggles; every marriage does over nearly a fifty-year period. But when I got up in the morning as a child, I saw a black man and a white woman get out of their bedroom, get up and make breakfast, raise the kids, and do whatever they were going to do. We always had dinner together at the dining room table as a family every night. So for me it was confusing when other people were fighting with each other on a racial level, because within my own personal four walls of the home, it was not what occurred.

In my family I am the oldest of three. I have two younger siblings, one sister and one brother. And in many ways I thought as a child that we were the strange family, in the sense of being the interracial family. But as I got older, especially when I got into college and met other families, I thought, "Oh, my God, we are Ozzie and Harriet" because we were literally the family that ate dinner together at the table every night. We were that family that went to church every Sunday. We were that family that had that suburban thing going on. So it was really this interesting realization that in a lot of ways we were very traditional, although in other ways we were very atypical. It was trying to figure out that balance.

As a young child we lived in Chicago. Apparently when my parents moved to that neighborhood in 1965, it was predominately white. When we left, in 1973, that same neighborhood was almost entirely black. So it was right at the height of major white flight. White flight was huge in Chicago. My mom remembers getting phone calls from people that would openly say, "Hey, the neighborhood is going to go black. It is changing. Do you want to sell your house?" And she would say, "Well, we just moved in." In any case by the time I was school age, I was living in pretty much an entirely black neighborhood. In school I remember the one white kid in the class because that kid was the *only* white kid in the class. When we moved into the suburbs when I was roughly eight, I went from an all-black environment to an all-white environment. And then I was the only black kid among my peers. So it was a pretty radical shift. There were some childhood things that I was upset about, like how white kids don't jump Double Dutch. I was *just* about to learn Double Dutch in Chicago, but we moved. If we had stayed in the city for one more year, I would have been able to do it. But there were definitely other and more important ramifications

[from] moving to the all-white suburbs that left its imprint on me. By high school it was much more crystal clear about navigating the racial obstacles that come with being one of the few. Or maybe it was the racial obstacles just being in our society.

In school or in your community did you get teased because you looked different?

I got called the "N-word," not a lot but I can tell you who called me it to this day. I don't remember getting teased that much, but I do remember feeling different. I think that as a little kid the fact that my skin was darker compared to the other kids' I interacted with was not as much of an issue. I do remember that once I started getting into junior high school and began liking boys and stuff like that, it became much more difficult for me because I didn't look like all of the rest of my classmates, even though within my own home of course interracial dating was acceptable. However, outside in the real world a lot of people did not find it acceptable. So it made it much more complicated. To make a long story short, eventually I dated outside of my high school because it wasn't really going to happen within the high school. There were some other complexities, given the few options of African American males in my high school, but let's just say that there were few options and not good options.

What centered you as an individual and young adult that allowed you to reach to academic and professional success despite the obstacles that you faced [from] society?

I think that part of it was my inner strength. I always just assumed that I was going to college. It was something that I was going to do. Part of it was my family. I always had my family's support. It was friends certainly. I also think, truthfully, moving to the suburbs for a better academic education was also a great influencer. The city school would not have given me the expectation to achieve, even though I personally had that expectation. Once I moved to the suburban schools it was just assumed that you went to college, regardless of race. Yes, there were a few teachers that you had to dodge—and that was one of things that you learned, that certain teachers would visually see you, and that was the end of your chance at excelling in that particular class. So you learned not to take certain teachers, right? And that was throughout my academic career. Among the few black students, whether it was high school or whether it was law school, it would get out: "Don't take so and so because this teacher or this professor will never give a black student an A."

Did you have mentors to help guide you through some of these obstacles? What did you do when you hit a roadblock or when somebody told you that you couldn't achieve a task because of your race?

To a certain degree my parents were always there, but that is not to say that they did everything correctly. For example one roadblock that comes to mind was when I was in junior high. The school administrators told my parents that I shouldn't take honors classes in high school despite having mostly As in junior high. And my parents listened to them. To make a long story short, I actually decided on my own that this decision was not appropriate for me, and so in my sophomore year in high school I changed my academic schedule so that I was taking honors classes. I think a lot of it is internal. It was an internal compass that said this isn't right, and I am going to change it. At a very early age I was always this headstrong child, which I probably learned from my father. It is actually interesting that I focus on race now, because back then I focused on gender. Another example: in elementary school I learned that there was a boys' soccer team but there was *no* girls' soccer team. I went ballistic. And in fifth grade I actually organized a petition. And they had girls' soccer the following year. I think that I got about two hundred signatures. I was, like, this is *not* appropriate, where is girls' soccer?

I also remember a time when I was a freshman in high school. I was sort of coaching the girls' basketball team, but I needed my father to assist me because there needed to be an adult. Anyway, we were at a game and somebody was messing around in the bathroom. The mayor, who was attending the game, came out onto the court—in the middle of the game, mind you—and proceeded to yell at the crowd about messing up the bathroom. I was livid. I actually said something to the effect of, "If this was a boys' basketball game, you would have at least waited to come onto the court after a dead ball. But, no, because this is a girls' game, you showed no respect and interfered with the play." Later the mayor caught up with me as we were leaving and said that I was a "snotty kid and disrespectful." My father told him, "No,

she is not a 'snotty kid.' She is correct in her analysis of the situation."
And so I am not sure to what degree I would say that my parents were
role models in standing up for what was right and to what degree it was
probably just who I was.

**Today you are a single mother of a beautiful son, who came to
you through adoption. What does that mean to you and for you?**

He is an amazing child, not just because he is beautiful but also
because he is charismatic and dramatic and verbal and opinionated
and variety of other things. I would say he is amusing. I think that it
is part of achieving one of the things that I wanted to achieve in life,
which is being a parent. I feel very blessed to be his parent. I hope one
day he will be able to say the same, to say that he is blessed to have
me as a mother.

What was it like to adopt your son?

I think that it was different for me than most people, partially because I knew too much about adoption, from being an adoption professional. I think to a certain degree I had to be pushed off the ledge,
like a lot of people who are considering adoption. You think about it
for awhile and finally somebody says to you, "You either have to do
this or not do this." More or less it was another adoption attorney who
pushed me off the ledge. Although I have to say, I was one of those
people, even as a child, who thought that I would adopt. As a child I
was *adamant* that I was only going to adopt, which ironically turned
out to happen.

I think the other way the adoption process was a very different experience for me was that, before adopting my son, I was connected with
an expectant mom who later chose to parent her child. I don't think
that I was as devastated, angry, or some of the other feelings that a lot
of potential parents have that come with a failed connection, because I
felt that it was her choice, number 1. I never really viewed her child as
my child until papers were signed, which they weren't. And number 2,
I didn't feel like it was the end. I felt there would be another connection. I didn't know when but that there would be. As it turned out it
was a cliché: What is meant to happen, happens. The right connection
was made for me in adopting my son. We are very much connected.
But I also say that in my connection with his biological mom. From

my perspective I am also tied to her for life through him. Therefore I feel like it was meant to be, in the sense that, if I had to be tied to a woman for life, I am glad it is his birth mom. I am happy to say that I like her, and I think that she likes me. I look at adoption like extended family. Just like when you marry somebody, sometimes you get great extended family and sometimes you tolerate them. I think that I have a pretty good extended family.

What narrative do you tell your son about how he came into his family?

My son is still a toddler. I am one of those "tell them the truth" parents. Also I talk to him like an adult, which might be problematic. But I break the story down basically to the level that he can understand. I have included in my library a lot of books on adoption. I think that my son and I are going to have a lot more conversations in the next year. He is just at that point where we will be able to have conversations. But he has always had children's books with people who are adopted or families with adoption. I have also made sure that there are pictures of his birth mother out. In fact somebody was in his room the other day and saw a picture and said, "Who is that?" And my son casually said who it was. He just knew. I always want him to understand that it is part of his story and part of his identity. It is not a secret. It is not something that is to be discussed only when he is older. It is what it is. Also, because of what I do and because of how I feel about adoption, I had been going to a lot of adoption camps, adoption conferences. So by age two my son had already been to, like, six adoption camps and I don't even know how many adoption conferences. I would just bring him with. And because of what I do through the multiracial community, a lot of my friends happen to also be adopted. If I need a babysitter, I call up my friends. They're there as adults who have experienced adoption too. It is just a part of his world.

Does your family support your son?

Oh, yes. My family completely supports my son.

Did you have a conversation with your parents when you decided to adopt?

Yes. When I told my parents, especially my mom, she basically said to me it is about time. My nephew, who was five, had to do an art project at school about family. My sister thought that he was going to do something about her. It turned out that his art project was all about his cousin. And he had not met my son yet. It's funny. In his art project he said something to the effect of, "This is my cousin from Chicago. He is black like me. He is African." It was so cute. My nephew and niece couldn't wait to meet my son. They call my son their brother even though he is their cousin. I think that as a whole my immediate family was very welcoming of my son. And he has a very close relationship with his grandma and had a very close relationship with his grandfather. Also I would say that some of my extended family was very supportive. What surprised me was that some of my extended racist family, which were mostly aunts and uncles, were also supportive. I would say that the whole family was welcoming. I was not one of those people that had to convince people about my decision to adopt or received negative feedback. And then, once you meet my son, your heart melts.

How did you become interested in transracial adoption?

I became interested in transracial adoption because of growing up in a multiracial family. I became a huge advocate for multiracial families. And I started getting involved in some multiracial organizations but didn't feel like they really covered biracial people very well. Hence I started my own social group for biracial adults. One of the things that I discovered is that easily 40 percent of the biracial people who would show up for anything were adopted and mostly transracially adopted. I think of all of the biracial people I met that were adopted, I think that I only met one who was adopted by an interracial couple. Because of that I started having a lot of friends who were transracially adopted; even prior to that, one of my best friends was biracial and transracially adopted. I think that my best friend and I connected on the multiracial level as well as some other levels. But that was actually years before I started putting groups together. So that's how I sort of tripped over into transracial adoption. And then I created Bridge Communications with a biracial transracial adoptee and then brought in another biracial transracial adoptee to Bridge Communications.

What does Bridge Communications do?

Bridge Communications focuses on diversity training or diversity parenting training. Most of our classes are geared toward transracial adoption. Although on occasion we do biracial identity work, or we do just general diversity training for corporations. But the majority of what we do is work with potential adoptive parents and adoption professionals to help them understand what it means to be a multiracial family and to make better choices for the children who will be living in multiracial families, through adoption usually.

Do you see progress in the transracial adoptive movement from the 1970s to the present time? What is different and what has stayed the same?

I do see progress, but I don't see it with everybody. Since the 1970s there are a lot of things that I see as different compared to today. Based on some of the research that I have read, conducted by scholar Gina M. Samuels [an associate professor at the School of Social Service Administration at the University of Chicago], and from my talks with her and other adoption professionals, it appears to me that a lot of the transracial adoption placements in the '60s and '70s were heavily biracial children as opposed to African American children with two African American parents. I see that now it is more African American children being placed transracially. I think that some of the parents today are consciously more aware that race is an issue in our society and are addressing that issue. I think that goes for some of the adoption agencies, although I see a lot of agencies still oblivious to it. And I think that it is a mix. Sometimes I talk to social workers, and social workers are really scared of IEPA, the Interethnic Placement Act. And so sometimes you can have private conversations with them, and they are much more aware of what is going on than what they are able to do. I like to call IEPA the affirmative action for white people to adopt black kids, frankly. And, yes, I realize I am misdefining *affirmative action*.

I think that provision within the IEPA Act of 1996 in relation to adoptions that concerned many social workers was the part that reads, "States and other entities that receive funds from the Federal Government and involved in foster care or adoption placements may not delay or deny a child's foster care or adoptive placement based upon the race, color, or national origin of the parent or the child."

Yes. Sometimes the things that I hear coming out of the mouths of some social workers, I am blown away at how uninformed they are about race in America. And because of the way things operate within the adoption system, I think that race is very low on the totem pole of things to be concerned about when placing black children. And that is today, especially in the private agency sector. For me there are different things going on. Everybody lumps adoption together, but I think that international adoption versus foster care adoption versus private agency adoption are three different segments of adoption. They overlap in some ways, and in other ways they don't overlap at all. So for example in international adoption, even though international adoption is tanking, [some agencies that handle] international adoption, because of the requirements of cultural Hague trainings, . . . are beginning to address issues of race.[2] They don't address it as race per se; they address it as culture. And I would argue that culture and race are two different things. But race gets sneaked into some of the training via culture.

What would you say are the differences between race and culture?

Every culture has the possibility of having multiple races. And every race has the possibility of having multiple cultures. I would argue to a large degree that race is a social construct based on how people look and group together. And that race changes somewhat from country to country. But ultimately we have an understanding in the United States of black, white, Native American, Asian, and Latino. I would question Latino['s] being a race, but that is how we operate in the United States so I am going to qualify them as a race for the purposes of how the layperson in America would define race. I realize that's not the way it is defined on any type of census or that the fact that Latinos come in every race and every combination of races. I would argue that they are one of the biggest multiracial populations. Nevertheless they operate like a race in our society. Whereas culture has to do with how a particular group of people do things, whether it is art or food or rituals like marriage or burials. It could also be the way in which they have language between each other. And I don't mean language in that people speak English or Spanish but in their body language and different cues that people communicate, like the way they greet people, how they treat the elderly, how they treat the disabled. Culture is how we operate within a group of people. [Like] most people we have multiple cultures because we have a bunch of subcultures. For example I operate as an American, but I also operate as a person in the African American community. I also operate as a midwesterner. I also operate as a woman. I have multiple cultures going on. I operate as being part of a multiracial family as part of my culture. So when I think of race, I would lump Nigerians, Jamaicans, African Americans as black, but they have very different cultures, even if they all lived down the street in Chicago.

Have you seen drastic changes in the challenges transracial adoptive parents faced in the 1960s and 1970s compared to those who are adopting today?

I do think that since the 1960s and 1970s racist things have become more subtle. I think that some of the things that the kids in the '70s and '80s had to deal with were very out in the open, and a lot of that stuff has now gone underground. The kids still have to deal with it, except that it is harder and more complex. One of the things that I do is talk at culture camps for teens. I am hearing twelve-year-olds, fifteen-year-olds telling the same stories that I am hearing forty-one-year-olds tell. In my Bridge Communications classes I put together a panel of adult adoptees to speak on their experiences. I try to get an age variation because I think, Rhonda, you're right, especially when you have adults who are in their thirties and forties adopting, listening to forty-year-old adoptees tell their stories. The stories of those adoptees in their forties may not initially seem to these potential and adoptive parents as relevant to their realities and to what their child is experiencing. That is why I also find twenty-year-olds to tell their story, to show that it's twenty years later and this is still going on. I don't use teenagers because they have not processed their experiences, plus you need to get parental permission, et cetera. But I personally know from talking to teenagers that it is still the same stuff going on compared to the families who adopted transracially, for instance, in the early 1970s.

I think that back in the early 1970s there was at least the civil rights movement putting fire under the feet of folks in this society to think about social justice and racial inclusivity. We had the Na-

tional Association of Black Social Workers (NABSW), who strongly addressed their clear concerns about children of color raised in white homes, especially black children raised in white homes, so there was at least from adoptive parents back then a recognition that maybe race does matter, and it is not just about color-blindness and love. Now I think some of our families operate in this "postracial" era.

I think you get a lot of people operating in a postracial era with some kind of color-blind religious stance. You know: "Love is enough." It is interesting to me because you also have the other group of transracial adoptive parents who are so conscious of their white privilege and of racism that they work overtime to make sure that their kid not only gets their history and heritage of their racial background but also the cultural pieces, that they have friends of color and focus on the more complex stuff. It is not like they are saying, "Oh, let's celebrate Kwanzaa with all of our white friends." They make sure that they have black friends around the table too. They make sure that there are black role models for their kids. So I am finding that in this new millennium that you have parents at both ends of the spectrum. I think that there are more parents now that are aware and are very conscious of race and adoption matters, and I also see that there are parents that are more naive than ever.

What are the major concerns that you find particularly white adoptive parents face today when raising their children of color?

I think that white adoptive parents need to face their own prejudices, which I don't think many of them have done. And therefore they don't have a comfort level of adult people who are the same race as their child. What I find is a lot of parents adopting transracially will navigate to support groups of other parents adopting children transracially, which, by the way, I think is really important, that transracially adoptive families and other multiracial families interact with each other. For adoptive parents we should find support on multiple levels. But what I find missing is the fact that many transracial adoptive parents are not comfortable going into environments where everybody looks like their child. One of the things that is fascinating for me is that on Facebook, there is a group that talks about how to do black hair. How many black salons are in this country of black women doing black hair?! The group that gets the most attention is these white moms who are able to do black hair. It is interesting to me that they are still not interested in adults that look like their child, which I find problematic because obviously the kids are picking up on that message.

How do parents make that transition into the black community, where they become comfortable communicating with adults that look like their child?

It depends upon the parent. I don't think that some parents will ever make the transition, which probably means that they shouldn't be adopting transracially and that the social worker should do a better job of screening who gets what kid. Not everybody should be approved to parent across racial lines. But for those who do, I think that for most parents they have to ease into it. By easing into it, they need to start with other multiracial groups and then move deeper into the community in time. I think that it helps if they have a good relationship with their child's birth family would be number 2. And number 3 they need to realize that their life does not have to radically change because they have become a multiracial family in order to find the resources of mentors and friends of the same race as their child. Sometimes people think that, just because I am adopting a child from another race, I have to now stop doing what I love to do. One of the things that I say in my classes is that if you love to bowl, instead of bowling in an all-white league, go find a multiracial league to bowl in. It's not like you have to stop bowling. Black people bowl. Black people go fishing. Black people knit. Black people do all the same things white people do.

Going back to your previous question, the other thing that I find that white adoptive parents are now facing that is different from the past because of openness [open adoption] is how *class* and *race* intersect. And so let's be frank: most birth parents are living on the edge and are probably near the poverty line today. And most adoptive parents, especially with the average cost of private adoptions being roughly $30,000, are at least middle class. So you have this intersection of class being forced because of the openness. In the past you had closed adoptions. So frankly you did not know one way or the other. But now you do, and so you have middle-class white parents meeting poor black birth mothers.

And they are digesting often, especially if they don't have black friends themselves, that black means socially and economically deprived. And some would argue that due to institutional racism that there are more socially [and] economically deprived black people. The truth is that most black people are not. And their kids are going to go to school with black middle-class kids probably, not black socially [and] economically deprived kids. Adoptive parents have this new challenge of how to integrate class in a positive way for their child, especially if their child is coming from a birth family that is struggling with economic issues, and adding in race on top of it.

There are always exceptions to the rules, but I would say, too, that one of the differences now, from what I have seen in the past, is that most birth mothers today are women already parenting. Most birth mothers of the 1960s and 1970s were perhaps the classic idea of a teenager getting pregnant or a very young woman getting pregnant, and this is her first child. Where[as] the realities of what I have seen as an adoption professional, now, is that, yes, occasionally I do get the teen that is pregnant, but most of these women are eighteen to twenty-six years of age and already have a child or two. These women slowly understand what it means to parent, and part of the reason that they are making such a difficult decision is the socioeconomics of being able to feed the two children or the one child or the three children that they are already parenting. It plays into this whole class-race thing going on. It is very different, I think, than it was in the past. Openness and the Internet have changed everything.

In your workshop sessions for adoptive families and those interested in adopting transracially, what material do you cover that helps parents understand the complexities of race and adoption? And what tools do you share that will help them navigate effectively through the triumphs and challenges of this type of family building?

Well, it depends on which program we are putting on, but usually in our standard class at Bridge Communications we break it out into three different sessions. The first session I like to call "Race + Adoption = Education." And we always do interactive exercises because it is not a lecture. It is about incorporating exercises to help people *process* their own feelings. The first thing that I need to get people to do as quickly as possible is to address their own prejudices. People do not like to admit their own prejudices. We have in this society been instilled with all of this institutional racism that we see on TV, newspapers, magazines, Internet, et cetera. It is in us. Whether we can actually name it or not, it is in us. We have to first address those prejudices. So I like to do exercises that both let people see their world, *world* meaning their world in the United States, and then see how their family members view their own world, specifically how they view a particular group of people. And then we explore how we talk about those issues that were raised and actually make changes within our families to help primarily our children.

The second class focuses on role-play[ing]. I use role-plays from either stories that transracial adoptees have told me or transracial adoptive parents have told me. One client who was in my class about two years ago sent me an e-mail that said, "Michelle, let me tell you what happened at the Walmart today!" And I said, "Thank you, great role-play." So I am constantly updating the role-plays because I want people who are going to the class to understand that this is not necessarily what happened forty years ago, but rather I got this e-mail two weeks ago or last year. So my role-plays are always contemporary with different scenarios of how to address sensitive situations adoptive families experience regularly.

Through the role-play[ing] we try to teach parents how to respond to different circumstances, what do you say to your child and to the person that, let's say, made an insensitive comment to you about your family? How do you address these situations as a parent? How do you do it with humor? How do you do it with setting boundaries? How do you do it with finding support systems? You need to learn how to work through the different ways because different scenarios need different responses, and different people need different responses. Not only do adoptive parents have different personalities but so do the kids. And sometimes an adoptive family will adopt three different kids, and they all have three very different personalities. So parents need to learn that with this one kid, when people say stupid things or ask stupid questions with regards to transracial adoption, you can use humor. If the kid thinks it is funny, he will play along with you. And with another kid in the same family, if humor is not the appropriate response, then you really have to set boundaries because this child does not want to be put on the spot. So it is about teaching parents that they sometimes have to step out of their comfort zone. Actually all of this is about teaching parents to step out of their comfort zone to make it comfortable for their children to navigate the world.

I know that idea of stepping out of your comfort zone can be scary for some adoptive parents.

Yes, it is very scary for some parents but not all parents. Some parents welcome the challenge. In my classes what is so interesting to me is that the parents who welcome the challenges are the parents who least need the classes, because they are the parents who have already been seeking out these cross-cultural and cross-racial experiences. And those are the parents who probably already had black friends long before they were thinking about adoption. The parents who are the most resistant [to] coming through my classes are the parents that need it the most.

Usually for many potential parents who want to adopt, this is the first time that they have ever had to address transracial issues. What is fascinating to me, too, is when you have white people come through the first class who are not familiar with race issues, a lot of them will tell me that these issues are not relevant to them so they don't need to address it. It is not personal. The reality is when you become a multiracial family, whether it is through marriage or adoption, all of a sudden some of the stuff becomes personal because it is no longer "somebody out there that I don't know," it is *my* child. I remember I did this one class where we had a couple in there who was adopting from Guatemala. This was about six years ago. They were very offended that their adoption agency made them go through this class. They were also very upset that they had to drive an hour to get to the class. Ironically I had people in the class who were flying in from Minnesota. That was easily resolved when I said in front of the class the family from Minnesota would get the award for coming the farthest. In the first class they went through the exercises having to do with their own perceptions and the world's perceptions of race. It was very uncomfortable for the parents. And I have actually had people in the first class never come back because it was too uncomfortable for them to deal with stereotypes and interracial stuff. They didn't want to address it.

This one couple, I remember the wife in particular, they went to the class. They really didn't want to deal with this class. By the second class they came back with a whole different disposition. The mother said, "Since this class I have been paying attention to what people are saying. Do you know what my cousin just said last week about Latino people?" And that is when the reality hit, that this was going to be her child having to listen to her cousin say this racist stuff about Latino kids, and her kid was Guatemalan.

I think that the hard part is, particularly for transracial adoptees, making that transition from home to society in living color.

I agree. I hear that from the kids that I talk with. These kids need to have tools to help them transition into the broader world.

So what are three or four of these tools that you talk about that transracial adoptees are in need of when navigating as a person of color?

One would be understanding that racism still exists. That is a huge one: putting a name on racism and giving your child the words to talk about racism, I found that to be true especially with junior high kids. Often their parents want to make the world all rosy and not let their child think about difficult realities in the world. And so they don't actually give them the words. I have actually been in classes where I have had to literally define words like *minority* to junior high kids. I don't think that black kids with black parents would not know what the word *minority* means by the time the kid is thirteen. It would just be a word you would know by then that you could define. But I have found sometimes that kids of color with white parents do not know that word yet. So it is about giving kids a language.

Number 2 would be understanding the nuances of racism. Not only does racism exist, but you can break it down into the subtle and the overt types of racism. I think a lot of times people get the overt. It is the subtle form of racism that I don't think many potential adoptive parents, in this case, get. One of the examples I use for parents, not so much for kids, is the University of Chicago study done a few years ago (Bertrand

& Mullainathan, 2004). In that study résumés with "black names," "Latino names," and with "white names" were sent out to companies. Each résumé included the same credentials. And the white-sounding names got more calls to come for an interview. So this is one of those things that is subtle because it is not obvious. The person who would have had the black-sounding name may have thought that there were better candidates. The person who had the white-sounding name may have thought, Well, I am the best candidate. This study is what I like to use as an example to show that racial profiling is still going on, even if you can't see it, and to help people develop an antenna for when it occurs. Not everything that happens is racist. And then I think the third thing, I would say, is explaining white privilege. There are different definitions to describe white privilege, but I would say the shorter definition is being white gives you benefits in this society for just being white—often benefits that are not recognized.

Like going into a restaurant without having a shadow of suspicion over you. I know that is a benefit that white people in my circles don't see. On the other hand I have been to a restaurant with my husband and other black friends, and I hear, "Here we go again, we are invisible."

Right. Or without the assumption that "Oh, this table isn't going to tip." And that you can actually be Caucasian and be considered an individual as opposed to a group. When often I think that if you are African American or from another group of color, if you do something bad, it reflects on *everybody*. Where the white guy who robs the store, it is just "Joe" who robbed the store. The black guy who robbed the store, [it is] "Those black people keep stealing." So you get to be an individual, especially with negative stuff, if you are white. The group identity stuff is not as strong. Ironically it is really strong, but it's the norm so we don't have to discuss it. So it is the same thing when you see on TV that they are looking for some suspect. Somehow the black man or the Hispanic man is always described by their race. But if it is a white guy, it is just a male. We don't need to put his race in there, sarcastically speaking. I think that is why there is this need for black magazines, Hispanic magazines, and other group identity media outlets, because what happens in those communities, especially the positives, are not necessarily reflected in general American media. And that is why you have to do some group identity activities.

But at the same time, if you are a black kid being raised with white parents, your group identity as a black person is not quite the same because you are raised in a multiracial family plus the adoption piece. And finding all those put together is important for the child. So when I am talking to kids, it is about understanding white privilege and understanding that some of the white privilege that your parents have, you are getting now sort of in a boomerang effect, because you are living with your parents so you get some of it. But once you go out on your own, you may not get that privilege. Even if that means that your parents have better jobs because they are white people, which means that they can bring in more money, which means that you can go on better vacations. It plays out in many different ways. Another example is that because everybody knows that you are that white person's kid, they are not going to follow you around in the store. But once you go to another town where they don't know that your parents are white, people will follow you around the store. And especially if you get kids—more in that junior high range as opposed to the teenagers—they haven't had the independence to know what it means not to be part of their family. They are still perceived as part of their parents because they don't have the independence, where the teenager who can drive might be in a different town now, shopping. So they haven't been seen just as the black face or just as the Latino face. They are still seen as, "Oh, you are Bob and Suzie's kid." And so there is this big transition going on. You have to tie all this into the transition of preteen, teen, and young adult. The other thing is for parents to talk to their kids about their own perception of race and adoption.

As I mentioned before, we live in a racist society and it is *subtle* stuff. For example cartoons are my big beef at the moment because I have a toddler who is obsessed with cartoons. And so I am now watching cartoons and dissecting them by race and adoption. The other night, for example, we were watching *Rio*. It is a cute movie. What was my problem? The white people in the movie are the good people, and the bad people in the movie have African features.

For most people they would watch this movie and not think about the racial overtones. *Rio* is a very cute movie, and it is mostly about the animals, frankly, the birds. It is colorful. The music is wonderful. And yet I am thinking, By letting my child watch this, what message is he subtly picking up? Every time he watches *Bob the Builder*—that doesn't have a single person of color in it despite the fact that it is located on a construction site—what message is he picking up as opposed to *Rescue Heroes* that have tons of people of color, white, and everybody?

That is something to think about.

I think most parents don't really analyze cartoons. On a side note it is really interesting to me how much adoption plays out in cartoons too. For example *Dinosaur Train* has a transracial adoption theme.

The T. rex, Buddy, accidentally ends up in the pteranodon nest. *Dinosaur Train* actually addresses transracial adoption pretty well. There are episodes that actually deal with differences, like the T. rex can't fly but the pteranodon can, but they are all a family, and they work together to make sure T. rex gets to where he needs to go—[in] a lot of ways they deal with it pretty well. Another cartoon called *Sheldon* has an adoption theme. We accidentally ended up watching the cartoon *Anne of Green Gables*. It has the orphan adoption theme even though it goes back to the 1800s. It is amazing to me how many times the theme of adoption actually comes up in cartoons. Sometimes it gets handled very well, sometimes not. I think most of the time it is the omission of stuff. But sometimes it is just how families deal with it. To me it is all very interesting.

Why do you choose to continue your work in transracial adoption?

I continue to do transracial adoption work for three reasons. The first reason is because of my friends and some of their stories. The second reason is I continue to meet transracial adoptees and parents that totally miss the race piece, and I think that we can do better. I do not want this new generation of children to go through the same things as the previous generation went through. That is not to say that every transracial adoptee has this horrific story. That is not true. But I think that we can do a better job. Some of the horrific stories that I have heard over time should not be happening again. I think that social workers should do a better job of screening potential parents. Adoptive parents, I think, should be getting continuous training and should integrate into a larger diverse community. And then the third reason is that we as multiracial families, whether by adoption or by union, sit in a very unique position in this society because if it is done in a healthy way, we have learned the ability to navigate different racial and cultural circles. Therefore we also sit in a very unique position to help different communities understand that we are all human and that we all deserve respect regardless of our race. I think that is why so many of us do this outspoken work. There are so many people who talk about the negative sides of it, but one of the benefits of being biracial or transracially adopted and being put out there is that we do have this gift of being able to navigate different worlds. If it is done right, we can feel comfortable in multiple worlds. Now it is not always done right, and not everybody feels comfortable in multiple worlds. But for those of us who do get to that point, it is amazing. We have the ability to talk to different communities in ways that can support unity. I don't just mean we as people of color going into the white community and being able to talk to that community about "black issues." I also mean going into the black community and being able to talk to the black community about "white issues." If it is done right, we can also break down some of the myths about white people in the black community too.

I am sort of digressing, but as part of the training I do, it is also about getting white people to realize there are all sorts of stereotypes about them. It is fascinating. I do a whole exercise on stereotypes. So many white people know the stereotypes of people of color, but many don't know the stereotypes about themselves. That is always fascinating, to get them to understand the stereotypes of themselves, which is really important because if their kid of color is connecting with their own racial community—guess what they get to hear? "Don't your parents call you the 'N-word'?!" It is assumed that every white person is racist. So if you are in a multiracial family, that can be very perplexing for a child, to have to defend that their parents are not the white racist people that another child or adult may think.

That is a huge task.

White parents think about how they are going to have to deal with race, but it is now about getting them to the point of how is your kid going to have to deal with race? And then also both inter- and intra-[racial situations], because if they don't have any black friends, then they are not going to be able to understand all of the cultural nuances going on in the black community—or black communities would actually be more accurate. Therefore how do you teach your black child how to navigate the black community if you don't know anything about it? Eventually, unless your child is going to stay in an all-white farming community in the middle of nowhere (which some kids do), they are going to move into somewhere where they will run into other black people, whether it is in junior high or college or when they move into the city, whatever. All of a sudden they are going to be interacting with black people who will look at their black face and assume that they know certain black cultural nuances.

Surprise!

Right. *Surprise*, exactly. One of the stories I like to tell is about one of my panelists, who did not know this, and when she got to college, she really wanted to connect with the black community. And because she did not know the black nuances, she had pissed off the black community there quite quickly. Ironically she had to have her white roommate, who grew up in a multiracial neighborhood, help her navigate back into the black community. So it is interesting to me: that story says yes, white people can learn this, because her roommate knew it. And number 2, how important it is for that black adopted child to know it because they should not be offending the people that they are trying to connect with. There are multiple layers of that story. That particular adoptee, too, also has a story of the cultural nuances where beauty became an issue. So when I am telling her story, I also talk about her going from an all-white neighborhood to going to a more diverse college, where the standards of beauty were different for the African American males compared to the white males from the white high school she attended. She also had to navigate the perception of who she was as a woman and what these black men were saying to her. In high school this particular woman was the "ugly duckling."

She went to college, and within a moment she became this beautiful Beyoncé, so to speak. That can be overwhelming at eighteen years of age, when you go from nobody is interested in you and nobody wants to date you to very full-on interest. That was a navigation that she had to deal with. I use her story, but there are many black women who have experienced that, whether they have white parents or black parents, if they grew up in an all-white neighborhood or not. You need to get places where the center of beauty is larger than blue eyes, white skin, and double d-flat booty.

What legacy do you want to leave your son?

I want him to be comfortable in his skin. I want my child to be comfortable eventually as a black man, as an adoptee, as being part of a multiracial family, and as an American. I want him to be able to navigate multiple communities to the success of whatever he should want to be professionally. I am pushing for neurosurgeon at this moment, but I may not win that one. But whatever he should choose to be, I want him to feel comfortable in who he is as a person. I want him to feel comfortable in the sense that if I dropped him into any particular place, he could drop and roll and be himself. He doesn't have to assimilate to the degree that he loses who he is as a person but that he can still communicate with other people and show them the respect that he needs to show them, as well as demand the respect he deserves.

That is an important lesson you can learn in your adulthood years too.

Well, I am hoping that he can learn it at a younger age. The other legacy I want to give my son is to respect all people and view people within their own lenses. One of the things that I am very cognitive of right now in the adoption community is these all-inclusive statements. "All adoptees are X." "All adoptees feel Y." "All adoptive parents are XX." "All adoptive parents feel YY." "All birth mothers are X." "All birth mothers feel Y." I just don't think it is true. I want my son to understand that, even though we can make some generalizations, there is not one view in any particular group. And I could expand that beyond adoptees to black people, to white people, to girls, to boys, to rich people, to poor people, et cetera. And then I want him to understand that people come from different experiences. He is going to have his own lens as an African American adoptee male child, who is raised in the Midwest with a loud, proud biracial mother that stresses education. So that is going to be part of who his world is and how he sees the world. His mother is a lawyer. If I have my way, my son is also going to have the experiences of traveling internationally. And I am doing my darnedest to make him bilingual. But my point is that he is going to have that lens. The legacy that I want him to see is that not everybody will have that lens. Not everybody will have the same educational level that he has. Not everybody will have traveled internationally. Not everybody will be an adoptee who has multiple families. Not everybody will have been raised in a multiracial family. So the knowledge that he has may be different than the knowledge that other people have. And sometimes that means taking people in where they are at and learning to communicate and work with them, even when you may disagree with them or have more, or different, knowledge. All of those things I mentioned I want to leave with my son.

Thank you!

MAHISHA DELLINGER
CEO and Founder of Curls
INTERVIEWED BY TELEPHONE, MARCH 30, 2012

Mahisha, thank you for taking the time to have this conversation with me. You are the founder of Curls, which specializes in multiethnic hair care products. When was Curls formed, and what products have you created?

We launched Curls in 2002. I was in a restaurant in Santa Barbara, California, with my husband—at that time we were dating. I was sharing with him that I would like to explore a new professional opportunity. I was working for a large technology corporation and had an amazing first few years there in corporate America. Then I ran across an extreme case of racism and discrimination at my job with the current manager. I was discouraged and surprised. At that point in my career I had never experienced that at all. Because of that experience I decided that I was going to do something different and control my own destiny. So my then-boyfriend and I were talking over a wonderful, romantic dinner and weekend about options for me. I told him that I wanted to explore this passion of mine—hair care.

On a personal level up to that point, I had a challenge finding the right products for my hair because the products that were available for the African American market were either relaxers or greasy, heavy products with synthetic oils that would smell awful and weigh my hair down, like a Jheri Curl.

But then the products from the main aisle or the mass-market products were too drying—the gels, the mousse, the hairsprays, et cetera. And so before Curls came along, I had to use a hodgepodge of products and kind of blend things together, like taking one shampoo from this line and mixing this and that from another line. And I was never set for great curly hair days. That is when I decided that I am going to embark on this decision and go ahead and form my own hair line. So Curls, Inc., was really born that night over dinner, and I had four products: Curls Shampoo/Conditioner, Curls Moisturizer, Curls Refresher, and Curls Lotion. Now we have four lines and thirteen products. So Curls has grown exponentially since then. It started as a very small, small business operating in my home, and now the Curls products are available in nationwide stores.

Mahisha, how would you describe the texture of your hair, and what makes it challenging to have the healthy bouncy curls you want using "ethnic products" [available] in the mainstream market?

Generally speaking, I have naturally curly, medium-textured hair. So it is not so thick, but it is not very, very fine either. My hair is midroad. I have definitely curly hair; it is not kinky, but it is not bone straight. Curly hair, no matter what texture, has a tendency to be frizzy. If you don't use the right products and then weigh your hair down with them, then your curls are going to droop, pull out, and look greasy. Really, it is about finding the right balance for your hair. Unfortunately a lot of the masses of products on the market for African Americans are not created *by* African Americans. They are created by big, large multinational corporations that put synthetic ingredients in their products because they are cheap to acquire, like mineral oil, which you see in about every hair grease jar. Synthetic or mineral oil is the heaviest and is *not* good for your hair. It totally destroys the hair shaft. It blocks out moisture, which dries out the hair. But that is what you will see if you go look on the main hair care aisle in the major grocery stores. So these types of hair products are cheap. They are easy to acquire. Basically these Caucasian-owned companies just throw that ingredient in there, not really caring about the quality of the product for the ethnic market. So that was the first generation of ethnic products—that is what I call it. The second generation of ethnic products includes my products, Curls, Inc., and all of those other great brands that are available now, *created for us by us.* You have probably heard of them: Miss Jessie's, Kinky-Curly, and Shea Moisture. There are a lot of new black-owned businesses that specialize in ethnic hair—I call them the next generation—which are now sporting better, healthier options because we care about what we are putting on *our* hair, and therefore we care deeply about what we are selling to our customers.

You have donated Curls products and partnered with adoption agencies and adoption-related groups to address the hair care needs of primarily black and biracial transracially adopted children. Why have you chosen to reach out to this particular segment of the population?

Working with foster care and adoption groups and organizations is very near and dear to my heart, and that is where we started ten years ago, and we still are very active in that community. I feel that there are so many kids that need great homes. As it relates to transracial adoptive placements, I am happy to see that black and biracial kids are being adopted and that Caucasian and non–African American families are bringing these children to their homes and giving them love. So they're doing that with their whole open heart to love them, but for some parents who may have straight, blond hair, for example, they can be clueless as to what to do with their African American or black baby's kinky hair. So my thoughts were, if you as parents are willing to provide a child a home but need assistance in taking care of their hair, then I would love to help you as parents with your children's hair care needs *because self-esteem is important for girls of color, women of color, and hair maintenance and health is a huge part of that.* These transracially adopted kids deserve it! They deserve not only the opportunity to have an amazing home and love, and I am happy for that, but they also deserve to have *their* hair cared for and maintained in a healthy way. Nine times out of ten, it has been my experience that these kids of color are adopted by Caucasian families who are not living or involved in black communities, so they do not have that help. Typically I have run into transracial adoptive families with black children where their daughter's hair is *horrible* looking because of the lack of care and expertise. I have seen cases where Caucasian families wash, shampoo, their African American daughter's kinky hair *every single day*! It rips out the natural moisture in the hair, and it causes hair breakage.

For my parents, and I know still for many Caucasian parents raising black children, maintaining good health for their ethnic child's hair is certainly a struggle. It requires a cultural and mental shift, I think, from what many Caucasian men and women are used to in maintaining their own hair. Can you walk us through how your Curls product line can help with this?

Yes. Black hair is not "wash-and-go" hair like Caucasian hair. That is the key difference that I don't think many Caucasian parents realize going into this, so they really have their hands full. With any product, not just with Curls, but with any product you are going to use, whenever you have an African American child, the hair care process or taking care of their hair is going to be much longer than taking care of Caucasian hair. So the shampoo process alone with Caucasian hair is basically wash, comb out, and go. When you are shampooing your African American kid's hair, you have that process of detangling the hair, which can easily take thirty minutes to get through, if it is really kinky. You do it with a large-tooth comb, section by section. And then from there to conditioning and styling of the hair—that can take you up to, at the minimum, another thirty minutes. So shampoo-conditioner days are about an hour to one-and-a-half-hour process. You don't shampoo African American hair every day. Usually we recommend one to two times a week; with kinkier hair it can go one time a week.

Caring for black hair can be considered a long process and a big shock to Caucasian adoptive parents. But regardless of what hair care products you are using, it is really about the hair type of the child when it comes to the process of detangling, shampooing, and conditioning the hair. It does take time, patience, and equipment. When I work with parents and do hair care presentations with Curls products, I do run across those parents that are clueless at first, but once they embraced their child's hair and learned how to care for it, they took it away. They learned how to French braid, corn row, and style their child's hair in many wonderful ways. They knew what they were doing because they invested a lot of their time in educating themselves on their child's hair and hair care needs. So every day of styling black hair is not necessarily long, but the shampoo day in a black home is like an all-day process, especially if you have more than one girl in the home.

Yes. I know for many of these families it is hard to rev up for a whole day of hair care. During a whole day on a Saturday, for instance, you can attend a soccer game or gymnastics practice with your child, listen to her piano recital, or allow her to swim in a pool with friends and still make time for a food break. Contrast that to a child who is getting her hair shampooed, conditioned, and styled all morning and into the late afternoon. It is certainly a reality and cultural shift that a lot of Caucasian parents raising African American children will need to address. I think, though, it is so worth it for particularly the child and adolescent to be proud of their hair health and style. It will instruct them how to take care of their own hair into adulthood in confidence.

Mahisha, I wanted to talk with you a little bit about how you progressed from your childhood to becoming a strong woman of color. Can you share any words of wisdom that have empowered you in your journey so far?

My father and his whole side of his family had an amazing impact on my life because they were a family of firsts. My dad and his family are a multigenerational mixed family, Creole. To me they were an amazing people because they made a lot of strides in society. Eric Holder is a cousin on my dad's side. He was the first African American attorney general for the United States, serving under the Obama administration. His career is quite extensive. Vivian Malone Jones is in my family, and she was the first African American to graduate from the University of Alabama. This was in the early 1960s, during a time when black students were vehemently discouraged from attending all-white institutions of learning. She had to be regularly escorted into the school because her life was threatened. She made it through and graduated. And then she became the first of many in her career endeavors after that. There is a building named after her at the University of Alabama because of the many contributions she made to the institution and to society, including her work during the civil rights movement and partnering with Dr. Martin Luther King Jr. and so on.

So in addition to these incredible people in my family, there are more people in my family that have also created an amazing legacy that I was able to see and watch and be inspired by. My family was, and continues to be, an advocate for education. A key question in our family is, What are you going to do with your life? Whatever that is, as long as it is noble, my family would say: "Don't sit and dream about it, go out and live it and make it happen!" That expectation was important to me.

The positive images in my family are what continue to empower me. I keep them near and dear to my heart. My father was also very big on reinforcing those images and insisted as I was growing up on making sure that I was exposed to my father's side of the family so I could see that example.

Was there discussion on either side of your family about how to move in society with dark skin?

Yes. Dad always said to me that you have to work harder than, be better than, and go further than your Caucasian neighbors or colleagues to get the same favorable attention. He said, "Remember that!" Personally I have *never* forgotten that, especially in my corporate America days. After I graduated from college and entered corporate America, I executed that belief accordingly. I did well, but even then you don't always know who you are going to get as a manager. That was the thing that threw me at that moment—that I was an amazing achiever, yet this one person wanted to get rid of me. I was a single mother and I had rent to pay. I had a daughter in private school. My world was almost going to be shattered for a moment. That was very scary for me. And I thought to myself that I would not be in that position again.

So you did realize, even before this sad incident [the manager who wanted to fire her], that people judged you solely because of the color of your skin?

Yes, absolutely. My dad would tell me that, obviously. He also was very active in the civil rights movement and was problack. He would definitely try to educate me about race and racism, but I personally did not see that before the event in corporate America impacted me. I was exposed to interracial couples. I dated guys from different racial backgrounds, including Caucasian, African American, and Asian. For me it was not really what color they were but who was compatible with me at the time. I worked and lived in diverse environments. My school was in a diverse environment. Up until then I simply had not experienced racism. So when I went to my very first corporate job, I recognized that there were not a lot of African American people there, but I came in knowing that I am who I am and I can make my mark because I am a good person, I am a good worker and have the skill set. This job was going to be a breeze, I thought.

The first three years at my corporate job were great. When I transferred to a different department, everything changed and I got a new manager. That was when everything went downward.

Do you think that the change in how you were treated by this manager occurred because of the color of your skin?

Absolutely. There was no other explanation for it. There was a very clear road map given to us as professionals on how to succeed at this corporation. I had a mentor. I excelled in everything I did for this corporation. Not only did I succeed at my job but I was involved in extracurricular activities and presented myself well before the board. I was on committees. I was delivering great initiatives on a regular basis. I was doing all of the things the corporation indicated that they would like for someone in my position to do, especially if we wanted a promotion. So I was exceeding everywhere I went, and then this manager came in and tried to fire me. Apparently he didn't think that I was working hard enough. This was a life-turning event for me. I was totally distraught because he put me on this crisis action plan, which was one of the most embarrassing punitive actions. I prayed about this whole nightmare. I knew that if I lost this job, it would be very difficult for me because I was a single mother then and I had a kid to take care of financially. I was so nervous. I could not afford to lose this job.

How did it end up turning out?

The manager left the department right in the midst of that drama. He actually got a promotion. I then applied to another position within the corporation and got another manager, a far better manager. From him I got ranked faster, got a promotion and more stock options. He was *amazed* with all that I was doing within my pay level. I always knew that I did great work; it was not a surprise to me.

And so to be treated inappropriately by my previous manager, it was clear to me what I was dealing with: racism. But in corporate America *you never know* who you are going to deal with, and that is unfortunate. This event changed how I viewed corporate America and how I viewed racism, and racism in the workplace specifically. Unfortunately I realized in my work setting that for some Caucasians, they are not going to always love me or see my value in the work that I do because they can't get past the color of my skin. My world changed. It was no longer an innocent world that I lived in. Now I was on guard. I told myself, "Mahisha, now this is real. Saddle up. Get ready. You might be hit with this again!"

What got you through this ordeal?

It was prayer. I prayed to God. At that point I had been at the company for six years. I loved the organization I worked for. It was an amazing company with a lot of brilliant people. I remember specifically praying, "Please, God, remove this man from this organization, and please enable me to move up and into another position!" Then God answered my prayers! At the same time I started working on Curls. That's when I decided that I was going to do something else in my career and not rely on corporate America.

The whole experience was [a] life-changing, devastating, and an eye-awakening experience because, one, you think, "That can't happen to me!" Reflecting on it, I can remember the situation and my feelings. The interesting thing in this whole job situation was that my boss that hired me [originally] was a Caucasian male who was married to an African American woman. Both he and his wife adopted two African American kids. I discovered this during the interview process when I saw photos of his family on his desk. So when it sunk in that his wife was black and his children were black, I knew that he was not going to be racist. I said, "Okay, he is married to a *black* woman and adopted *black* children—I am good. I am good."

I'm glad that you worked through what sounds like a very difficult situation. Given the experience you just shared and what you have learned as a parent, what values are you and your husband teaching your children?

For all of my kids I teach them the importance of education, working hard, thriving, and giving. In this household we do not allow anybody to do things just halfway. Just yesterday my six year-old son was working on a writing assignment for school. My husband and I want to make sure that our son's sentence structures are correct and that he is writing neatly. That's the most important thing right now that we focus on with him in his schoolwork. Actually our son is very smart. But he was rushing through his writing assignment to do something else. My husband ripped the paper up because it was not written neatly and made him start all over again! It took my son a long time to get to the point that he was at. My husband is strict. He is a little bit more hard core than I am. I probably would not have ripped up the paper. For us it is about teaching our kids to do the very best they can, all of the time. Now for my seven-year-old daughter it is about saving and investing and working hard. I bring her to work with me during her school breaks—spring break, summer break, and winter break—so that she can see how hard I work and to give her hands-on experience working in an office environment. It is not a typical job a seven-year-old would be doing but rather a twenty-five-year-old or twenty-six-year-old. It certainly is nurturing a sink-or-swim mentality. I am giving her that real-life experience. I didn't have someone in my family who started a business. They were mostly either attorneys, doctors, politicians, or pro basketball players. So for my daughter this is great for her because she gets to experience the behind the scenes of the Curls business. She is traveling with me and works the phones. She gets to put in marketing time. She does a lot of stuff. I want her to learn that the key to success is hard work.

You have the heart and vision of a teacher. That is very impressive!

While you are on such a roll, I want to get your motherly advice on dating. It is probably a topic that all parents hold their breath

on when their children turn sixteen or seventeen years of age. What have you taught your oldest daughter on how to navigate the dating scene? I want to also touch back on the transracial adoption piece for Caucasian parents who are raising black daughters who may be interested particularly in dating inracially as well as interracially.

My oldest daughter is young and beautiful. She is a popular girl. So I have really frank, honest conversations with her about boys, and her father does too. She is definitely sheltered and a little bit naive. I have to meet every one of the boys that she wants to date. I have a very good sense of character. I will determine yes or no as to whether she can date the boy. It is not easy.

I am curious to know what that checklist looks like for you when determining what young boy is acceptable to date your daughter.

He needs to have a good upbringing, a good family structure. I definitely want someone for my daughter that is God-fearing because at least he will have a sense of morality about him. Unfortunately there are a lot of young boys out there that don't have a sense of morality. I saw this one brother walking hand in hand; he had one girl holding one of his hands and another one on his arm. Two! And they were both okay with this! When it comes to dating, I work with my daughter to teach her what characteristics to look for in a boy and emphasize to her that she needs to always have a strong sense of self.

A strong sense of self-esteem is so important because when she turns sixteen, from that point on, it is almost too late if she doesn't have it already. In our family we have close conversations about trust with our daughter. How do you build trust in a healthy way when you begin a relationship with a boy? We monitor all of her relationships as a way to guide her and to help her make wise choices. Some people may say that I should give my daughter privacy. I don't agree. She is a teenager. I monitor everything. If she is on Facebook or any other social sites, I expect her to give me her passwords. I may monitor her sites every day, every week, or every month—regardless she knows that I have her passwords. It is not so much about her, but it is about other people and what they are doing and who she is out with. Again, we are very strict about who our daughter can go out with on a date. It is all about monitoring and being very active in your child's life as a parent. For me nothing slips through my fingers because I am a very active parent. My words of advice to parents: Before any kid gets to the dating process, parents, you need to establish in your daughter's strong self-esteem. If not, when your daughter starts to date, she will give in to any boy and have the potential of becoming a victim to any predator or any guy that wants to explore that intimate part of his life with her.

How does a parent give the gift of nurturing a strong sense of self-esteem in a black girl in particular? A healthy self-esteem seems to be a key answer to addressing in a healthy way life issues. That's huge!

In college I had a Women of Color class I took that was amazing. What I remember from that class was this study conducted with a group of nine-year-old black girls. These girls were given a black baby doll and a white baby doll. They were randomly asked questions about each of the dolls. The results of the study showed that the majority of the black girls preferred the white baby. And the interviewers asked the black girls why they didn't like the black baby. These little girls of color said that they did not think that the black doll was beautiful or cute. They also said about the black baby doll that she looked sad and mean, that she was not nice. And for them the white baby doll represented all of the pleasant things.

Yes. I remember the Clark and Clark Doll [Tests]. [They were] conducted by [Kenneth and Mamie] Clark . . . back in 1939. Since then I believe there have been other, similar doll studies conducted with slight variations in the results. The Clark and Clark Doll [Tests] remain such an eye-opening study even today when we look at the value (or lack thereof) placed on someone solely because of the color of one's skin.

Exactly. That study was about self-esteem in black girls, basically. When I was taking this course in college, where I first learned about this study, my daughter was only a few years old at the time. I really took that study to heart. I made sure first that she had a lot of images around that looked like her. My daughter's pediatrician was African American. Her dentist was African American. The books that she had included black characters in them, and her baby dolls were also black. There was a preteen TV show called *That's So Raven*, which featured the little girl who was on the *Cosby Show*. I actually took my young daughter at the time to the taping of that show so that she could meet Raven [Raven-Symoné] and see someone who looked like her. I wanted her to see images of herself in all of these good places so that she could build a good sense of self. My daughter attended a mostly white private school so I had to bring all of these extra images to her of black people so that she could see like images of her. From that I constantly told her how beautiful she was: her character, her skin, her hair—even though she was different, she was also beautiful!

My youngest daughter, who is now six, she has brown skin but has bone-straight hair. She doesn't have any curls in her hair. My husband is Asian, so she has interesting features. It can be hard to determine what her racial background is. I tell her all the time, because she is also attending a mostly Caucasian school, that she too is pretty and that there are a lot of people that pay to look like her. Most of her friends are Caucasian, and I don't want her to feel horrible because she does not look like her friends or wish that she wasn't who she is. Now she says, "I have the prettiest skin in my whole school."

You have to give your children images of themselves everywhere you can. That is what I had to do with both of my daughters in particular.

You have a young son. How do you raise him?

It's a little different. Girls have the biggest issue with self-esteem. I remember reading a lot about that and paying attention to studies on this subject. That is why with the girls I take a very aggressive approach. With my son it is a little more lax. For him I encourage him to be a good person, but I don't emphasize to him that he is so handsome and that his skin color is beautiful, et cetera. It is a little bit different. So I am not overt with him with that piece. It's more about teaching him to be a good boy, a good son, a good student, a good person.

How does your husband guide your son as he gets older and is moving in society with dark skin?

My husband and I, we are an interracial couple, so he has not had the same experiences of course as I have. He is part Korean and part Caucasian, so he doesn't see the issues of being a person of color because he has the white skin privilege. Asians, as you know, are the "model minority." Therefore we have to balance that because he does not see really how different the experience could be for our son, who looks black.

I like how you are able to see and assess the strengths and challenges within each of your children as well as their realities, given the society that we live in. You certainly, though, have a beautiful family and an engaged one!

Before we end our conversation what is your advice to white adoptive parents who are raising children of color as it relates to how they can connect with the black community, to gain the kind of experiences that you have talked about here?

I think that it is extremely important for transracial adoptive parents to definitely seek out people in the African American community for themselves and for their children. Also there are many adoptive parents who are already doing this, but I think it is a great opportunity to sign up their kids with transracial adoptee play groups. With my six- and seven-year-olds, I put them in a play group with kids their age and who are multiethnic. They are a part of a group of six, three boys and three girls. They all go to the same school. These kids formed their own alliance and get to socialize with kids that look like them. In her play group my daughter Isabella sees somebody like her, Kayla, so she is not the only one. So my daughter forms this strong sense that "I am beautiful, Kayla is beautiful." Play groups are a great place to start for parents, especially if they do not have an official organization that their kids are participating in. Also, if parents can bring other positive imagery to their family illustrating kids with dark skin, ordering—online, if necessary—storybooks with African American kids and other kids of color in it and dolls et cetera is another wonderful option. These seem like little things that we don't always think about, but they matter in a huge way. If you grow up with dolls as girls, a lot of times you wish you looked like them. I know that when I grew up, I didn't have a lot of black babies. I had an identity crisis myself. That's why I decided that I was going to do it differently with my daughters. I gave both of them a totally new experience, especially Isabella.

You have clear vision for your blended family and for your life. How can Caucasian parents who have adopted multiethnic children gain from your blueprint?

That is a really hard question to answer. I can definitely say to adoptive parents to take some of the things that I said here and try to implement them. For some parents who are adopting transracially, it is a world that is unfamiliar to them so it may be hard to think about how important it is for their black sons and daughters to see positive black images. You know who I think does a good job at this? The answer is Angelina Jolie (and Brad Pitt) with their Vietnamese son and their Ethiopian daughter. They take them back to their home countries, their homeland, and keep them connected. I know that they don't do it often, but at least Angelina and Brad are aware of the importance of that connection for their kids. So I think to be cognizant as transracial adoptive parents of the fact that their children of color *need* to see that imagery and really *appreciate* it is really important. In their minds they may feel that they are giving these kids a loving home so why does it matter? I go back to, because it is important to their son's and daughter's self-esteem. So being cognizant that their children need that is the number 1 step to implement the things that I said I did for my daughters. I think the same principles could apply to Caucasian parents who are raising children of color—because, although I am not Caucasian, I still live in a Caucasian environment, and I needed to make sure that I was able to supplement my children's exposure.

I think that parents can really look at supplementing their children's education, their exposure to a diverse group of people, their surroundings, as a really great way for providing for each member of the family the needs and cultural experiences that help each one flourish and be essentially valued.

I want to thank you, Mahisha, for sharing so much in this discussion and for your generosity in time and knowledge.

Curls is now available at all Target stores. Curls products are also available at nationwide Sally's Beauty Supply stores. We are also at Rite Aid and CVS stores. Next year Curls will be in Walmart stores. So we have our retail line as well as we have Curls professional, Curls for kids, and Curls for babies. So Curls is growing phenomenally. So what we would like to see, or what I would like to see in the next five years, my goal for the company, is to double our sales and to continue our exposure into other international markets. We are already in the U.K.

and Brazil, but we want to go into other markets as well, including Africa and including other South America areas. The retail line is doing amazing. We have hit our sweet spot. It took a lot of work because, as you know, when you come in doing it yourself, learning as you go, it took a while to get to where we are today. They always tell you in business school, when you are prepping to be a business owner, . . . don't prepare to make any money the first five years. You will be in the red. Expect that. Well, we made money out the gate the first year and every year after that. We started small, but we kept growing financially every year. And then in the fifth year, really, Curls shot through the roof and things really shifted for us.

DENETA HOWLAND SELLS
Physician and Civil Rights Advocate
INTERVIEWED BY TELEPHONE, JULY 12, 2012

Dr. Sells, I am thrilled to talk with you about race, marriage, and adoption, as well as your incredible passion for civil rights. I've seen a photo of your wedding to Bryan Sells in the *New York Times*—you are in church and holding hands with your Caucasian husband as you are getting ready to jump the broom, which is a custom practiced by African Americans as well as other groups.

My husband, Bryan, and I were married on October 7, 2007, at the Memorial Church at Harvard University, where we met. Three weeks later the story was featured in the *New York Times*, as you mentioned.

What were the events that culminated in that picture in the *Times*?

Bryan and I had met in 1989 when we were students at Harvard. I was immediately attracted to him, but I had decided that it was not a good idea to date or marry someone white especially. Back then I had some racial allegiances that I felt I owed to someone or something to have a black family and black children. I wanted to be like the *Cosby Show*. I felt that that was something that could be fun, to be successful and have a black family. As much as I liked my white friends, I thought then that I should date and marry inside of my race. Fast-forward ten years: I had dated other people and Bryan had dated other people. We reconnected through one of my college roommates. Since we lived in different states, we communicated through e-mail. At that time I was in Memphis in medical school, and Bryan was in Montgomery, Alabama, clerking for a federal judge. [Bryan] was getting ready to leave his position because it was the end of his clerkship. Anyway, we were chatting about civil rights issues one evening. I was a civil rights junkie. I had read many books and watched movies about the movement. So when he asked me if I wanted to come to Montgomery to visit him, I was excited. I had never been there before. Montgomery was where in 1955 Rosa Parks refused to give up her seat on the bus to a white passenger.

I can imagine visiting Montgomery, especially given your passion for the civil rights movement, was an incredible experience.

It was definitely that! Bryan had always been interested in that kind of thing too. He took me around Montgomery, Birmingham, and Selma, all landmark civil rights sites.

But when I arrived in Montgomery, I remember, surprisingly, that we drove the same car. Then we were just hanging out, and I am looking at his bookshelf at his home, and he had a lot of similar books that I had on my bookshelf. We spent a lot of time that weekend reconnecting and talking about a lot of topics, from global warming to raising children, all against the backdrop of driving the back roads of Alabama. And I realized that we had more things in common than things that separated us. I recognized that race was a big thing, obviously.

What were traits that you found common between the two of you?

We believed in the same things. We found the same things important. We had the same life goals. I joked in the *New York Times* article that here I reconnected with this wonderful man who has a great appreciation for civil rights like I do and the passion to restore the civil rights movement but also reads the same books, drives the same car, and recycles! I was like, Deneta—you have just been an idiot for not jumping all over this guy ten years ago. And so I did that weekend! And so we have been together ever since.

Tell me about your childhood.

I was born in Illinois. My mom is from Washington, D.C., and my dad is from Illinois. They both met when they were in college. When I was born, they were seniors. We lived in Illinois for the first fourteen years of my life. It is sort of complicated. My parents divorced when I was around four years of age. And we, my mom and siblings, moved to Washington, D.C., for a little while to live with my grandparents. Then my parents reconciled and got remarried. After that I started kindergarten in Maryland. And then we moved back to Illinois, and I spent the next ten years in Illinois. It's strange.

It's funny—I feel like I was very much of a midwesterner. I remember growing up near cornfields and relatively small towns. Then, with my grandparents being from Washington, D.C., we spent as a family a lot of time visiting them. I have always had this fascination of being in the Washington, D.C., area. On some of our visits there I remember spending a lot of time at the Smithsonian museums. Also I remember my grandmother and grandfather graduated from historically black colleges. Alums from these institutions, they would have a Dr. Martin Luther King Jr. breakfast every year around King's birthday in January. There were intellectually bright icons speaking at these breakfast events. So I grew up with an acute emphasis on learning and understanding our black history and going to museums and going to historical sites and going to this dinner and that breakfast. My great grandmother on my mother's side was the first woman president of the NAACP chapter in Charlotte, North Carolina.

So things like knowing and celebrating our rich black history and heritage were important to my family. Being involved in our community was also another value that was important to my family. I was a Girl Scout, where they teach you to leave things better than how you found them. That was definitely a basic tenet that our family tried to uphold.

From everything that I read as a child, including picture books about the Montgomery bus boycott, to being a youth member with my siblings in the NAACP and participating in social justice rallies and Labor Day picnics—all was a huge part of my upbringing.

When did you move back to Maryland?

I moved back to Maryland halfway through my freshman year of high school. I literally came from Springfield, Illinois, with 100,000 people. In my middle school in Illinois I was one of two black students who was placed in what they called the talented and gifted track. Then in Maryland we were zoned for Northwestern [High School in Hyattsville], so I started there in January of our freshman year. It was terrifying. My mom was about to pull me out and put me in a Catholic school. I was stunned and overwhelmed by Northwestern—the playing—the kids in the hallway—slamming the doors when you're sitting in class trying to learn—I could go on. For some reason the counselor assigned to me didn't understand my transcript. So she put me in basic English for freshmen. That made me mad. Fortunately after a few weeks the teacher realized that I did not belong in that class. The teacher agreed with my mother, and I was moved into a more advanced class. It was really, though, a French class that saved me at Northwestern. My French teacher took us to Belgium that summer. I met upperclassmen and made some friends slowly. By the end of the summer I was prepared to go back to Northwestern, but I was really scared when I first got there.

When you transitioned from middle school to high school, how did you view yourself as a black girl? Did you value yourself? What did you think about yourself internally?

That's a hard question but a good one. In a sort of way I think that I thought I was beautiful and could accomplish anything that I put my mind to, and of course I knew that I was going to go to college. I am among the fourth generation of women in my family who went to college. My mother, my grandmother, my great grandmother all went to college. So the message from my family early on was, You are going to go to college, you are going to have a career, because you are going to take care of yourself and be independent! Still, I did have some problems with other black girls when I was young. I think that it was not only because of my skin but also because of my hair and because I was slim in size. In my immediate family there was just an acceptance of who I was and how I looked. Both of my parents are African American, but you go back a few generations, and you will find some things mixed in, right? That is just part of being African American. But when my sisters and I went outside of our house, the black girls in our neighborhood would say to us in a derogatory manner, "Oh, you think you're this and you think you're that!" "Are you an Oreo? Why do you look that way? Why does your hair look like that?" I had reddish fine hair. My sister had very dark thick long hair, and my youngest sister had blonde hair. So they didn't know what to think about us. My brother was a boy and nobody paid attention to him. His hair was short. It was different for him. He never got the trouble from these girls. Our hair was put up in pony tails, which did not look like the black girls' hair in our neighborhood at all. It was crazy how we were treated. That's why I think I found myself, when I was already very young, hanging out with white girls and Latina girls because they did not give me grief about my hair. Or ask me all the time, "Are you white? Are you mixed? Are you black? What are you?"

How did you maintain your hair when you were young? Did you and your sisters go to a hairstylist?

No, we didn't get our hair professionally done when we were young. It was a big deal when I was thirteen years old and *finally* able to get my hair relaxed. It's funny, you look back and you realize that you didn't need your hair relaxed, like you thought you did at the time. Anyway my mom insisted that the hairstylists keep my hair long enough so that I could still put it in a ponytail, which I did often in my teenage years. There were three of us girls. You can imagine that there was a lot of hair between the three of us. So to maintain our hair my mom essentially washed and brushed our hair back and put it in a ponytail. In the summer months we would wear our hair in cornrows so that we could go swimming and not worry about having to manage our hair every day. As far as hair care, it was definitely cheaper to pull out the hair dryer and take out the straightening comb to make our hair straight and more manageable.

Northwestern High School was a very diverse school socioeconomically and racially as well as culturally. How did you navigate that terrain as a student?

I think I learned how to talk to the white kids, the black kids, the Vietnamese kids—you just had to figure out a way to talk with each individual person. It was not easy for me. I had an Illinois midwestern accent so I sounded like a white girl to them anyway. I was smart and cared about my academics so that was always a problem, sadly. However, I think that it did help that I had a black boyfriend during my sophomore year; it actually *legitimized* me at Northwestern in a strange way. I think that I was a really friendly person in general, which helped. I smiled a lot and was able to make friends somewhat easily. Getting involved in student government was another positive factor that helped me connect with other students. In my younger years and adolescent years especially, I was judged by how I looked. I didn't like that feeling. So I personally worked hard not to judge others in that way. If you were nice to me and smiled at me, then I was nice to you and smiled at you. If you recall, I was student president of our class in our junior and senior years at Northwestern High School. I intention-ally tried to be inclusive of everyone. Yes, initially when I saw all of the white kids, the black kids, the Vietnamese kids, and the few Latino kids that were at the school, I was like, "Oh, my God, it is so different!!" But as I got over the hype and accepted the differences, I was okay and not as intimidated by the diverse group of people.

From there you chose to attend Harvard. How did you not only survive but thrive in that environment? What lessons did you learn as a student and as a black woman?

It obviously had its challenges. At Harvard, when I was a student, you could feel the sense of privilege in the air. My first week as a fresh-man, students were talking: "We need to buy a sofa. We need to get a refrigerator. We need to get a TV for our common room." Fortunately I had worked all summer so I came up with some money. But I remem-ber being conscious of, What if I had not worked over the summer and earned additional money? What about students who didn't have the extra money to help purchase these expensive items? I had some friends who were intimidated by the assumption that "of course you are here, so you should be able to afford to chip in $50 for a sofa!" You can't assume that. I was a work-study kid. It was definitely a positive that my friends cared. I had friends that had to work while they were students at Harvard, and I had friends who didn't have to work while they were at Harvard. I wouldn't have been friends with them if they made me feel badly about having three jobs to make it.

Also I found it an effort to make it at Harvard; I had to get to know people like I did at Northwestern High School. There was still a good amount of racial and ethnic diversity at Harvard. I was there in the late 1980s, at a time when the emphasis was all about having a racially diverse campus and focusing on diversity training. Our freshman week orientation was about learning how to embrace your differences instead of using diversity as a way to separate yourself from others. At the same time I think that there was a lot of pressure, at least in the black community, to not forget where you came from and to make sure that you still had black friends. There was the expectation that you move between the different communities. In the dining hall, for example, you would sit with your white roommates sometimes and sit with your black friends sometimes. It was expected that you be a part of the black student unification and the freshman black table, as examples, as a way to sort of "prove yourself" by having the right friends and belonging to the right clubs at Harvard. I don't know if we were as tolerant of some of the people of color who didn't integrate themselves in the way we thought they should then. You look back on things with more perspective and maturity, and I think that we were too hard on each other for that. There was some artificial criterion we used to judge whether you were "black enough." And that is silly, especially when you look back twenty years later. But we felt strongly then that we should think the way we did and owed it to the black community to be strongly a part of it, not just when we graduated.

What brought you to Harvard?

I wanted to go to the best college. When I was in high school, I read this book about Harvard, not thinking that I could ever possibly get in. I saw pictures of Harvard and said, "This is what a college is supposed to look like: all of the old buildings and the changing of the colors in the fall." When it came down to it, I went to Harvard for a visit and loved Cambridge. I loved Boston. I also thought the college was easy to get to and from Washington, D.C. The things that you think about when you are seventeen. And then, once I got in, I realized that I would have regretted it if I didn't go there, even though it felt so different than where I was coming from. Harvard was the best college in the country. The institution accepted me so I was going to go.

What were you interested in studying as a student at Harvard?

Initially I wanted to go to law school with the idea of doing something in government or social studies. Then I read the descriptions for the classes for sociology and thought, This is great I can learn about race, identity, and urban development. It was a neat blend of psychology and social studies, and so I switched to a major in sociology.

How did your college experience help you grow as a professional?

In college I thought more about what kind of life I wanted to have. I was really concerned with what kind of family I was going to have, so much so that I turned my back on who ended up being my husband. Also I wanted to make a difference in the world. For years I was working at a summer camp for kids in public housing in Cambridge. It was important to me to make the world a better place for all kids, including disadvantaged kids. I didn't know how I was going to do that down the road professionally. So I got some advice about going to law school. I toyed with being an elementary school teacher. Finally I heard about how kids being healthy made a huge difference with their success in school. Also I had an opportunity after college to work with the Georgetown Pediatric Mobile Unit in Washington, D.C. I was doing more of the outreach social work kind of stuff for them and got to know the director of the unit, who was a pediatrician. I saw him working with kids and their families during his days in the clinic, and then he would go to conferences and talk about what kids need from a more community-wide advocacy level, like better schools and better parks, et cetera. People listened to him because he was a doctor. So the combination of me already having this idea in my head that being healthy makes a difference, and that health care is a social justice issue connected to seeing a pediatrician actually implementing these same values in his life's career, was compelling for me in deciding what I wanted to do in my career. What better advocate for children than being a pediatrician and what an awesome job? I could work independently. Be my own boss. Run my own show.

I went to medical school at the University of Tennessee College of Medicine and earned my degree in 2003. And then I started a practice. It started with just me, a medical assistant, and a practice manager–receptionist. It was my husband's idea. We live in a section of town close to downtown Atlanta that has been undergoing economic renewal, with people buying houses in the neighborhoods and fixing them up, that type of thing. Most of the pediatricians are outside of the city. Literally my neighbors went out of their way to ask me why I don't open up a practice close by to where we live. I thought nobody starts their own practice right out of residency. My husband Googled some consultants and said to me, Sure you can start your own practice, look! It's crazy. And now we have a staff of fourteen—four providers, six medical assistants, a couple of billers, and a couple of receptionists in *six years*.

Speaking politically, what effects, if any, do you see Obamacare having on your practice and children specifically?

I am supportive of Obamacare (also known as the Affordable Care Act). I think that there is more to be done. I don't think that it is perfect. For children anyway, Obamacare has done a lot already. It allows coverage for children and families with preexisting conditions. It allows children to stay on their parents' health insurance until they are twenty-six. It was not long ago [that] I remember being a young person without health insurance through my twenties. My mother had great health insurance and would have kept me on her plan as long as she could; that just wasn't an option twenty years ago. Once I was done with college, I/you are out there on your own, right when you are trying to figure out who you are and planning on going to graduate school or [need to] budget for things, and that is definitely the time when you *need* health insurance. There needs to be minimum standards for what insurance companies should cover. For instance every day in my practice we have families whose insurance does not allow them to have certain amounts of vaccines or well-[child] visits per year. These are routine scheduled well-[child] visits that the American Academy of Pediatrics recommends for children to have in order to monitor their health and development over a set period of time, in months and years. Obamacare establishes that children will be covered for these well-[child] visits. On top of that, it doesn't make sense [that] families who have insurance, who work every day, whose children get sick and then have to worry if they are going to be able to pay for the treatment. That just doesn't make sense that you can be paying for insurance and it doesn't do what it needs to do when you actually need it. And so Obamacare puts into place necessary reforms that ensure that people actually get what they are paying for and actually get something that makes a difference for them when they need it. If you don't need it, fine. But if your child gets leukemia, and all of a sudden you are look-ing at hundreds and thousands of dollars in medical treatment, what are you going to do? That's why Obamacare is so important: it ad-dresses these critical, costly, and life-defining situations for families.

In your medical practice and in your social circles, have you come in contact with families who have transracially adopted, par-ticularly black children?

Yes, in my practice I have several white families who have adopted one or two black children. It is interesting to see the difference be-tween them. I have a couple of transracial adoptive families who are concerned with helping their black children develop a strong racial identity. And I have another transracial adoptive family that does not even think about race and identity and what it means to their child and to them. For me it is a challenge to find a way to bring the topic up, and I need to do so because I do think it is important for these parents to be aware of the challenges that they may face as a family and the challenges that their child may face today. I think that it is great that you have taken on as your life's mission to write books and develop other adoption-oriented resources that look at this issue criti-cally. Today, in my opinion, we as a country are not postracial, even with a biracial man as our president.

Are there any medical issues white parents who have, or are adopting, black children should be aware of that are unique to the race of their child?

No, not generally for U.S.-adopted children. Certainly if you are adopting a child from abroad, like from Haiti or Ethiopia, then there are some nutritional issues, there are some infectious disease issues, particularly like intestinal parasites in Ethiopia, for instance, and vaccine coverage, whether they were adequately vaccinated and whether there are reliable records to know these things. In fact I think that the recommendations for some of these countries are to start over, since in many cases the records are not as reliable. But once these children are here and for U.S.-adopted children, there are really not any significant differences. You want to know whether your child has sickle cell, the disease or the trait. There are several different types of sickle cell, but just broadly it is a blood disorder in which the red blood cells are misshapen so they don't function as well. Therefore the body throws these red blood cells out because they are misshapen, causing fewer red blood cells in the body. The people who suffer from sickle cell anemia are at risk for infection. They are at risk for what we call sickle cell pain crisis. They can have very painful exacerbations in their arms and legs. They are at risk for certain kinds of lung disease and stroke. So very significant health risks and [they] must be followed up by a hematologist who specializes in sickle cell disease.

For those parents who have children with this disease and live in places other than Atlanta, Georgia—like, let's say, Sioux Center, Iowa, or Moscow, Idaho—how can they find a really good hematologist in their community?

Fortunately we are getting of the age where telemedicine is very helpful. I know that some of our cardiologists, and I think some of our hematologists, too, will do some really interesting things with remote medicine. They have special clinics where you can do appointments/consultations via basically teleconference. And I think pediatricians in places like Iowa, for instance, would know to have the children start medication in order to monitor their anemias and hopefully be in contact with a hematologist wherever their closest tertiary medical center is located. You can do a certain blood test and have close blood test monitoring where you are; it's just making sure that those things are being followed up and that these families through their pediatricians are in consult with a hematologist. I think that most pediatricians and family doctors would know that, but as a parent that is definitely something that you want to advocate for your child, if they find out that their child has the disease, to make sure that they get the best comprehensive care.

And do you see a value for white adoptive parents with black and brown children to seek out African American doctors and dentists for their children?

Yes. In fact my transracial adoptive families said this to me, that they appreciate being able to bring their children into an office where they see people who look like them. It's funny—it's not always cross-racial. I had a little white girl who was in our office who has very curly hair. She loves Princess Tiana, the Disney character who has brown skin and curly hair. For this little girl Princess Tiana reminds her of herself because she has curly hair too! And so I think that having those role models in their everyday lives is important. It does not necessarily have to be their child's pediatrician, because they may not be able to find a black pediatrician where they live. But having, like you did, a godparent or mentor or Girl Scout leader or someone where it is part of a routine. It's not simply something special or rare, like a trip to the Smithsonian museums when you go to Washington, D.C., but rather someone who is a part of their lives, literally, that looks like them and/ or resembles them in some way, shape, or fashion.

What words of advice can you give to black and biracial adoptees that are growing up in white homes across this country, about how they can build a healthy self-esteem while walking in society with dark skin?

In most of your daily life or activities, what you look like on the outside probably is not going to matter as much, for instance, if you are driving in your car, doing your laundry, making your dinner, et cetera. But having a good understanding of who you are in the inside helps when you are judged by someone based on how you look on the outside. It is important to know that there will be people who are going to judge you, assume things about you. And unfortunately those things can get under anybody's skin. But knowing that that is their issue is an important perspective to have. And that it has to do with who they are and how they were raised, not who you are and how you were raised. At the same time we all tend to judge people by what we see. Sometimes we need to learn to forgive people when they make the wrong assumptions when they first meet you and be willing to try to still be open to see people for who they truly are. Because that's what you want people to do when they meet you. Now it's about knowing when to have that tougher skin to deflect someone's negative attention toward you and also knowing when to turn that off and be kind and open to meeting new people.

Being in an interracial marriage opened my eyes to those principles I just mentioned. Bryan and I don't talk race every day. I don't wake up and say, "Wow! This is my *white* husband!" Out in public other people around us sometimes give us an extralong stare—I don't know, maybe it's because they like my shoes?!

[*Laugh*]

I don't know. And then I think, maybe they are not used to seeing a couple like us or are surprised or intrigued by what our connection is. I do think, however, that people are getting better at understanding boundaries. Interestingly I was just talking with somebody, and they asked me, "Why are you married to that white man?" I think to myself, Don't be concerned about the person I love. Worry about the one that is going to love you. Those are boundaries.

You are very wise.

Be happy that people find someone that they can connect with, who can care for them, and vice versa—that is what is most important.

I really think that adoptees in general struggle with boundaries in particular because we are straddling different worlds and trying to please our family and figure out who we are simultaneously.

It is such a big issue for a lot of us. You don't have to necessarily [have] been adopted to have to worry about being alone or abandoned. Of course when you have the reality of being abandoned or placed into foster care at such an early age, that pain can stick with you. I think that trying to realize that that reality is not who you are is key. Rather that's what happened to you. It was your circumstance. Who you are and how you deal with it is much more important. It did not happen because of who you are as a person. I'm finding that to be born in the first place is an achievement. And then opening yourself up to a new family and to new parents and siblings is an achievement. Allowing yourself to feel good about that, and to allow yourself to accept this new family, is important because that will go a long way towards your healing and feeling accepted and safe internally, even as an adult.

I know adopted children. Adopting a child or two is something that Bryan and I would like to do someday. Understanding that for a lot of families who adopt children, that child is a blessing. And for those adopted, that family is happy and grateful to have you, and so you, as the adoptee, should feel worthy because you brought so much into their lives and allowed them to be parents and for their other children to be brothers and sisters. You could, as an adoptee, feel unworthy because you may not know why you were adopted for starters, but hopefully you would realize what a gift and joy you are to the family who brought you home.

What words of advice can you offer to white adoptive parents who are raising kids of color in a world that is still arguably not postracial and who receive the stares that you are talking about in public and even negative comments?

I would say to them, Love your child! That is the most important act. If you are dealing with someone, for instance, who is black or white that is asking you questions and not respecting your boundaries, you can tactfully and confidently tell them, "We chose to have this child in our family and we love them like our own." I do think you recognize, too, that there is some higher level of cultural things that children need to learn. On the basic level it is all about loving and caring for your child. And then you do the extra things, like making sure that you have diverse books in your home and diverse toys in your home, diverse dolls in your home. As well as try to have people of color in your home—not just the same race as your child but from other racial backgrounds too. I think that it is helpful for children to see black, brown, and white adults loving and caring and part of these children's lives as good role models.

Thank you for that. I do think, too, that comments are made to families like these from the public out of genuine interest for the child. But there is still that concern, I think, from white adoptive parents of, "Am I raising my child of color right? Am I okay as a person and as a parent?" These parents are also working to develop a sense of confidence in their own parenting skills. It is not always easy with the pressure of outsiders looking in.

That's exactly right. You don't have to do it alone, either. There is a great story a couple of years ago about this couple that adopted a child from Ethiopia, right when they were about to have their own biological child. So the wife could not go with her husband to Ethiopia to pick up their daughter. Once in Ethiopia the father had to take it upon himself to learn how to do his child's hair. For any father [knowing] how to do their child's hair is an accomplishment. Our dad never did our hair. But you can learn. Another example: one of my best friends in college is biracial, and she has a white mother. Her mother had to ask the question "How do I deal with my child's hair?" I think that if you recognize where you need help and aren't afraid to be vulnerable—and you have to be vulnerable to say to someone who might know better, I need help with this child's hair—people will help. That is something that I need to learn too. I can improve on how I do my own hair. A key, too, is recognizing that there is a lot of politics with black hair, and I think that there is some judgment, particularly in the black community, about cutting your child's hair all off or not maintaining it properly. That child having well-cared-for hair is going to have more esteem as well. Part of your job as a parent is to build up your child's self-esteem and help them feel good about themselves. That includes *consciously* figuring out how to help them do their hair, especially if you are going to adopt a child of color.

Your words have inspired me throughout this discussion. I thank you for that. Finally, who are you and what kind of legacy do you hope to leave society?

As I said in the beginning of this discussion, I am part of the fourth generation of college-educated African women in my family. It is huge. I am very proud of that. It is a legacy of valuing education, being intellectually curious and smart. I am a wife, and that is about being supportive of my husband, his travels, and his career. I am a neighbor and enjoy being a part of the community and helping to make my world and the bigger world a better place. I am a doctor and a business owner and try to do right by my employees by providing them with an enjoyable place to work and in compensating them in such a way that they can care for their own livelihoods and raise their own families.

The one thing that I haven't done yet is become a parent. That is something that I would like to do and something my husband and I are working on. I look forward to, in one way or the other, having children in our lives. Bryan and I are good people, and that's why I think we have an obligation to influence a new generation through raising a child or two. I think that we would enjoy it. I also think that I am leaving a legacy through working with my families in my practice, by trying to help them raise healthy kids and good kids. I would like to think that I am also a role model to my nieces and to my friends' kids. At the end of the day I would like to be known as someone who cared for and made a difference for kids.

TABITHA
Child Welfare Bureau Chief
INTERVIEWED BY TELEPHONE, JANUARY 22, 2012

How did you get started in child welfare services?

I started my career as a therapist in children's mental health. I never dreamed that I would do public child welfare, until I began to see that, as a therapist, I couldn't achieve the change I wanted to for children and families; [that] was beyond a fifty-minute session. I felt extremely limited. So I began taking on case management, where I began to learn the multifaceted problems and the complexity of the issues that children and families were dealing with. I just was so struck and compelled to change over from therapy to public child welfare, because I thought that is really where I was needed. Plus, child welfare is an extreme passion of mine. I couldn't see myself doing anything else.

You are based out of the Washington, D.C., area and have seen the issues facing children and families in that locale. What would you say are the top three areas the public child welfare system is dealing with in that respect?

The system is dealing with extreme poverty, substance abuse, and neglect. The magnitude of it is pretty staggering. The way in which the crack epidemic changed the city is incredible. You have a whole group of kids who may have been born addicted to drugs, and now they are in middle school and high school. This is the time you're seeing parents who don't know how to deal with their children's behaviors or parents who are doing horrific things to their children because the addiction has overwhelmed their life.

What is the state of the children in the foster care system in the Washington, D.C., area?

There are so many youth who have been in the system for a long time who weren't given the full opportunity to be reunified with their families, for one reason or another—maybe the families were unable or unwilling to provide a home for a child or the system did not dig deep enough to identify family members. And now you have these youth languishing in the system. In part black families don't really know about adoption the same way as, let's say, white families do. Black people tend to do informal adoptions rather than going through a court or formal adoption process. For many black people the system is a very scary place, and therefore I'm not sure that the black community is as educated about how to navigate the court system to make adoption a legal thing versus everybody just going over to Grandma's house when you need help. So now you have this big group of youth [aged] ten and above—that's primarily the age of children in foster care—and then you have teenagers who are now saying, "Well, I want to be on my own." This idea of "independent living" is really a misnomer. Who is really independent? You always need to be tied to some kind of family connection. When adoptive parents are traditionally thinking about adoption, they don't think about teens, they don't think about older youth; they think about babies. So you have thousands of kids in this area who are without permanent families, and they are just waiting.

How did you get introduced to transracial adoption?

One of my most memorable cases involved ten children from the same family placed in foster care. These children were all placed in different foster homes. A Caucasian lesbian couple became interested in two brothers of this African American sibling group. I thought, whoa, this is ripe for conflict!

Definitely room to have good discussion.

I began to talk with the couple about their experiences, about just being different in the world and what that was like. What did they know about black people and black children? I was really unafraid to broach the hard issues with them. I really felt like; if I didn't do it and ask the questions, they would hear it elsewhere and be shocked, be unprepared, or feel as though we did not do all that we could as an agency in terms of our due diligence to help them make an informed decision.

And so we talked about how do you comb these black boys' hair? How do you explain who you are to these black boys? The scenario was that these black boys would be with Caucasian females and stick out like a sore thumb, and then in addition they would also have two mothers. That is a tough road to pave.

I appreciated that these two women were not afraid to respond to my questions and ask their own questions of me. They were thinking early about the issues and what these children might face in a family with them. I am saddened that they, too, experienced their own "isms" in the world. I appreciated that they lived in a multicultural neighborhood that was more accepting of diverse families; they didn't just go and get black friends as they were thinking about adopting these boys—they already had them. And so this couple was further along in their preparation than a lot of potential adoptive parents.

I hear a pause.

As you can imagine, we began to experience some opposition from other professionals who dealt with children and families, like attorneys, judges, therapists, and other social workers, teachers, et cetera. Everyone had an assessment and an opinion. And so quickly I began to really ponder my stance on transracial and same-sex parenting, particularly when there was another professional who started quoting scripture. This person did not feel comfortable being helpful to the process of them joining as a family. I had a visceral reaction to that. In my mind you don't need to use God against anyone.

I so agree with that!

I really had to ask myself, and this professional person, Who are you? What do you believe in? And how are you going to, as a social worker, a system mover, really help this family and educate others on this team? It was pretty difficult. We had some heated moments. Our charge was to find a solution that was in the best interest for these kids. They are black boys, who are the least desirable, unfortunately, when potential adoptive parents begin to look at who they want to adopt. So I began to look at these two boys' reality if they never join a family. Who am I to deny them an opportunity for having a fulfilling life with a family who could provide them both with love and with limits? That was it for me. I concluded that these children deserve the chance to have the positive, prosperous life.

Can you share any other experiences with transracial adoptions that worked out well?

[Yes.] Over time I have learned that transracial adoption can be multifaceted and complex but yet so simple at the same time. At some point the human heart and spirit seems to guide the process. I can say that because of the extraordinary families and child welfare staff with whom I have worked. Let me tell you about two more families that will challenge your thinking about adoption.

A single African American woman who raised her children decided to become a foster parent with our agency. We placed twin Caucasian toddlers in her home who captured her heart. This was a quiet unassuming woman with deep faith in God and a strong Baptist Church family. This foster mother dealt with such public scrutiny from other parents in the girls' school. Once the Caucasian parents in the girls' school discovered that she was not the nanny, they began to voice doubt that a black foster mother could successfully raise white children. Several of the families even contacted the agency with the expectation that we would place the children with another family. Nevertheless she adopted the girls and even maintained contact with the twins' birth family, including their three other siblings. The twins' brother was nonverbal and diagnosed with autism. Our agency recruited for an adoptive home but was continuously unsuccessful. After seeing their brother featured on Wednesday's Child and other outreach events, the mother decided that she would move into larger housing to accommodate a larger family. Years later she moved from her condo into a single-family home with the full intent of adopting the twins' brother. Today she is the proud African American mother of three Caucasian children. The girls happily sing in the choir at their predominately African American church, and they speak openly about the joys and challenges of transracial adoption.

Three small children entered foster care after their mother had a psychiatric emergency that left them unsupervised and in danger. Child protective services staff placed the children with a Latino family who had no birth children. Staff was able to locate and engage the father of two of the children. He quickly gained custody of his children and returned to their home country. The youngest child, only nine months old, was left in this country without biological connections to provide her with a permanent family. The foster family felt an immediate connection to her and devoted their time and energy to attend to all of her needs. The foster mother operated an in-home day care center. They formed a quick and deep attachment to each other. The family understood the cultural differences and sought out people of African and African American descent to support them in bridging the cultural gap and helping them to braid her hair! Staff quickly realized that the foster family was the only family she knew. Staff worked with the family through language barriers and issues with citizenship status to ensure the adoption could take place for this child. Today this toddler from Nigeria speaks Spanish and is flourishing in their family.

Those stories are such an inspiration and make the case that transracial adoptions come in different combinations.

So . . . you got involved with transracial adoptive placements professionally and have had to ask some hard questions in that process: Why is it important for white adoptive families in particular to connect with African American families? How exactly do they make these linkages, and why do you think that these linkages are important?

It is critical because children have to see images of themselves in their day-to-day life. I tell families that they need to be intentional. In most cases that means that they must insert themselves in the black world. You should, for instance, go to a black church and join a ministry. You, as an adoptive family, should begin to establish yourself in a different community that can embrace you, where you are not afraid to connect and ask questions in a safe setting.

Hopefully these transracial adoptive families already have black friends and have had black people in their home. It's a funny reality.

You can see black people and white people at work, but mostly these groups are divided. Many white people have never had a black person in their home and have never entertained that idea. The goal is to really be intentional about having people over for dinner and you going to their home also. Other activities you can do in the black community are to go to community events, concerts and church activities, so that you can get immersed into a community that will support you. Now some people in the black community will confront you. They will confront you, but they will also support you in raising these children. One of the values, Rhonda, as you know, in the African American community is the popular saying "It takes a village to raise a child."

That is a very firm value in the black community, and the black church is the great place to start that. Transracial adoptive families need to be ready to do the heavy lifting.

How do you prepare families that are interested in adopting transracially about the realities of this choice?

Again, adopting a child from a different racial and ethnic background is different. These children cannot just pass as your birth child. I think interested parents need to think about how their family will be forever changed. It is not just the family in your home, but it is also your extended family network that will forever be touched by the difference. Let me be clear and say that the difference is not deficient—it is adding value to your family.

Very good point.

So I think that [it] is really important to accept that love is not enough. You cannot simply think that love is enough and that color-blindness is the way to go. Actually the family that has that mind-set scares me more than a family that is really able to sit down and say that this will be different, this is another layer of parenting on top of the regular developmental things. This child will experience driving while black. This child will experience being called the "N-word." This child will have to deal with images of race and of skin color and the complexities of different textures of hair. A transracial adoptive parent needs to think, I need to be ten steps ahead in my level of awareness so that I can be of use to my child.

Amen!

I am a firm believer that color-blindness has been the enemy to forging progress in transracial adoption for so many years. You cannot be naive [about] race and skin color. You must prepare your child to go out confidently into the world, to be safe, and to have a healthy sense of self. Color-blindness does not facilitate that type of growth and preparation for children.

I want to talk about, as much as you will allow, your personal life. I think your background will help, especially many transracial adoptive families and those touched by this phenomenon, to see through your eyes walking this Earth in dark skin. What was your childhood like? What were the values that you were taught?

I came from a working-class family in rural Georgia. In the early 1970s the town I lived in was very racially segregated. In fact black people lived on a few streets in my little town in Georgia that everyone called Brown Town. My family are hard-working people. Everyone worked at a carpet mill, the biggest industry in the town. The steady force in my upbringing was the deep religious faith in God that has centered my family. Because there was not a lot of money in my home, there was a lot of resourcefulness that had to go on to make ends meet and to take care of everyone.

My mother had some very bold thinking, and she entered into the military. And that helped her to kind of break the cycle of the conditions we lived in. However, during that time in the military my mother couldn't take me with her. So I lived with my grandparents and my aunt. And so my living situation was really a kinship environment, or a village. My grandparents and aunt took care of me while my mother was trying to become more upwardly mobile and create a better life for me. And when she was able to get stationed at a place where I could join her, I would join her. So I lived with my mother and with my extended relatives periodically. My father took no real interest in me. Interestingly my grandfather was the man of my life. He taught me about God. I saw him pray. He took care of the women in the family. He was a good, honest man of integrity, and I watched him treat my grandmother like a queen. He actually treated me like a queen. My entire family believed in me so much that they wanted me to go to school and do better. So I was pushed academically, very hard, particularly by my mother, as a means of creating a better life for myself. Her belief: You get a good education. You get a great job. That is your focus.

So that was my aim: to strive for a quality of education. I was the first in my family to actually go to college. I knew nothing about how to apply to college. Nobody else in my family knew how to do that, so I had a lot of figuring out to do. I thought my mother had college money saved for me, and to my surprise, when I got my acceptance letter in the mail, I asked her how much money she saved. She said, "What? I was just trying to feed you all of these years." So I knew that I had a lot of figuring out to do in the financial area.

I applied for every scholarship that was available to me. People took an interest in me. Let me go back a bit. At that point I was living in Texas. I had moved eleven times throughout my childhood and lived in different countries. I experienced different cultures and heard different languages and had the opportunity to be immersed in different things. I appreciated differences, and I was not afraid of those differences. It was all actually pretty intriguing to me. Anyway, I was graduating from a high school in Texas. There was a school counselor asking me where I was interested in going to college. I had no idea. She said, "Come in my office." She sat down with me—she was a black woman—she said, "You're smart. I think that you should look at this black women's college." I liked the idea. I thought, I am from Georgia. I could be close to home. The climate is warm. It is a southern city. I can do this. I can be around black people. It works for me!

What college or colleges did you apply to?

I applied to Spelman College. Period. I could not afford application fees at other places. I never visited the campus prior to the day of my arrival. I could not afford a college tour. I had to go on a brochure in my counselor's office.

Now reflecting back on your college experience, what would you say are some of the advantages of attending a historically black women's college? I am asking this question in particular for the young black women who grew up in white homes and are struggling with self-identity issues.

Well, even though I was a military child and lived so many places, I was still hungry for positive imagery of myself. When I arrived on Spelman's campus and saw two thousand black females who were smart and beautiful, well dressed, from different cultures and of different shades of color with different hairstyles, it was just amazing to me. I was in complete awe.

I mean, what a powerful experience to see positive images of yourself everywhere you walk. And then of course you had Morehouse College for men across the street, as well as the coed Clark Atlanta University, all historically black colleges. So it was this bubble I was immersed in for four years. I saw so much talent and energy. I soaked in everything. It was the first time ever I saw dreadlocks—coils of long hair—in my whole life and people debating social and political issues until the sun came up in the morning. The experience, the wisdom and values—and the confidence that I got there was incredible.

At that time Dr. Johnnetta B. Cole was the president of Spelman. I tell you, she makes me to this day feel like I can fly. What better way to feel, as a young girl, trying to figure out the world and navigate life—is to believe that you can do anything, that the sky is the limit. I heard that message every day. That experience of being on a campus with teachers who told you that powerful and uplifting message was edifying. I also saw political figures and celebrities on the campus. Spelman was what they called the Black Mecca; people navigated there. For example I could walk down the street and see the Reverend Jesse Jackson, Sr. Dr. Cole was jogging around the circle. I could bump into [the late] Betty Shabazz [educator, civil rights advocate, and widow of Malcolm X] in the elevator, for God's sake.

The richness and the history and the pride that I gained from going to a historically black college were enormous. Right now I have goose bumps thinking about my experience at Spelman.

Just listening to your experience and what you gained from it is definitely food for the soul.

And that is exactly what it was. It was food for the soul. It was nourishment for me during that time in my youth, and it continues to keep me steady today. I just loved the experience. Do you remember Spelman is where they taped the sitcom A *Different World*?

That is the sitcom created by Bill Cosby based at a black college in the South. I didn't realize that it was taped on the Spelman campus.

Yes. So Thursday night we had TV night at the dorm. A bunch of us would get into a room and hover in front of the TV, just looking for our experience fed to us on film. Our Morehouse brothers would come over, too, and we would talk about the TV show and current events. I think we all were hungry for our own image or likeness. Very cool.

After Spelman you moved into the professional arena. How did you begin to navigate as a black woman in a strikingly different society that did not recognize your experience and racial and ethnic heritage?

Yes, I was immersed in this bubble for four years. But the belief in myself that I now have and the confidence in my ability really help me to be audacious today. My Spelman experiences taught me to open up my mouth and be noticed and not fade in[to] the background. So that has helped me even right now. It has not always been easy, but if I didn't have that experience in college, my reality and outlook in life would not have been as bright. I was a very skinny girl with buck teeth and glasses. I needed affirmation! My family affirmed me, but, my God, when I got to Spelman it was magnified by who I came in contact with and the messages that I heard about myself every day. It shows me today that I can do that, I can do this. If one door closes, another one will open.

Tabitha, you are now a wife and a mother with two beautiful children, and they are a shade of brown.

My children are a deeper shade of brown than me, yes.

So how are you and your husband raising your children?

We are raising them on purpose and with purpose.

I hear you loud and clear! How old are your children?

Malcolm is three. Our daughter, Camara, is nine. She has already been on Spelman's campus. We make sure that our children are in environments that are positive, that affirm them, and that they feel safe in. I have many friends from college that have relocated to the Washington, D.C., area. So our children can see a black woman come into our house who is a school principal. Our daughter and son have the opportunity to see black doctors, black attorneys, and black teachers.

They see black couples and black families and black fathers. Those
images are really powerful!

**What is the parental plan that you and your husband abide
by in raising your children, particularly given how society can be
harsh towards black boys and black girls and can portray them in
negative ways?**

I used to be afraid of having a son in this society because of how
cruel people can be to black boys and black men and [because] society
expects very little from them. So my husband takes a very active role
with my son, who is only three. We look at our son in terms of how he
interacts socially with people. We are at the stage of teaching him how
to share, not yell. We are teaching him how to regulate himself and to
build friendships. We teach him that it is okay to experience emotion.
Just as important, we try not to get into some of these stereotypes that
we as a society put on our children. There are girl toys in our house
because we have a daughter. Girls and boys both wash dishes. Girls
and boys cry. Mommy drives the car just like Daddy drives the car.
We have some traditional ideology, but we are also very flexible in our
roles. My husband cooks. My husband cleans. My husband washes
clothes. He actually cooks better than I do. My husband sews. All of
these things our children see. We believe these images are powerful for
both of our children. Yes, you should share in the household chores,
and it is a partnership for all of us to be flexible in this family. We
don't pay my daughter an allowance for chores. We pay her for reading
books so that she can be exposed to different things through reading,
and we incentivize that. We participated in Martin Luther King Day
as a family because it is important for our children to know that we are
blessed and that we should also give back to others. Those are things
that we are being intentional about.

Also we do talk with our daughter about hair. She has extremely
long thick hair. [*Laugh*] Of all of the people who do not know how to
do hair, I am one of them! I pay someone to do that child's hair. So
when transracial adoptive families are struggling with hair care, find a
person or a beauty shop that can do some braids. I can do a little bit,
but the majority of the time, my daughter is taken to a hair salon once
a month and they braid her hair.

Well, that is a huge secret. I know right now there are a lot of particularly white women and men who have adopted black children who are struggling with their child's hair: What can I do? How can I learn? You just made it easier for a whole lot of families.

I used to be embarrassed as a black woman that I could not do hair. Let me tell you, that hair salon is amazing. I go to a hair salon that is designed for children. They have mini shampoo bowls and mini chairs, et cetera. This salon is for children. There is a waiting room for the parents. There are typically no seats. So I am not the only one who is inept in this department. I have grown to the place where I am actually okay with paying a hairdresser to do my daughter's hair. But I tell my daughter, as we are taking braids out and trying to find new hairstyles, that her hair is beautiful, that her skin is beautiful. Camara has seen parts of the movie *Good Hair* so it is a good place to continue having conversations about hair.

She has a scripture on the mirror in her bathroom that says, "You are wonderfully and fearfully made" (Ps. 139:14). So there are books that talk about black hair that are designed for children. So she has a couple of those books. Camara is really, really in a good place right now in where she is with hair.

I want to tell you this one story. My daughter's in a swimming class. Her hair was starting to break off from the chlorine in the pool. And so, when I told her that she needed to get her hair cut, she began to cry. I thought, Oh, no, here we go. I told her that we are not going to have unhealthy hair hanging on the edge just so that she can say she has long hair. So I went to my hairdresser, and I had my hair cut off. I was purposeful about sending the message that it is just hair. And we had a conversation about this before I had my hair cut. I told her that I was going to cut my hair first, and she could see that it is just hair and it grows back. She didn't think that I was going to do it, and so it had to be a dramatic haircut! I thought I needed to do this for my little brown girl, so that she could see that this is only hair, and it is not a big deal.

So the values you said that you learned from your family as you were growing up, like the importance of God in your life, education, and the reality that it takes a village, are they today the same

values you rely on, now that you have stepped up the educational and economic ladders?

You know, I spend a lot of time thinking about this. I have been told by people in my hometown that I am the one that "made it." I am in a big city now. I have this four-bedroom house with land, et cetera. It looks all pretty on the outside. Actually that bothers me because when you "make it," if you aren't careful, you can lose yourself, especially if you are not grounded with good values. So as I age, develop, and am raising children, the values of my childhood are the things that keep me centered. I am proud of who I am, where I came from, and where I am from. I used to be embarrassed that I was this black girl from the wrong side of the tracks: that I had no money, that my family really did not have a lot. We didn't have a lot, but we had what we needed. So when you look at this society of wealth and waste as you're raising children, the question my husband and I ask ourselves is, What is the legacy that we want to leave our children with? It really is, for us, have God, understand a power greater than you, be kind to others, have integrity, say what you mean, mean what you say, be *proud* of who you are, you only go through this life one time. I love that I have the home base that I go back to because it helps me in my decision making at work. When I think about the many disenfranchised, vulnerable children, exploited families, families who just need a step up, I realize I am only here, I am only in this middle-class society now, because I am on the shoulders of the people who helped me. That's it. It humbles me, and it brings me down when I think I am getting too "high sadity." I am humbled by the sacrifices of my ancestors and [by] my family values. I am not better than others; I am simply blessed.

I love how you use the [term] *high sadity*—**acting important; putting on airs, acting like you think you're better than the people around you. You, Tabitha, truly exude a spirit of humility.**

My childhood values really guide me. I have worked for everything I have. I wish it was easier, but you know that grit and that tenacity has helped me to advocate for myself, and it has helped me to advocate for vulnerable children. So I honor that.

What do you want for children in foster care?

For children in foster care who are waiting for their permanent family, I want families to step up for children, to wrap a circle of support around them. If it's not your parent, let it be your godmomma or your auntie or your grandparent. And if they can't do that, for these children, then please give these children permission to love another family through adoption.

A lot of transracially adoptive families tell me about the stares they get from people when they see them with their children of color. Some people in fact will walk up to these parents and ask if the children are okay. Are they babysitting? Have these kids been kidnapped or are they lost? Some also state how saintly the adoptive parents are for adopting a child of color, et cetera. These questions are asked particularly from people in the black and white communities. My first question is, What more can be done to educate the black community about transracial adoptive families and normalize this reality?

That is an uphill climb. It really is, and that is unfortunate that I would state that. Transracial adoption is still, like you said, it is a bit taboo. Families must be ready for the stares, for the ridicule, when they walk down the street, for the curiosity of, How did this happen and where are the other set of parents, what is the situation?

Is there a response for when these uncomfortable events happen? I think so many adoptive parents are looking for a guide to how to handle these situations.

I don't think that there is a textbook response. I think that families have to craft their own responses that they feel are appropriate to share at that time in their life. You need to remember that the children are listening and waiting for their response. So these kids take the lead from the adoptive parents. They will mirror that response. Children can sense the anxiety a parent might feel upon answering a question like that. So I think that it is important to begin thinking about how best to respond. In fact there are [a] few resources that we use for families in foster care that talk about the tough issues and how to explain those issues to children. The WISE UP curriculum through CASE [Center for Adoption Support and Education] gives the language to respond to curious or negative people in the grocery store, the library, or the book clubs. Parents really need to model and craft the message in developmentally appropriate ways, particularly when they are with their children. Also you don't have to respond to everybody's inquiries. It is quite okay to say it is none of your business, and this is a private family matter.

I think adoptive families feel like they have to answer everyone's questions. And that is far from the truth. In terms of the black community, there is a lot of just straight talk that needs to happen about waiting children in general and the need for families to adopt. Adoption is not a subject that is broached in the black community often enough.

We are talking about formal adoption through the child welfare system?

Yes. I think that in the black community there is a healthy dose of fear of the government imposing itself in their family system. Let's think about—

Slavery—

Yes. Think about when systems get involved with people of color. It usually goes badly, such as incarceration, hospitalization, sterilization, like the Tuskegee experiment [in which black subjects were deliberately injected with syphilis].

It really is a historically ingrained distrust of systems because of the disparate treatment of people of color. Truly there is a healthy dose of fear and a huge dose of distrust because it plays itself out. So when you think about a court system or a child-serving system getting involved with your family, it is definitely a scary thing. Oftentimes, when you think about adoption, particularly private adoption, it can become political and it can become a financial issue. You know, a lot of people cannot afford to formally adopt. There are a lot of complexities that go into these conversations in the black community. I think a lot of it starts with peeling back the layers of distrust so that you can sit down and have a healthy dialogue so that there can be some education around the need to adopt children. A lot of families in the black community don't really know how many black children are in foster care, how many children are waiting for homes, or even how to get matched with a child so that you can have a child join your family.

How are adoption agencies broaching this issue for the most part—or are they?

Private adoption agencies must do more. [*Pause*] Many private adoptive agencies are located in affluent, predominately Caucasian neighborhoods, with little access to public transportation and so forth. People who can afford to adopt through a private agency, obviously, are in a higher income bracket. So you're going to get a large Caucasian group of people. Therefore there has to be deliberate outreach in communities of color in the faith-based communities. Adoption agencies typically don't do that type of legwork and put that much outreach effort into it.

If adoption agencies are struggling to build these linkages into communities of color, how are white adoptive families going to have the "how to" of finding resources like you? In other words, where are all the smart, value-grounded black people that these families can go to that will help them feel safe?

I think that when you are in an urban city, of course there are many more cultures, many more types of people coming together, so it is easier to find any ethnic group. You can go to different cultural events that are advertised in the paper and on TV or are advertised in your libraries. If there are colleges nearby, particularly a historically black college or university, those are really good places to get linked in with. Your churches are going to be a huge help to any prospective adoptive family. Again, I am hoping that these parents have formed even a small network of support within a community of color so that they can lean on their own friends. With word of mouth you can build a support network. You have an Asian friend. You have a Native American friend. You have an African American friend. They all can help with linkages into their community. Of course, reach out to the local department of social services in your area.

Where do you see transracial adoption going in the future? Do you think adoptive parents are going to be savvier and do the heavy lifting that you are talking about?

I am hopeful, especially if we can get past the political correctness of people and the whole idea of color-blindness. I have seen some incredibly savvy families who were moving into, or already live in, a diverse neighborhood. For example the children who have been in foster care, if you as parents continue to stay linked with that department of social services and attend support groups, you have a natural network. The child's previous foster care parents may have been of African American descent, and so that becomes a resource for that family for support, for questions, for respite, even. It is like an extended family. I have seen that happen. I have seen that adoptive parents are extremely conscious that they don't know about black hair care so they will attend a seminar on black hair or, if a local community college has a braiding course, they will attend. Certainly there are events that you can attend to be purposeful about the journey they are going to take.

How can transracial adoptive families become more flexible in how they raise their families, particularly if their extended family members are not so supportive? I know unfortunately that is not always the case, that extended families are receptive to this type of family planning.

That is a sad reality. If your family cannot be your biggest cheerleader, then you better have some good friends that become pivotal in your life. As a military family I moved to a lot of different places so my friends became a network for me. And for my mother who was a single parent, she had to form relationships wherever we went so that she could have support for herself. I would venture to say that we need that anyway as parents. Particularly if you are an adoptive parent, you are going to need a level of support, if not from family, definitely from friends or from coworkers or from the previous foster family, if possible.

Adopting older children can make the issue even more complicated, I can imagine, in working to deliberately develop good support.

If you are a parent who is adopting an older child, you can never underestimate building linkages to their birth family as a meaningful resource to you. That, I know, is not a popular view. But when you are adopting an older child, maintaining their kinship connections so that they can know something about who they are, where they come from, is huge. Their genetic history is critical. Every child needs to know critical information about their health!

How can families nurture relationships with their child's biological family members with appropriate limits or boundaries?

It is definitely an art, not science. Adoptive parents can start out as slow as getting a P.O. box and sending cards and letters, then gradually move up by having visits at the local agency or at McDonald's or at a park once every couple of months. Some adoptive families are fine with birth parents or the birth family, even sharing holidays or Sunday dinners. It really takes time, and it does take the adoptive parents' feeling confident in their own parenting, such as knowing this child is a part of my family and here are our rules and our expectations and you, the biological family member, can enter into our home or into our family life to the extent that I/we can handle at this time. Birth family members need to understand that the relationship can ebb and flow as the child ages. Rhonda, you know, every young person is eventually going to ask those questions of who am I? How better to be prepared than to have their birth family connections available to them? And if they are already in a transracial adoptive situation, and it's a black child, you already have a natural linkage to the black community right there.

What final words can you share with transracial adoptive parents?

Transracial adoptive parents must know that their work is ahead of them in this journey. My advice to them is to laugh, to learn from their mistakes, to admit mistakes, and to keep on trying. We all do the best we can as parents every day. With love, a healthy support system, and intentional work, you will be alright. Enjoy your family!

Your insight is invaluable, Tabitha. Thank you!

BRYAN POST

CEO of the Post Institute for Family-Centered Therapy and Adoptee
INTERVIEWED BY TELEPHONE, JULY 16, 2013

When we as progressive practitioners, researchers, and society think about transracial adoption, so often we think about teaching parents and children how to navigate the racial terrain, which is critical. However, Bryan, I want to talk with you about the *emotional* impact on the child who has survived the traumas caused by

foster care and adoption and how children and families can move through the emotional pitfalls successfully. What is it about adoption that can create such anxiety and trauma in a child?

It's a multilayered answer, Rhonda. First and foremost it is important to look at the neurophysiologic experience of this infant. So what we know is that, as early as the fourth week after conception, the fetus is capable of hearing. As early as the second trimester the fetus is capable of physiological processing. Essentially from conception the fetus in the womb of the biological care figure is experiencing and processing all of the messages and communications that go along with placing a child for adoption. So the reality is that for a fetus, i.e., an infant, for the first nine months of their lives [they are] repeatedly exposed to messages in energy. It doesn't take any words for the fetus to understand what is being communicated. It is energy. Even *thoughts*, Rhonda, create energy. This phenomenon has been measured in birth and prenatal studies. Just a thought from a mother can cause a fetus to have a reaction. So thoughts, feelings, as well as experiences—all of those are essentially being processed and internalized by the developing child. And what that does is that it stores the messages literally in that child's DNA. And those are messages of abandonment and rejection at the core.

From a personal perspective, being adopted myself, I asked my biological mother, "At what point did you know you were going to have to place me for adoption?" She said, "When I was about three months pregnant." I then said to her, "At what point did you really start to disconnect?" She said, "At about seven months into the pregnancy I knew that I was going to have to give you up, and I became depressed and I tried not to think about you being inside my stomach."

Whoa.

As a developing child in my birth mother's womb, I was essentially bathed in that negative experience. So I came into the world as a very sensitive infant, completely vulnerable, with all of this encoding already that essentially says that I am at risk in the world. I am not safe because I am not with the person who I have known all of this time. I have all of these messages of insecurity. I have anxiety of being abandoned. These messages get stored in the DNA. We, as the adopted child, cannot conceptualize the impact of that experience. Our adoptive parents cannot conceptualize the impact of that experience. Mental health professionals can't do it. Physicians can't do it. We as a society cannot even begin to feel what that is like for an infant, much less that infant that grows up as a child who has those messages that live within them. As a therapist myself, doing my own self-analysis and doing my own therapy, even at forty years of age I am still longing for things that are direct antecedents from my birth and from my in-utero period.

Let me stop you for a second. Are you saying, then, that once a child is birthed and *immediately* placed into a good adoptive home, that that child has already received an encoding saturated in fear and anxiety?

Yes, potentially irreparable damage. I am going to be blatantly honest with you. I don't know if that gets repaired. I don't know if that wound ever gets healed. I think that it becomes a part of that child's personality.

This is so intense to wrap one's arms around and understand. Still, today I talk with parents who have adopted and are adopting, particularly infants. Many of them speak in terms that convey that the slate is clean and the clock gets reset the moment these infants become a part of their family. And this is what they tell me they have derived from the information their adoption agency has shared with them in their adoption process and from the information that their agency omitted.

That is asinine. We are a whole decade beyond the decade of the brain. And for scientists and for therapists to continue [to] perpetuate this tragic myth upon these children and upon these families, it is just not okay.

I agree with you. It is not okay. What we have established so far is that the infant's development is already occurring in the womb. So when we talk about ways to help, especially our adopted children, we have to recognize that there is an embedded history that is a part of each infant before he or she even comes to the adoptive family.

Yes—blueprints that will follow them for the rest of their life. We talked about the first layer of what creates trauma in an adopted child.

The second layer that creates trauma for a child is the environmental/experiential part—after the child has been adopted. Think about it: the potential frequent moves that the child goes through being in foster care or just the learning the child must do, even if the child comes right into his or her adoptive family's home, which is so unlikely [in] these days and times, is enormous. Just learning the new physiological sensations of the new environment is overwhelming for the child. Many people don't realize that moving is one of the top five most stressful events that we ever encounter in life. Imagine what that must feel like for completely helpless infants. The reason why moving is so traumatic and so difficult, especially to the adopted child, is because the child has to adjust all of his or her sensory system to a new environment, to new people, to new sounds, to new temperatures. All of that is different. So you have an infant who has spent nine months where the womb has been their world; it is their sole experience. All of a sudden they are now in a completely different environment. Everything has changed. That is trauma number 2, in addition to the emotional experiences that the child has had in utero. Trauma number 3 are the terrors that the adoptive parents feel when bringing a child home and the rippling effect that has on the child.

For instance my parents really struggled especially with my [younger] sister. They were not able to have biological children themselves. I refer to my adoptive parents as my parents because they raised me. They really struggled. My sister had in utero exposure. She came to them crying. They were completely helpless. They didn't know what to do. It was probably a day after they adopted my sister that they had left me with my mom's parents, my grandma and grandpa, so that they could go off and buy stuff. That is all fine and well. That doesn't seem harmful. But when you have an adopted child, those intricate moments, they all become potentially traumatic experiences. From the beginning I was connected to a biological figure, and all of a sudden that person is gone. And now here I am with another stranger. So from the point that that infant comes into the adoptive home, whatever that infant or child has experienced before he or she has come into the home matters and will have an impact. Rhonda, the point I am making is that children of all ranges and ages get adopted, so there is the gamut of experiences that go into the making of a child *before* the child ever comes into the home.

Thank you for addressing this. It is huge. I think that this is a piece that does not get talked about, much less thoroughly, on the grassroots level and in the trenches within adoptive communities. Without question this dialogue is absent in mainstream settings. I do know that there are books, like *The Primal Wound: Understanding the Adopted Child* by Nancy Verrier, that touch on this subject, but, Bryan, you are the only one that I know and have talked with who can break this trauma phenomenon down clearly for me as an adoptee. Bryan, I just talked with a parent who adopted two kids from Haiti. And they cannot understand why the kids are acting up. To them they are providing their children love, their own bedroom, and vacations. They should be happy, they said to me. And all I am thinking about is that these children are living in a remote, predominately white farm community.

You know what? We are woefully ignorant. It is beyond my ability to fathom how we can continue to allow parents to bring kids into their homes without any or adequate education.

I know, and that is why it is important to talk with you here. Parents need support and guidance, especially when their kids are going through trauma. We are fixin' to go on a roller-coaster ride in our discussion.

What personal experiences catapulted you into the work that you do for children and families?

I was adopted as an infant. Now that I know this information, I like to always include it because it is a part of who I am. My biological mother and father were two young individuals that fell in love. My biological mother was already in a relationship. She had three small kids, ages three, two, and one, when she became pregnant with me. Her husband was in Germany, enlisted in the army. He had told her that he was not coming back. She had met my biological father and they fell in love. It turned out that my biological father left her pregnant. Well, she was faced with the choice of basically not knowing if my biological father was going to be available to be a dad—he was only eighteen years of age at the time—or [whether she was going to be] . . . a single parent with four kids. She talked with her husband and he told her to have an abortion. This was in Oklahoma in 1970. It was not a good position to be in. So other than having an abortion, which everybody except for her sister thought my biological mother did, my biological mother made the decision to come to full term with me and place me for adoption. I spent a few months in foster care as an infant, and then I was adopted into my adoptive family. A year after my parents adopted me, they adopted another child. And that was my home growing up.

My adoptive father was a Vietnam veteran. He had posttraumatic stress disorder (PTSD). Both my mom and my dad were children of alcoholic parents. They were both the oldest of sibling units of ten and nine. My mother was the oldest girl of all of her siblings. My father was the oldest boy of all of his siblings. So they were both very "parentified," hyperresponsible individuals. And so here they are, bringing in these two babies to raise. It just didn't go well. Parenting was a challenge for them. I was a challenge, not so much that I know of as an infant or toddler, but as I got older I had behavioral issues. My sister was a challenge for my parents from the very beginning. As I said earlier she had sensory integration challenges from the beginning that they had no idea about how that really affected their relationship with her. My entire life growing up was kind of like World War III. You have the kid who is crying all the time, the mother who feels completely helpless, and the father who is triggered by his PTSD. On top of that they practiced old-school parenting. They knew how to yell, whip, isolate, shame, and threaten. That was my life growing up. They did the best that they could as parents. They did what they thought they were supposed to do. Bless their hearts, they even asked for help. I remember having a counselor come over to take my sister out for ice cream. My parents tried. That was back in the late 1970s, early 1980s. It is unfortunate that not much has changed for adoptive parents since then. Adoptive parents today continue to face the same issues and struggles. That is what compelled me to do the work that I have done over the years to try to educate adoptive parents, first and foremost about themselves and their own reaction patterns and then, secondly, to help them understand their adopted children, their struggles and behavioral challenges. It is personal. That has been the crux of my work. I have been helping adoptive parents help their children to get through this fear of living and to create more loving environments.

You touched on what seems to be a common theme, which is that much has not changed for adoptive parents and children compared to thirty or forty years ago. How is your therapeutic approach to parenting different and how does it yield a better result for children and families?

If people are not educated, they simply don't know. They are just going for a ride, making assumptions about their kid without education. The basis of my teaching is education, which is helping people understand the dynamics of adoption, trauma, and stress. I teach them to understand the dynamics of family roles and how each member's role in the family is impacted by their own history. And then from there I teach people how to learn different parenting approaches to not create more stress and fear for their children and instead create love and more oxytocin-rich opportunities. This way parents in particular can help their child's brain heal and develop along a trajectory that will help their child to understand more about themselves as they become an adult. A big piece of what I do is really helping parents create an environment where their children grow up having some *self-understanding* of their own struggles. If I could have had just the beginning of understanding that revealed how stressed I was as a child or how fearful I was or how sensitive to rejection and abandonment I was as a child, I could have grown up into that knowledge in a way that I would have more control over my emotional reactions and my patterns and behaviors into adulthood. So I really spend a lot of time helping to create that framework for parents.

Here is a scenario: There is a child of color who has been adopted into a white family. Let's say this family is also living in a predominately white neighborhood. This new environment is different than what the child knows. He starts acting out. He throws temper tantrums. He throws dishes and toys at anything or anyone that moves. He even starts physically hurting the cat. How do you as a professional intervene in that kind of stressful situation?

First I want the parents to stop putting so much focus on the fact that this child is of a different race and in a different culture, because his resistance to relationships is rooted in that. I want to get the parents out of that mind-set. Let me be clearer: I want the parents to be aware of the child's culture and race and all of those important matters, but *I want them to place their relationship with their child above and beyond everything else.* It gets them to a place where they love that child as parents love their children. And it has nothing to do with race. It has nothing to do with the culture. I don't want race and culture to be the first handicap. A lot of times with transracial adoption, the parents want to use that as the first area for relationships. For example, "Oh, we are having these issues with our fifteen-year-old black son. He is in this school with all white kids. You know, he is the only black child in the family. He has all of these identity issues. He is listening to rap music and dressing weird." This is the first thing that they want to do, make it about race. But the reality is that the child is rejected at a core level. The child does not feel accepted *in the core unit of the family.* And so when the child does not feel accepted at the core unit of the family, it doesn't matter how many black churches you take him to. It doesn't matter how many black friends he has. *He does not feel accepted.*

I want to move beyond that place of being arrested in a relationship and get back to just connecting with this child as a child. This child is stressed out. He is overwhelmed. The central way that I like to say that is "A child who is acting out is a child who is stressed out. Where you got an acting-out, stressed-out child, you've got acting-out, stressed-out parents." First of all, what I want the parents to do is get themselves calm, pull themselves together, and look at what some of their reactionary patterns are and then start thinking about how they can create more soothing and more calmness in their relationship with the child.

How do parents calm themselves down when their child is throwing things and acting up?

The first step is to just sit down and take a deep breath. And shut the hell up.

Wow! I got it.

It is that simple, Rhonda. Shut. The. Hell. Up! Sit down! Stop being so scared and so overwhelmed. Don't worry about that kid in the moment. Just calm the hell down. You know, it is not that difficult but we make it so hard. We make it so hard. We want to get all technical, theoretical, and psychological. It is just not that serious.

Once parents have calmed themselves down, how do they then discipline the child? It can be so easy to turn the volume back up. I remember my African American godmother, Myrtle, at times looked at me with that *eye* when I was beginning to get out of control. Part of that had to do with the cultural differences of how she was raised to parent, compared to how I was allowed to act freely or wild within my adoptive family. Myrtle intuitively was able to discipline me effectively, but there were a few times when she would get upset with me and give me that *look*. If I still acted up (which did not happen often) she would make a gesture, like she was going to take off her shoe and throw it in my direction. It definitely put a fear in me to *stop* my nonsense immediately. What would be a better approach?

You have to rule by modeling, teaching, and discipline. And discipline means to be an effective disciple. So you have to discipline from a heart and a spirit of love as opposed to one of fear. You can't just threaten, hit, yell, and scream and expect the kid to do anything different. Kids don't understand anything different. With your example, once your godmother calmed down she could have said, "Rhonda! Come over here and sit down." She doesn't have to be in a good mood to say it. And as she was getting herself calm, she could have said, "Girl, what is wrong with you? What is going on?" Then it is not coming from a sphere of trying to shame you. I don't believe that parents need to be fake. I believe in parents being just as real as they possibly can. If you are upset, you're upset. When I say, "Calm down," really what I am talking about is the brain. When you are stressed, your thinking becomes confused and distorted, and your short-term memory is suppressed. When I talk about calm[ing] down, I am just talking about getting to a place where you can think clearly without being completely overwhelmed and therefore completely overwhelming your child. It is that simple. Then you can be in a place where it all comes back to teaching. That's when you can teach your child what she can do differently. You can tell your child to stop doing something, but then you can tell them how to stop doing it or how to do it in a more effective way.

Bryan, I would describe myself as hyperresponsible. I have always had a lot of responsibility, even when I was a child. And so anytime anything happened in my family growing up, where there was a huge forced transition, all of a sudden my breathing increased drastically into short breaths, and my anxiety took over. I always felt that I had to fix the problem to survive. So after the parent has calmed themselves down, how do they then help the child to start breathing in a normal, calm way?

Here is the magic of our neurophysiologic communication processes: The moment the parent starts calming down, they then start communicating and sending the vibrations to begin calming down the child.

Tell me more about the neurophysiologic process.

Just the process is interesting. It's called a neurophysiologic feedback group. It's basically made up of these energetic feedback groups that get created by these vibration loops. And it is really the communication of each person's amygdala. It is your alarm system in your brain. It is where stress originates. When a child is agitated and escalated, they are sending off a stressful signal, which alarms the parent's brain to start to react in kind. The parent has to be able to calm their brain down to send a countersignal back to the child that doesn't amplify the child's stress response. Here is the counterdynamic. I should be writing this out on a diagram. But the counterdynamic is the very process of the parent calming themselves down and therefore activating a hormone within their brain called oxytocin. Oxytocin is the brain's antistress hormone. It is also called the hormone that makes love and relationship possible. So when the parent is calming themselves down, actually what they are doing is turning on their oxytocin response. While they are turning on their oxytocin response, they start to trigger the oxytocin response of their child. And when that oxytocin response has occurred in their child, the child cannot continue to escalate. It is physiologically impossible that a child escalate in the presence of a calming parent. A child can only escalate in the presence of an escalating parent. It is so simple, Rhonda, but it is so not easy because the exchange at the growing base level is literally painful. The reason being: the moment the child escalates and amplifies, it jacks the parent's brain up. And depending on what happens, what that parent brings to the table, what their experiences have been, what their parenting interactions have been, and what their blueprints were like, that is what is going to drive their own reaction. When that child's brain gets amplified, it amplifies the parent's brain and from there it is kind of *on*. For me, if my brain was jacked and my daddy's brain got jacked, then the next thing that is going to happen is that I am going to get yelled at or I am going to get whipped. And there is not a lot of variedness in response. However, for my own children, if their brain gets jacked and my brain starts to get jacked, I have learned to teach myself to calm myself down a little bit and turn my oxytocin response down a little bit to be able to step away from the environment, to be able to create less stimulation for myself in that moment, so I might have to move my kid away from me to create some more soothing for myself. And then actually through that process, I can start calming the child's brain down. I am no longer escalating their brain. And then I can go back to my kid and say, "Look, we can do better than this. I don't know what is going on right here, but we need to work through this situation."

That makes sense but it is heavy. I can visualize what you are saying. I can clearly see why you focus on the education piece with the families you work with, because it is so easy in the heat of the moment for our brains to turn off and behaviors get escalated.

There you go. It escalates on both sides of the relationship. The parent's behavior escalation doesn't look like the child's behavioral escalation because the child is not well equipped to suppress their energy the way a parent does. But that vibration that kid is sending off is huge. That's why your godmother could give you the evil eye, and it felt like you had been whipped.

True. It was all in her eyes and in the strong vibrations she sent my way.

Oh, yes, she could feel your vibration and tell your brain, "Girl, you better back up!"

Let's talk about bonding. Why do some children not bond with their parents, even if the child has been adopted into a family as an infant?

Think about it as attachment and bonding. Attachment is the behavior of the child to the parent. Bonding is the behavior of the parent to the child. It is a two-way street. Children have a difficult time attaching when they come from perennial environments that say attachment and connection are not safe; attachment and connection lead to pain; attachment and connection breed insecurity and anxiety. And they have all of these experiences in their brain that tell them that the first human connection that they had was not good. Essentially their brain is automatically wired to have a fear reaction in the midst of an addiction of attachment. We have that. Then we have the parents. This is what I realized early in my career. Nobody was talking about it. You have parents who bring their own history to the table. The moment that child is crying, it is dropping that parent right back into the mix of what that parent experienced as a child. For that parent their window of tolerance of how much stress they can handle starts to wear out. Pretty soon they are not thinking of their physiological environment or bonding with their child. They are not creating or providing a physiological environment for the child to attach to. I used to say in my lectures: "Kids don't want ugly parents. Kids want pretty parents." What I meant by that is kids want parents who are emotionally attractive: Parents who are fun, parents who are loving, and parents who are understanding. That's what kids are attracted to. They don't like a parent who is negative, mean, and always critical. There are not opportunities for secure attachment to happen in those situations.

And so does that emotional reality carry into adulthood for a child who has struggled with attachment issues with their guardians, and, if so, how does that look in adult relationships?

Absolutely. It looks no different than it did in childhood. It looks exactly the same. I remember interviewing Marti Glenn, who is the founder of the Santa Barbara Graduate Institute in California and a longtime prenatal and perinatal professional. And I asked him, "Marti, how do attachment challenges and disruptions show up in adulthood?" He told me, "Bryan, they show up the same way they did in childhood." People are afraid of relationships. They are afraid of vulnerability. They are afraid of intimacy. They are afraid of rejection.

They are afraid of abandonment. They get anxiety around all of those issues. They get fearful, and when they get fearful they can't communicate, and they act out in an attempt to soothe themselves. I would not be surprised if adoptees disproportionately experienced divorces, acted out, and suffered with sexual dysfunction and substance abuse more than those who are not adopted. I think, all around, adoptees have more challenges. In general I think that adoptees are doing the best that they can based on what they have experienced throughout their lives.

Sadly I would argue that for most adult transracial adoptees who are struggling in the areas of trauma, stress, and anxiety, they most likely do not know where to access strategic help from someone who also understands the deep-rooted complexities of their life experiences because of adoption and transracial adoption.

No, they don't have a clue because they have not been educated. Their parents have not been educated. Professionals aren't educated. Yes, there are some professionals that are doing some great work like yourself, but when you are no longer a child, when you are an adult, there are not many places to turn to. To be honest with you, some of the places that are out there for adult adoptees to turn to, Rhonda, they are some nasty places. There are some online "resources" even offered by adult adoptees who have had bad experiences and do *nothing* to offer support and consolation and understanding. It's like they are feeding the negativity. I know because I have gone on a few of these sites. I used to run into that same thing in my work with children diagnosed with reactive attachment disorder. It's like where there was a child diagnosed with reactive attachment disorder, you would find ten parents who would gather and say nasty, negative things about that child. There is no healing in that. You cannot get better in that dynamic. And I have had to stop having interactions with these kinds of people on the Internet.

I think for adult adoptees who especially have not dealt with their issues—if for no other reason than we weren't taught how to do it—we can get so desperate that we will reach out for anything or anyone that will promise us relief, even if it is not healthy. Many

of us are walking wounded. How do we as adult adoptees learn to pause, discern, and make better decisions for ourselves?

The first step in that is to realize that what they may be struggling with and the challenges of their struggle are directly related to them being adopted.

That is a hard realization to arrive to. Many of us are taught adoption is love. So often we don't get the other side of the story. Even in my upbringing, my family and I did not talk about the loss that also comes with an adoption. To my parents' credit they were not taught that piece. Any learning they did was by trial by fire. It certainly did not come from a social worker or a mental health professional.

Absolutely. The child, now an adult, can give themselves permission to say, "Wow! Maybe this adoption is not the rosiest thing in the world." I think for the adoptee it is important to do a little investigation about what their life was like before they were adopted and then for them to honor those experiences. To me, Rhonda, I believe that there are really some very core challenges the adult adoptee struggles with. And I believe at the basis of those are rejection and abandonment anxieties. I think so many of our struggles are rooted in that—that need for approval and to be good enough. And we try to be good enough to prevent feelings of rejection and anxiety from happening. But it is happening again because it is like we are stuck in a perpetual cycle of trying to be accepted. We are stuck in a perpetual cycle of trying to be okay. We are trying to be good enough to bring healing to a wounded person in us. I just believe within me that that is the crux of the challenges we adoptees face.

And in that mix we must rise. So how do you build a healthy self-esteem with all of the inherent challenges that we are talking about?

What you are talking about, Rhonda, is a lifelong process. Building one's self-esteem is not something that occurs in a three-day intensive workshop. What happens is that you begin the process of self-understanding. You move from the process of self-understanding to the process of self-processing. So now that you are at the point of seeking to understand yourself, you begin to process the challenges, the pains, and the feelings within you. And then you move into a place of self-acceptance. You cycle between those three stages all of the time. Really, that is the process of growth. As adult adoptees we have to understand that we have a fiber moving inside of us that needs attention, honoring, mindfulness, and sensitivity. When I say *sensitivity*, I mean that there are some kids born with autism. Some kids are born with spina bifida. And many were adopted. In my opinion the undercurrent of challenges that an adoptee faces can be viewed in a way like a disability. You have to grow up with it. You have to learn how to adapt to it without allowing it to take over your life like some negative baggage. Instead it is not baggage at all. The emotions that each person faces because of their adoption and the underlining realities make each one of us unique and special. It is what sets us up to do great things. There are quite a few remarkable people who have been adopted. Some of the richest people in the world have been adopted. He has passed on now, but Apple cofounder Steve Jobs was adopted. Wendy's founder Dave Thomas was adopted. Former president Bill Clinton was adopted. The list goes on—their woundedness, depending on who they were and what they experienced early in their lives, led them to accomplish great things.

Okay, so now that the adoptee is practicing the three steps toward a healthy self-esteem: self-understanding, self-processing, and self-acceptance, how does the adoptee continue their growth if they are operating within a family system that suppresses it?

You know what? We cannot be held hostage by any institution, by any person, or any culture. If we choose to do that, then we have embraced a victim's mentality. We have to be committed to our own growth. And assuming the more love that we can generate within ourselves, the more other people are going to be okay. They are going to be okay *however* they're going to be okay. You are not responsible for how other people feel. You just have to do the best that you can.

For some adoptees there is the fear of the "what if": What if I take control of my own growth and my parents feel uncomfortable? Bryan, for many they have already been abandoned at least once

and then to rock the boat as it relates to our adoptive families is a huge risk. I have spoken with adult adoptees who have said to me that if they go against the grain in their families, or don't show that they are grateful enough, they fear that they may be kicked out of the family, will or not be viewed as a full-class citizen within their family tree—

If getting kicked out of the family or not receiving any trust fund money is directly connected to you getting better and being okay and being a whole person, then that is a family that you didn't need to be in anyway. That family has done their job. And that is money that you don't need anyway. That is dirty money.

Good point. We as adoptees deserve to be whole people and thrive! Anything less, I am learning, is not acceptable. In your book *From Fear to Love* **you talk about two major emotions that all behavior falls under, which is fear or love.**

That's it.

Let's say I am arguing with my spouse and filled with anxiety, ready to walk away—that reaction comes from a place of fear?

Yes. That is it. Again, it is very simple. People might want to call it "up high in the sky." But the truth is, *love is patient, love is kind.* There is always trust, there is always hope, and there is always truth; outside of that is fear. It is as simple as that. The best we can do is try to be the most loving somebody that we can be in any given moment. And when we are not in a loving place, the best that we can do is try to get back to it just as soon as we can.

I love that. Yes.

Nobody is perfect, Rhonda. We are all doing the best that we can. People have to understand that about one another. Parents need to understand that about their children. In those moments of strife and struggle, that child, just like that parent, is doing the best that they can. If they could do something different, for the better, they would. They are not equipped. They don't have the understanding. They don't have the knowledge. It is not there. If it was there, they would be doing something different.

What is your best guess why some potential parents make the decision to adopt a child of color without gaining education and

understanding of the child's racial and ethnic background or history?

You don't know what you don't know. If the professionals don't know, we sure can't expect the very parent who has love in their heart and desire in their heart to be a parent and to create a loving place in their home for a child to know.

Bryan, how did you change your course as a social worker and therapist focusing on children and families from a traditional model of behavior analysis to where you are now?

I changed my course through constant questioning, first and foremost. I questioned all of the sacred cows and I asked myself, "What makes that true?" I questioned it and questioned it until I came to an internal understanding of why that was true or why it was bullshit. If it was bullshit, I came up with a new answer, a new understanding. My knowledge and my experiences stand on the shoulders of a lot of great people before me who have done a lot of amazing research. Rhonda, you are one of them. Before you came along, Rhonda, I don't think that I gave five seconds of thought to *transracial adoption*. I grew up in a transracial environment. I was one of very few black kids in a predominately white town. My family was black, but we were the only black family in the whole town of white people. Your work is very useful to me.

Thank you. That means a lot to me.

What legacy do you want to leave your children?

At its core I want to leave to my children that it is okay to be happy. It is okay to be the most loving person that you can possibly be. And it is okay to take responsibility for your life. As my kids lie back and think about me, my ultimate example is for them to say, "Dad may not have been a lot of things, but Dad is all about showing us that it is okay to be happy. Dad is all about showing us the importance of taking responsibility [for] our life and showing us the importance of being loving people." Rhonda, if I can do that for my kids, to me that will encompass everything.

I know you mentioned to me that your adoptive father passed away eight years ago. What would you want to tell him about who you are as a person if he was here today?

I would like to tell my dad that I am proud of who I am. I am proud of what I have learned. I am proud of the lessons he taught me. I don't have any regrets.

Thank you, Bryan. I really enjoyed talking with you and learned a lot in this conversation!

SHILEASE HOFMANN
Spouse of a Transracial Adoptee
INTERVIEWED BY TELEPHONE, NOVEMBER 10, 2013

Shilease, I am thrilled to talk with you to get your perspective on parenting and transracial adoption. Of course I also want to talk with you because you are the wife of a transracial adoptee. But first tell me about your background.

I was born in Toledo, Ohio. I grew up in the inner city of Toledo during the 1970s and 1980s and went to Toledo public schools. I have lived in Toledo my entire life so far. I have one brother, who is four years younger than me. My brother and I grew up in a home with both of my parents. My life was pretty normal.

Where did you meet your husband, Kevin, and how did your relationship evolve?

I was a teller at a bank. Kevin was one of our customers. I met him because he was in the bank quite frequently. One day he sent me flowers and asked me out to dinner. I agreed. Pretty much, after that the rest is history. We went out for a few years and then we got married and have been married for more than twenty years.

You and Kevin are the parents of two sons. What are their names and how old are they?

Our son Tai is seventeen and our younger son, Zion, is thirteen.

I am asked, often by white parents who have or are adopting children of color, particularly black boys, about how they can raise their children in a way that will protect them from the harshness and racial injustices of today's society. So let me ask you, since I don't have children: How do you and Kevin raise black boys in today's society?

I don't think, going in, we put a lot of thought into how we were going to raise our boys. We both brought our own experiences from our families and applied lessons from what we liked and did not like or what we agreed with or did not agree with. But with boys we did realize early on that we were going to have to teach them that they were going to have to be better to be considered equal to their white peers. We had to teach them that what people around them might find acceptable for their white kids to do would not be acceptable for Tai or Zion. In other words their friends could do things that they could not do, and that would not be fair, but it is what it is. We taught them: *if you want to be successful, you have to be better.*

Can you give me some examples of what it means to be better?

We pretty much have told our sons that whatever is successful for your peer group, you must be better than that success point. If everyone around you is getting Bs, and it is great for them, then you have to get As. If everyone around you is saying please and thank you, then you must do the same and also say, ma'am and sir. You have to stand above, just to be on an equal playing field.

I think that is where there can be a lot of confusion, particularly among white adoptive parents raising children of color. Why is it that you feel it is important and necessary to raise your kids to be better and behave better, compared to white kids?

In our opinion we teach our kids to be better so that they don't appear to be a typical black kid as perceived by society. We teach them that so that they can hopefully overcome the baggage that people throw at them because of the color of their skin. And then, even when you do stand out to be above and beyond, you will be seen as possibly equal.

You said that when you got married, you didn't necessarily think about how you were going to raise your two sons. As your boys got older, did they confront, as black boys, racism in their schools, on the streets, or in their communities? If so, how did you deal with those realities as a parent?

They have both unfortunately had negative racial experiences. It started when they were both very young in school, where they were called derogatory names by their classmates. Our boys have attended primarily white schools and were picked on because of their skin color. And the way that we dealt with it was we addressed it case by case. We always taught them that someone else's ignorance is not their fault. And also we pointed out that they too had to take responsibility of whatever ownership that they may have contributed to the situation—because sometimes you can contribute to that situation. One of our biggest struggles we had was addressing the "N-word" and teaching our kids that if you don't want to be called that word, then you can't say that word. You can't use the "N-word" as a friendly term between your black friends and then get angry that your white friends use it. If you don't want the word used, just don't use it.

Did you and Kevin have to address the racial incidents that were directed to your sons with the school system or the parents whose children used racial slurs against your children?

We have had to do both. We have had to meet with principals, teachers, and staff within the school system and address with them that this is happening and communicate with them that we need to know what the school system is going to do about it. We have had to address parents and let them know what has happened and ask them what they are going to do about the situation. At sports leagues our children have been insulted by racial slurs in the middle of games, and we've had to address the sports league. And so it has come up in different areas of their lives.

This country has not always been kind to black boys. How did the case of Trayvon Martin [the seventeen-year-old fatally shot by a neighborhood watch volunteer in Florida] hit your family personally?

That tragedy was very hard for Kevin and me, being the parents of black boys. Trayvon Martin did what I would have told my children to do. But with the incident involving Trayvon Martin the whole game changed. It was confusing. Before we told our kids, "Don't run because you will look guilty." Now maybe had Trayvon run, he would be alive. The whole "hoodie" thing is the issue that they knew beforehand. Hands free. Face clear. And hopefully that keeps you out of trouble. In this case it didn't matter. So it just holds a lot of confusion and questions and reinforced some of my beliefs that you always have to be vigilant and you always have to be aware, because the rules can change on you.

Even though I grew up in the Washington, D.C., area, which was diverse racially and culturally, I lived in a white family and experienced white privilege. So I didn't realize early on that, for so many black families and other families of color, there is a constant cloud of suspicion and pressure over them because of how society perceives blacks and other minorities in America. Now, living away from my white adoptive family, I find pushing through the stereotypes and suspicion can be quite exhausting. How have you had to condition yourself for that reality as a parent—a reality that many white parents of kids of color are confronted with but don't always know how to address effectively?

For me it really wasn't a conditioning that I had to do because I grew up in it. My parents had these same conversations with myself and my brother. We saw racism in action. I saw my parents experience it. So being a voyeur into their experiences prepared me for parenting in it. And of course Kevin's experience was totally different, because he didn't see his parents subjectively experience racism. He did however get to see his parents fight against racism through their active involvement in social justice issues. For me racism is one of those realities I expected would happen but hoped never would happen. So when it happened, I wasn't surprised. It is the world that we live in.

From your perspective how did Kevin respond to racism as it affected his own children, especially given his upbringing, versus how you responded to racism?

The way that I saw Kevin respond to racism when it came to our kids was that he was more vigilant than me. It seems like things were newer and fresher to him than they were to me. For me dealing with racism on a personal level was very, very, common area. For him you could tell the reality of racism wasn't as ingrained into him as it was in me. I think because of it he was more vocal and action oriented when there were racist insults done toward our kids. I was more matter of fact when it happened. For instance my mind-set was, "Okay, this is what happened. This is what we have to do going forward from my child's point of view." Where he was more, "This is what happened, and this is what we have to do from the *outsider's* point of view." The differences in our approaches to how we dealt with racism may in part have to do with maternal versus paternal instincts as well. I was focused as a mother on my child's hurt, his experiences and his pain. Kevin was like, "This is wrong. We have to fix this systematic problem!"

Transracial adoptees like me and Kevin who were raised in white families grew up with a sense of privilege, which we got simply by living and being within our white families. Granted, growing up we may not have known that was privilege, but it was. We witnessed our white family members moving in society as true members of society or welcomed participants at the table of power instead of feeling like so many people of color, at one time or another, as uninvited visitors who are tolerated at best. Have you seen cases with Kevin that aligns with what I am saying?

Yes. I can still see incidents where he is ready to take action that I wouldn't consider need action. But he comes from that advantage of growing up with that privilege. For example: "If I have a privilege, then I have a right to speak, be heard, and do." My thinking is that I don't have that place in society, so I have to protect my own. I have to do for me. So I can see where growing up in that privilege really gives you the mind-set that you can go out and change and fix a problem. Whereas growing up in racism you learn to grow and fix only what you can in your space.

I have been married to my husband for over thirteen years, and I am still struggling with grasping the reality he sees through his lens. He definitely holds the same perspective as you do. I am more like your husband, Kevin. When there is racism that comes to the surface, I don't want to just address it within our family. I want to talk to, for example, the head of the corporation and address the systemic problem. I don't like revisiting stuff, especially if it is crazy.

Can you remember your first interaction with a transracial adoptive family and what your initial thoughts were when you interacted with them?

Yes. I can remember. And my first thoughts were, "You are in for a rude awakening." What they portrayed to me was [a] "roses and sunshine and we are going to take on the world kumbaya attitude." I felt, like, oh, my goodness—this is going to be a hard road to travel.

How did you come to that line of thinking?

This family told me that they were going to love their child, and it didn't matter what the world thought. Everything was going to be okay as long as they loved their child. I thought that was great. I am glad that they loved their child. I just come from the camp of thought that love is not enough. I mean, I love my children. And I am black with black children. If all I did was love them, they would be in trouble. I need to love my children and prepare them to thrive in the world that they live in.

When you talk about preparation, what would that look like for white parents raising a black child in a predominately white community like in Perrysburg, Ohio [an affluent suburb of Toledo]?

I think that white parents adopting black kids or any kids of color need to be educated. And I don't mean simply learning that Rosa Parks sat on a seat on a bus and Martin Luther King Jr. gave a good speech. I am talking about parents' need to educate themselves about the world they live in and the perceptions that people might have about their children and their family. I say *might* because everybody won't. I tell adoptive parents not to *always* look for the bad but always be aware that the bad is possible. Another way of saying it is you can't always assume that people are good, but you can't always assume that their intentions are bad.

Do you think that transracial adoptees need to connect with their ethnic communities of origin?

I do believe that transracial adoptees need to connect with their ethnic communities, and how they do that can take a lot of shapes, but it is important. As far as how you go about doing it, going to church is an option, joining social groups or visiting a barbershop or beauty shop where there are a lot of people are all good options. I would recommend that parents find out what their kids are interested in. Usually, depending on where you live, if there is a sport or a social outing, there is generally somebody else of color present. Connecting with them is a starting point. If you practice connecting with people that look like your child and going out of your comfort zone, you will get so good at it that you will be the one that extends your hand to somebody else and be the one who starts up a conversation and develops a friendship.

You have seen transracial adoptive families develop over time, given your unique position. Do you think that transracial adoption is good policy? And do you think that we as transracial adoptive families are gaining better understanding of how to deal with some of the complex challenges?

I think that transracial adoption is very good and very necessary. I think that most of the parents that I have interacted with seem to be much better on how they tackle some of the issues they are confronted with because they are multiracial and have adoption in their family. I think that in general the transracial adoptive community has made big strides in coming from a "love is enough" mind-set. There is awareness on the part of transracial adoptive parents that there is some work involved in fostering and nurturing a child of a different race and culture to live in the world that we are in.

Why would you argue that transracial adoption is necessary?

I say it because the numbers say it is a necessity. For the most part the adopting population is white, and the adoptable population is not. So the numbers say that it is necessary or kids in the system are left without homes.

How have your kids embraced transracial adoption?

Transracial adoption is normal to them. They don't even think about it. It is commonplace to them that their grandpa and grandma are white. And when they see other families like that, they say, "Oh! They are like your family, Dad."

Given the twenty years of marriage to Kevin, how has your relationship with Kevin's family developed overtime?

My relationship with them was very easy from the beginning. Kevin's parents were very open to me, and his parents and my parents got along. It was all organic and good. For me it was a good transition.

Wow. That is excellent. There are families, though, where that transition is not as smooth. In my case, while I think that my parents would like my husband's family, they have not met. It just hasn't happened. In other cases it is simply hard for some transracial adoptive

families whose children marry into families of color to push through the "un-comfortableness" to create meaningful relationships.

For us what worked was the time spent with Kevin's family and my family. I had a family that didn't have any issues with me marrying into a multiracial family. They did not have issues with white people in general. Kevin's family did not have any regrets about him marrying me or building relationships with black people. It's like with any relationship: it takes time invested in one another.

What words of wisdom do you have for transracial adoptive parents, particularly those who are adopting black and brown children, seeing that this form of adoption is on the rise?

I would encourage adoptive parents to look at the adoption process as a "special needs situation," even if and when the family continues to grow. In my opinion there is nothing negative about the term *special needs*. It means your child (and family) has special needs. If your child is of a different race compared to the rest of their family, then the child now has a special need. And you need to address it like you would *any other need your child has.*

When you say "any other need your child has," what do you mean by that?

What I mean is that if your child was musically gifted, and you knew that your child craved the ability to create music, and you had the ability of getting them in a situation where they could do that, you would seek out the music teacher or the piano teacher for your child. You would go to garage sales to seek out a piano if you couldn't afford a new one. So it doesn't even necessarily have to be if your child has autism—no, it is *any* need your child has that is special, which means it is different than anybody else's need might be. You owe your child as a parent to do whatever you have to do to seek out filling their need. So if my child is African American and I am not, then I need to tell myself that since I don't know how to be African American, then I better find some African Americans who can help me make sure that I am not missing something. It means that as an African American parent who, let's say, adopted a Latino child and doesn't know enough about being a Latino, I might miss something. So therefore I need to build a Latino community to make sure I don't miss anything for my child's sake.

I was at an event recently, speaking to adoptive families. This one couple said to me essentially that they did not feel comfortable asking an African American parent for help because they wouldn't want them to think that the only reason why they are asking them questions is because of their black child. How would you address that question?

Parents have asked me that question too. I have told them that they probably are desperate. You might start out in a position where you are kind of using them. It is what it is. But if your child had any other need, you would do what you had to do. You should think to yourself in that case, "Whatever relationship I must make, whatever bounds and steps I must take for my child." So that you can get the courage to say to the person in front of you, "I have this child and I don't want to miss something." Like I said, parents may have to be desperate sometimes when helping their kids. It's just us being adults and putting on our big-boy and -girl pants.

Who is Shilease today? And what do you want for your kids?

Today I consider myself a mother in a multicultural family. I want for my children to be able to pursue their passions. I would love for them to pursue that on a level playing field, but they won't because of being black in America today, and that's a reality. I don't want them to lose sight of who they are and their values. And I want them to remember that, if they want to be considered equal, then they really need to work at it and for it. I want them to pursue their passions so that they can be happy, productive citizens. And I would like to graduate them out so that I can have the second act alone with my husband.

What is it that nurtures your family's worth?

For our family we function not on our self-view but our God view, how God sees us. It is our faith in God that keeps us functioning the way that we do. We do not put our worth into how others view us based on stereotypes or media but, again, on how God views us. Our worth means so much to him, like it does for all of his children.

Researchers, adoption agencies, and parents have certainly made strides in moving the transracial adoption movement forward over the last fortysomething years. What can adoptive parents in particular do more of in terms of bringing clarity and cultural inclusiveness to their families?

I think that what needs the most work within transracial adoptive families is their connection to communities that reflect their adopted child's racial and ethnic background. It is important of course that the adopted child connect with others, whether they are mentors or friends that look like him or her, so they won't feel alone. But when the *family* as a whole connects with the community, then it is normal for *everybody*. Therefore as a transracial adoptee creating a family through marriage that is multiracial or resembles your ethnic community of origin, your own cultural nuances that so many adoptees seem to face for the first time won't be new and different anymore. It won't feel like an eye-opening experience because your transracial adoptive family connected with it when you were of younger age.

Where does the problem come in for families when they don't connect as a whole to others that are from their child's ethnic community?

I believe that if there is a white family that adopts a child of color and even makes sure the child is connected to his or her ethnic community, but *they* don't invest in that community themselves, then when the child develops his identity and interests and the adoptive family doesn't grow, it will create confusion and pain for the child. Essentially that child will grow up as a black child in a white family and *not* as a child in this multiracial-cultural family who has all of these cultural experiences that they can now take and build within their own family later in life. That's why I think it made it so easy for Kevin and me. His family was at ease being around me and my family and other people of color. They did not have to aggressively work at it.

My understanding is that Kevin's father was a pastor in Detroit. Correct.

I think that it makes a big difference to be able to interact with people of color on a regular basis. It deepens one's ability to move into a wider range of venues and opportunities. I of course think it is beneficial for all families to reach out to a more global world.

I agree. My parents purposely put me in situations where I was not only among black people but had exposure to people who didn't look like me or have my same experiences.

I want to go back to parenting. Many transracial adoptive parents are now realizing that the societal consequences for their black sons and daughters' acting out are more severe than if it were their white sons and daughters exhibiting the same behavior. As an African American mother, what is your philosophy on how to best handle society's rules when it comes to how your kids are perceived?

We started at the very beginning with our children, sending the message that being out of control and unruly was not acceptable behavior. There is always a threat. The [parental] threat that, "You know what? I might beat you within an inch of your life." That threat alone kept it from ever being necessary. But they always knew. And they saw the situation that if they ever—ever—acted like that, they would pay dearly. And so it was a threat. Honestly I can count on one hand how many times my kids got spanked. And how many times did they get beat? Zero.

Can you take me through, step by step, the parenting strategies you and Kevin applied and continue to apply [in] raising your kids?

Honestly our parenting strategies have been the same since day 1. As soon as our kids walked, talked, and understood what we were saying, it was "No!" The first time my kids asked why, I said to them, "Why is the answer no? Because I am your mother and the authority, and I said it was no! And as a child you need to accept that my answer is no." Rhonda, I know that when I get into this same conversation with white moms who have adopted black children, they say to me that they cannot speak to their child like I do, because they do not have the voice and that they feel like their child should be able to participate in the conversation and express themselves. I disagree. I say that these are black children living in the United States of America. And if they do not understand and learn how to respect authority and operate in a disciplined manner, I would argue that white privilege is going to get them into trouble because everybody else does not see them as white. So my job as a parent is to teach my children how to respect authority. When my children were growing up I taught them that there is a time and place for their questions, and in the middle of administering that authority is *not* that place. In other words I could tell my kids no, but later on we could have a conversation about why Kevin and I think A was a good idea and why B was not a good idea. For example, when our kids were little, I would say, "No, I don't want you to have another cookie because that is too much sugar." Later on we could have a conversation with them about it in more detail. But in the middle of the situation, that is not the place for a question. They had to learn that you accept what it is and move on so that they can live another day.

I think that this is an important piece to discuss when it comes to disciplining children. I know that when my husband has gone with me to adoption events and has seen little black boys, especially, hitting walls, throwing objects at folk, and jumping off of couches with no intervention from their parents, he is very concerned about that because he recognizes the consequences for these kids in society is more serious than it is for white boys and girls, generally speaking. He, like you, is supportive of transracial adoption. He was informally adopted himself. But poor behavior, especially by kids of color in public, I think that he finds [it] unacceptable and dangerous.

It breaks my heart because I see that child that you are talking about either dead or in prison. There are no other options, except for death or prison, for that child.

It is not fair, but there still continues to be unwritten or hidden rules in this society if you are white and different ones if you are black. Case in point: When a little white boy or girl hits against a shelf in Walmart or pushes carts into people, I have seen it perceived by the people watching as cute. That same behavior can get a young black boy into the juvenile detention center.

Yes, as I said it before, a black boy or girl has to be better to be equal. If you are black and want to be cute, then you need to say, "Yes, ma'am, yes, sir." At work I interact with white parents who tell me about their children. They say to me, "I don't know what to do with my son; he is always talking back to me. I can't get him to do what I want." And then they stop and say to me, "I don't understand why your two sons are so good." And I am thinking loudly to myself, "Well, when your son was two years of age and telling you to shut up and did bad things and you giggled, you taught him who he was and what allowances he had. So now when you say something to him, he is going to tell you to shut up because it has always been okay." It is too late now. But, Rhonda, in that instance their mother-son relationship may not be great, but her white son knows how to go out into the world, and he has allowance to do some of that stuff, exhibit those same behaviors, without getting penalized. On the other hand the consequences for the black child who gets to do that, run around recklessly and say whatever comes out of his mouth to his parents, he grows up to be not that cute little black kid anymore but now this grown black man who doesn't understand that you can't just do whatever or say whatever because you will land yourself in prison.

When parents are raising children in a blended family situation, where there is a black adopted child and white nonadopted siblings, how do parents set boundaries and rules for their kids? Should parents set different boundaries for the black kid and different boundaries for the white kids?

You, as the parent, have to set boundaries for the *whole* family. There has to be an expectation. And even if it is uncomfortable in a transracial adoptive family, you have to make it the family expectation. When I grew up, it was the Hightower family expectation. My mother said to her kids, "You will not disrespect our family. This is how we act. So out in public this is how you act." Transracial adoptive families can adopt the similar mind-set: "This is how we act." This is how everyone should respect everyone.

Thank you, Shilease, for a great discussion.

CHELSEY HINES
Foster Care Alumna and Transracial Adoptee
INTERVIEWED BY TELEPHONE, MAY 11, 2013

Chelsey, I am happy to spend time with you here. You transitioned from your biological family support system into the U.S. foster care system and ultimately, years later, into an adoptive home.

Can you talk about your family background and how you entered into the foster care system?

I was born in 1992 and lived in Aurora, Colorado, with my biological grandpa and grandma, my mom and my dad, and my brother and two sisters. My mom and dad were smoking crack and had a hard time taking care of us. My grandmother was also smoking crack. She was the one who actually called Children's Social Services to come take us out of the house. Social Services found that my family really could not take care of me and my siblings. They took my brother and me and put us in one foster care home, and then they took my two sisters and put them in another foster care home. I don't remember the exact age that I was first put into the foster care system, but I was young.

Do you remember the first foster care home you and your brother went into?

Yes. The first foster care home we went into, the adults were really strict on me and my brother. Sometime after we were there, I remember their son—he called me and my brother a nigger. We both got mad and beat up on him. That's when Social Services came in and separated us. My brother, who was four years older than me, knew more about what they were doing to us, where they were taking us, and where my sisters were living. He knew.

How would you describe how you felt when you were placed in your initial foster care home?

I was scared. I was angry. I was upset. I didn't want to be with the people that they put us in foster care with. I didn't think it was fair because most of the time I felt me and my brother were being judged for what my biological mother and father did. They just judged us off of that.

Were your foster care parents white or black?

They were white. All of the foster care people I had were white.

After you and your brother were separated, you went into another foster care home. How long did you stay there?

It was probably less than a month, and then Social Services came in and switched me to where my sisters were living. That home was okay. We were doing pretty well, and then something happened with my younger sister, where they sent her to a "crazy home." She was mentally and emotionally not there because we were taken away from our parents. So they sent her away, and then my older sister started to act out. So she was moved into another foster care home. I was the only one left. I was there for maybe three or five more months. I guess the lady lost her fostering license so they had to move me into another foster care home. I just kept on moving from foster homes to foster homes. Really, I can't remember all of the foster care homes I was in because it happened so fast.

That's incredible to me. Nobody set you down to explain what to expect as you were moving from one foster care home to the next?

No. Nobody set me down and explained to me that I had to move here and how many weeks I had to plan for the move and what the family would be like. It was that day. The social worker came and got me and my stuff and took me to another foster care home after another foster care home after another foster care home—I have been in so many, it kind of just blurs together.

What was the most difficult part of your experience in the foster care system?

The most difficult part of my experience in the foster care system was being separated from my siblings and then also not knowing these people I was living with and them not caring about me. The foster care parents told me that they were doing it because God told them to do it. Personally, based on my experience, I think that most of these people who run these foster care homes are doing it because of the money. I don't really think they spend much time in getting to know the kid and the kid's background. And then they don't bother telling the kid about their background or where they came from.

Were you in contact at any point with your biological parents during your time in foster care?

Yes. There was a year where we were able to do these visits. It was in a room. Supervisors would watch all of us play and talk. They would always be constantly watching. At the time I wasn't really quite sure what that was about. But I felt kind of awkward, like why do I have to be watched while I am visiting my brother and my sister and my mom? And then after a year my mother couldn't get her stuff together, so they took her visiting rights away. So then after that, I couldn't really see my brother and sister. We just fell off.

I am having such a hard time getting through our discussion. This is so painful.

[*Pause*]

During the time of your visit with your biological family, how did you feel about your birth mother and birth father in particular at that point?

Well, my biological dad, I really didn't like him. I didn't mention him. I hated him because he was not there for his kids or for my mom. When he was around, he abused my mom and he abused us kids. It was bad. As far as my mom, I really missed her. I really loved her. I didn't understand what the social workers were saying about her and why we couldn't see her. I was really upset about the whole situation.

What for you worked in the foster care system and what didn't?

In the foster care system I had a roof over my head. I had food to eat. Those were good things. I was blessed that I didn't get physically abused in foster care. When I lived at home, my dad physically abused me and so did my grandpa. What didn't work was that the foster care people that were to oversee me and other kids in the foster care system did not pay attention to us. It is like favoritism. They favored their biological kids over the foster care kids. The foster care kids that I saw weren't shown much love. And I think that's what most kids who are in those situations are really looking for, love and somebody who is actually going to be there for them and not leave them or judge them.

How were you doing in school during the time you were living with your biological family and functioning within the foster care system?

In the beginning I was not going to school when I was living with my biological family. Then, when I went into the foster care system, I kept moving from school to school to school. Really, that wasn't any good education for me because I had to move so much that I would get behind in my classwork. It was really hard.

What age were you when you were adopted?

. I was adopted when I was nine years old by Chuck and Sarah [pseu-donyms]. I lived with them first a few months, and then they decided to adopt me. I remember they asked me if that was okay. I was only nine years old, so I really didn't know what that meant at the time. In my mind I was thinking, "Adoption, okay, what does this mean?" I was kind of rushed into making a decision, and I told myself just to say yes.

Similar to your foster care guardians, your adoptive parents are also white. You came, Chelsey, into your adoptive family with a strikingly different family background and experiences: You were biracial. Your hair was different. Your views were different. Your history with your own biological family and your experiences in the foster care system were different, to name a few examples. What did your adoptive family do with that information?

In my opinion I don't think that my adoptive family did much with the information about my background or even how I looked. When I came to Chuck and Sarah's house, I was little and I really didn't know how to do my hair. And they definitely didn't know how to do black people's hair. The products that they used for their hair were not made to be used on my hair. In general, black people's hair requires more time to manage and can be kind of more expensive to care for, com-pared to white people's hair care needs. And my adoptive family was on a budget. It seems like all of the foster people I had, and Chuck and Sarah, were always on a budget, but it didn't include what I needed to take care of my body and my hair. Yet they could afford what they needed. At one point my adoptive parents actually cut my hair all the way off and made it into a little boy's style. It was okay because I was a tomboy, and so I didn't mind. But wow! You shouldn't put a mixed kid with nappy hair into a home where the parents don't know how to deal with, or want to deal with, hair like mine. It's like my adoptive parents really didn't know anything about racially mixed kids or African Ameri-cans. They didn't know. Later I told them what I knew about my hair care needs. They did do some research, but I don't think that they did as much as they could have.

Did your adoptive parents share with you why they decided on bringing you into their family permanently?

No. It was more like they said to me that they wanted to adopt me so that I could be a part of *their family*. I can't remember a conversation that you are talking about happening with my adoptive parents.

You also have nonadoptive siblings in your family.

Yes. I have a brother, Alex, who is now sixteen, and a sister, Nicole, who is thirteen [both are biological children of Chuck and Sarah].[3]

Did you feel like your adoptive parents treated you and your siblings equally or fairly?

No, I didn't feel that way. I think that they favored their biological children more than me. They would participate in activities that Alex and Nicole enjoyed. I also noticed that the consequences of their negative actions were not the same as my consequences doing some of the same things that they had done. I felt kind of left out and alone, still—even though I "had a family."

Can you give me some examples about how you believe your parents treated their biological kids differently than you?

Yes. When I got in trouble, I would have to go to bed early. I wouldn't be able to have my lights on in my room. They would take the hinges off my bedroom door and take the door away. I would not have any privacy. They didn't care. If their biological daughter did the same thing that I did, it wouldn't be as big of a deal; her consequences wouldn't be as strict.

So you are in your adoptive family. Do you call them Mom and Dad?

I did because I felt obligated to because they were helping me. They had a roof over my head. Also if I didn't call them Mom and Dad, they wouldn't respond to me. So if I said, "Hey, Chuck or Sarah, can I do this?" they wouldn't try to listen to me. If I said, "Hey, Dad and Mom, can I do this?" they would listen. That is another reason why I felt obligated to call them Mom and Dad. I wouldn't be heard.

Tell me where you lived when you joined your adoptive family.

We lived in a small town outside of Denver, Colorado. Most of my adoptive parents' family lived near us. In the town we lived in, it was mostly Mexicans and white people. There were a few black people but not many. So in that situation I also didn't have any black friends.

I lived in a small town where I stood in the background. It was not where I came from.

How did it work for you to be in your adoptive family?

It was okay some of the time, but most of the time it was hard for me to do what they were doing and be a part of their life. For example, when I went out with my adoptive family, it was hard because I always stood out because I was a mixed kid with a white family, and everywhere I went people stopped and stared like, "What are they doing with her?!" As I got older, I didn't want to do things with them as a family because I felt so awkward. I didn't really want to be seen with them because I didn't feel like I fit in.

As you know, I was in Colorado a few years ago at a speaking event on transracial adoption, and your parents invited me to their home for a visit. I spent time with your entire family and had good memories. When I spent time with you, what was that experience like for you?

I was very happy and excited that you came to the house. I appreciated you also taking me out so that we could talk privately. I felt like you understood where I came from and didn't judge me. Because you lived in a white family and were honest about your experiences, I felt that you knew and understood what I was going through. We had a connection. It was really sad when you had to go.

I enjoyed getting to know you too. I saw, and continue to see, so much potential in you. Chelsey, were you then able to express to your parents how much having somebody you could relate to, especially given your experiences, was helpful to you?

Yes, I expressed that to them. But in my opinion they did not try to do anything about it after you left. I don't think that they saw the importance for a mixed kid to have a positive African American role model that looks like the kid.

After I saw you in Colorado, I lost track of you for a couple of years. Your life took some abrupt turns. Tell me what happened.

Yes. My life did take some abrupt turns. I went to jail.[4] After I got out, I asked Chuck and Sarah if I could live with my biological parents. They actually allowed me to go live with my biological family in

Denver. I was messing up there. I was not really doing anything there that was helping me put my best foot forward.

Let me stop you. Why was it important for you to go back to Denver?

In Denver there was more of my background there. Where I was going, it was in a more diverse community racially. It was not all white people or all black people. There was a mixture, where I was going, of people who looked like me. And I felt more comfortable in Denver. I felt like I could be myself. I needed to show that I was a mixed child and not be ashamed of that truth.

[I was ashamed of] . . . being in foster care and then being in an adoptive home, where I did not feel like I was seen. I felt like I was an object that just kept on getting moved around. I did not feel like my adoptive parents helped me to figure out who I was as a person that was also mixed race.

So you went back to Denver to live with your biological family. How did that work out?

It was rough, definitely tougher than I thought. I thought we would all be happy again to see each other. But actually stuff went downhill. My older sister and I didn't get along, and we started physically fighting. That caused more problems. My younger sister started fighting me. My brother, he didn't really care. He was just mean. It was not as great of a deal as I thought it would be. I struggled through it.

Did your adoptive parents visit you in Denver during this time?

If they were coming to Denver, they would try to get a hold of me, like, "We are coming to Denver for such and such. We just wanted to see if we could stop by." It wasn't because they wanted to visit me as the main reason. It was because they already had plans to come out to Denver, and I was just on their route.

How did you make the move from Denver to Tennessee?

When I was still living in Denver with my biological family, I went to . . . a Christian school that helps at-risk kids get back on track with their schooling. I really enjoyed it. But then I got kicked out. There was this white girl who was in one of my classes. She would talk shit in my ear. I stood up and got loud. I told her, "I'm not the one to be messin' with because I'm not about to sit back here with you whispering in my ear. So you just need to shut up because I am not tryin' to deal with what you are saying." This girl was saying some weird stuff to me. The administrators thought that I was being mean to her, so they kicked me out of the school. I was on my last warning there, and that was the final one. But it was at that school that I met my girlfriend and had my chance to leave Colorado. My girlfriend and I first moved to Kansas and then to Tennessee.

Do you feel that you are in a safer place with your girlfriend in Tennessee?

Yes, I do. I am accomplishing my goals. I feel like a stronger and better woman. I have been through a lot, but I am still here standing. A lot has happened in my life, and I feel like I can be heard now. I feel like I can change other peoples' lives through my story, through my journey.

What advice would you give to other foster care kids who are struggling with their identity and trying to make it day by day?

My advice is that they continue to keep on pushing on. I am not going to say that life will necessarily get easier. That would be a lie. You go through trials and tribulations each day. But if you keep strong and trust in what you believe in, then there will be a way for you in this world—in this world there is a way.

I want to go back to our discussion on adoption. Are you supportive of transracial adoption?

I am supportive of transracial adoption, but then again I am not. The "I am" part is that I am so glad that there are people who believe that they can handle having an African American kid step into their family. What I am not happy about, and what I am angry about, is that too many of these families are not prepared to raise a black child or any child of color. They think they know what it takes, but many don't have any idea, and the child is the one that gets hurt the most. You can't just stick a kid in a placement home and expect them not to be angry but be grateful all of the time. I can tell you that many times, for these kids like me, their smiles are fake. I know because when I was smiling it wasn't real. Foster care and adoptive parents need to try to relate to and understand the kids that they are taking in and be there for them and actually touch the kids' heart. They are not doing a good job.

Did you feel that the social workers in your life were listening to you, particularly as you were making transitions into different homes?

Oh, no, the social workers weren't listening to me either. They were there to do their job and check up on me. After they spent the required hour with the family, they would say, "I will see you all next week." They didn't even pull me or the other foster kids aside one on one to determine what *really* was going on in the house. It would have been even nice if the social workers, for example, put all of the family members in a circle so that we could all talk honestly about what was going on in our lives. Then I would have begun to believe that the social workers respected all of our opinions, including the foster care kids'.

Chelsey, how did you feel when you were in foster care and then when you were in your adoptive home?

I felt alone. I felt like no one understood me. But yet I knew that I had to keep pushing on anyway. I had to still be, I would say, grown. I had to have a grown mentality of survival because in foster care I could not survive as a child. Then in my adoptive home it was the same thing. I just did not feel right. Inside I felt sad. I felt depressed. Outwardly to my adoptive family I expressed anger at times. I didn't like it. I did not want to be there.

Where did the anger come from?

Where did the anger come from? I really don't know exactly, but I think it had a lot to do with all of the hurt and pain I felt on the inside — of not knowing what was really going on. Why was I in foster care? Why am I in this adoptive home? The foster care system and my adoptive family kept so much that impacted me a secret. That was and is *my* life! There should not be any secrets about my life, even as a child. I think that the foster care system and my adoptive family lost what really was important. It is about the child's life. It is not about the system making money off of kids or just the comfort of the adoptive parents.

Do you consider your adoptive family your family?

Yes. They are still my family. I love them very much. I have respect for them. However, even after years of not living with my adoptive parents, I am still angry with them. I believe that I have that right.

Why are you still angry?

I am angry with my parents because I do not think that they are helping me or guiding me as they should. For example, if you call yourself a mom or a dad, to me, then, I think that I should be able to call you with any and everything, and you should be there for me. For the most part, if I communicate with my mom, it is because I am the one who calls or texts her. And when I do contact her, she gets angry with me because she thinks that the reason why I call or text her is because I need something. But I think that is her job as a parent, to fulfill the needs of her child's life and show the child the right direction. But if you just stop when it is painful and then say, "Well, I guess you can go back to your biological parents," then you really don't care about raising me. In my mind I see that you, as the parent, aren't taking the time and energy that you committed yourself to when you chose to adopt the child in the first place. The commitment part when it came to me, my adoptive parents failed. They failed.

What can adoptive parents do differently that would be supportive of the child and his or her needs?

What adoptive parents can do is actually participate and invest in their child's life and, like I have been saying, try to understand the child and what that child has gone through before he or she is placed in their home. Instead of so quickly making it seem when there are troubles that it is the *kid's* fault, that the kid is the crazy one, and then putting him or her on medication so that they can walk around like zombies. That's not right. Parents need to be there for their child. When you are looking to adopt, you should know the responsibility of actually adopting a kid and what that means long term. If you think it is fun and games, it really isn't. If you are choosing to adopt, you should be trying to change the kid's life for the better. The goal should not be for this kid to be sad and depressed and just the same way as they came into your home from the foster care system. I think that when you adopt a child, it is no longer temporary. It is a whole different page. Adoption should be supportive and permanent.

You are definitely making a way for yourself despite incredible obstacles. What, if anything, do you still want from your adoptive parents?

I want them to acknowledge that I am a human being, just like they are. I am still here. I want them to try harder. They call themselves parents so that is what they need to be for me. When I turn thirty, forty, if they are still the alive, then they should be the parents that they said that they were going to be when they chose to adopt me at the age of nine.

Now that you are in a relationship with your girlfriend, how has that relationship helped you to grow into a more effective person?

Now I am freer about things. I really don't care what people think or say. Being gay, I don't hide it. I am just out there. If somebody does not like that I am gay, they do not have to be my friend. This is who I choose to be.

Being gay is who you choose to be?

Yes. I feel much safer in my relationship with my girlfriend. She treats me good and is supportive of me and my goals. Earlier, in my years before I went into foster care, I was raped by my uncle. In general I am not fond of how guys that I have been around treat women. I think that they are very disrespectful toward women. I think because of how many times that I have been raped by guys, it made sense for me to switch to a girlfriend. Plus, my girlfriend and I have so much in common and we enjoy spending time together.

Do you feel that you are in a better place now than you were years ago?

Yes, I do.

As a black woman how do you feel?

As a black woman I feel strong. I feel that people are intimidated by what I have been through and overcome. I can speak my mind in a positive way, and I think that threatens some people. There is always truth behind what I speak, regardless of how people look at me or talk about me.

One of the things that I think about when I navigate in my white adoptive family, nuclear and extended, is whether they will accept all of who I am.

I think about that too. But now, as I have gotten older, I don't think about it as much. If people who I care about don't accept me for who I am, yes, it is going to hurt me deep inside, but as a woman I have learned to have a strong outward appearance and brush it off. It is sad, but I have learned that I can't change somebody else. If somebody decides that they don't want to see the good in me and only bring up my past, then maybe I shouldn't be around them.

What would you say makes Chelsey amazing?

My life story. How I have handled my challenges and obstacles. And how I have become the woman I am today which is a beautiful, tranquil, African American individual.

Where do you get your support and encouragement from?

I get my support and encouragement from my girlfriend and her mom. They have really helped me. I really don't get it from my family. I am not confident that they are going to give that to me because they have their own biological kids that they are more concerned about and their own concerns. I also don't think that they understand what I have gone through. They communicate to me through their words and actions that everything about me is a bummer. And then I don't think that I will find support with my biological family because they are insecure about many things from within themselves.

When your family needs guidance and support, are you there for them?

Yes, I am. I am here for everybody, no matter if I am mad at you or if you have frustrated me. I will get over that quick and try to help if we can connect. That is one thing that I can say about myself: . . . I don't stay mad at people for too long. I have been through a lot. I do wish I could help my adoptive siblings more. I have given them my cell number so that they can contact me. I have apologized to them for not being there for them as much as I would have liked. I had to figure myself out.

Where do you get your inner strength from, Chelsey, that positive energy?

It comes from inside me. I don't think that kind of strength comes from anybody outside of me. I thank God that he has given me that wisdom, strength, and power.

Chelsey, you are an inspiration to me and, I am certain, to others as well. This discussion has been emotional for me to get through, as I hear what you have gone through. I personally can empathize with the pain of abandonment and deep transitions in your life. But

what an inspiration you are. I am so sorry that you have had to go through what you have.

It's alright. My struggles and my journey have made me who I am today. It has made me a stronger and more powerful woman. I don't regret anything that I have been through. I don't look at it in a bad way. I just keep on pushing forward. And I think that is what anybody should do, adopted or not, push forward. You just can't sulk in misery or else you will be sad for the rest of your life. That's no good.

So what are your goals? What are you looking to accomplish?

My goals in life are to continue to help others. I want them to understand that life is not as bad as it seems. Anybody can make a future.

I wanted to talk to you because I wanted to know your experience, going through foster care and being adopted into a white family. You are so incredibly honest about your experiences. I think that it is important, in stories like yours, to see where families can do better. We have to get a handle on treating everybody equally and fairly. I don't know why, in society and in some of our families, we differentiate between how people came into the family and place value on that.

Exactly.

That is what needs to change. Yes, we need to know how people came into families and we must embrace them. What we shouldn't do with that information is make them any less human or with less privileges than others who came into the family by birth, for instance.

That is how I feel. Social workers need to do much, much better. They need to figure out how to place kids in an environment where the kids will actually feel comfortable instead of in an environment where these kids feel like a ghost, not a part of the family, whether they place them in foster care homes or in adoptive homes. Yes, social workers should want to place a child in a stable and good home, but I also think that they need to realize, and open their eyes to whether, that potential foster or adoptive parent has been through or understands what the kids have been through. If not, then it is really not a good placement for kids. Social workers need to place these kids *correctly* in foster care homes and adoptive homes. The future of these kids' lives depends on it.

In my foster care homes and adoptive home, my parents would tell me in one way or the other that they were fostering and adopting me because of a calling from God. I say if that is the only reason why you are doing it, then you are not helping me or other kids. Don't just do this for God, but do it for yourself and the kids that you are committed to taking care of.

What would have made you feel more comfortable in your adoptive family when you lived with them?

I would say that I would have been comfortable if we as a family were exposed to African American people who were both gay and straight. They could also be Christian. I would have appreciated attending a cultural heritage camp with other black people and kids who had experiences like me, living in a white home. That all goes to what I was saying, that white parents who are adopting kids of color need to get involved in the communities where their kids come from and understand their background and history. For starters, if these parents know that they are going to get a black kid into their home, it is important for them to find out what the kids' needs are for their hair and skin care. As I said earlier, they need to find these products and have them in the house when the kid arrives at the home. That step already will help the kid feel more comfortable. The feeling is like, "Wow—they actually have the shampoo that *I* need to use for my hair." Also, when you have kids of color, it is not enough to live in white communities and spend time with all white people. What message is that sending to your child of color?

For me, Rhonda, one thing that did help me when I was living with my adoptive family was basketball. I didn't feel so alone when I was playing that game. I could *see* myself when I played. I was really good at the game and that really helped my self-esteem. I knew that if I got into trouble, my adoptive parents wouldn't allow me to go to practice or play in a game. Playing basketball helped me stay out of trouble. I would definitely recommend that other adoptive parents get their kids into a fun activity that the kids like and can be good at.

But, yes, the foster care system sucks. I dislike it still today. That is all I can say about the system here in America. It does cause more problems to the kid than it creates solutions. If the foster care system was managed right, where it looked at the best interests of the child instead of trying to make money off of these kids, I think less kids would go from foster care to prison or be left out there on the streets to fend for themselves.

From your experience in the foster system, why is it that for many foster care kids they transition so easily from the foster care system into prison?

Basically foster care is prison. They both feel the same. When I was in foster care, I felt locked up like a dog in the backyard. I felt alone. So that is basically what many foster care kids feel, alone. Some join a gang so that they can feel like they have some kind of a family. In foster care I had to do whatever the foster care system said. I just tried to follow their rules, and their rules were strict. In order to spend the night at somebody's house, they had to be certified or I couldn't spend the night. Foster care is prison.

That is why it is so easy to make that transition from foster care to prison, because if you are a foster care kid, you are already in the system? Is that what you are saying?

Yes, you are already in the system. Prison is just another system, but it is a system, right?

You're right. I was in foster care until two years of age. I don't remember a lot mentally, but emotionally just those two years has created trauma within me still today.

Being in the foster care system is traumatizing. The system acts as if kids can switch just like that—like a light switch that goes on and off—but really we can't. Our bodies are not meant for all of that stuff, moving and moving. There is so much stress on the body and mind that it can mess somebody up for the rest of their life. I have bad memories and good memories being in the foster care system, but the system messes you up.

What makes the moving so traumatic?

You never get a connection, and you will never feel safe, because who knows when that next day will come where you'll have to pack your bags and leave again? You never get a connection. That is how I felt. I never got a connection. And when I became an adoptee, there was some connection, but it was not all the way there. So I didn't even know what this adoption word meant when I was nine. At any point I remember thinking that if they don't want me, I could still go back into the system.

That is a roller coaster. One that is not fun to be on.

I never felt safe. I always had to watch my back. It was just me, alone in the world. I really didn't have the ability to care about anybody else at that time because of my own abandonment issues. I just didn't trust anybody. Today I am working on that. My girlfriend is really helping me with my abandonment issues and my trust issues.

What makes you smile?

Having a job makes me smile. Getting my own car makes me smile. Helping people makes me smile. I love to help people and make other people's day. That really makes me smile. Being myself and being able to trust somebody like my girlfriend makes me smile. Being able to come this far, that I don't have huge trust issues, still is amazing to me. Though, I still have abandonment issues because I am still scared. But the way that I look at it is, I have made it this far, I can make it further, no matter what happens. Any obstacle that comes my way will just be another lesson learned in life. It's hard. I know it is really hard for, especially, foster and adopted kids, given what we all have gone through emotionally. To them I say, You can't change the past. All you can do is look at the future and see how you can make your life better. You *can* change the future. What you are going to do in the future *is* you! You can't change the past. All you can do is look back and wave and keep on walking forward.

Your wisdom and grit are amazing. Thank you, Chelsey, for spending time with me.

DEMETRIUS WALKER
Entrepreneur and Cofounder of dNIBE Apparel
INTERVIEWED BY TELEPHONE, JUNE 28, 2012

You grew up in the heart of the inner city of New York in the 1980s. What was the black experience there then, and what were your day-to-day realities?

Actually I lived in Brooklyn, New York, until I was about eight years old. Then I moved up to the Bronx. Going into my early experiences in East New York, Brooklyn, it was known as "homicide central" at the time when I was very young. I could recall things that most children probably have never had to experience, such as witnessing a break-in of my home. Coming home and there is this guy in our living room "stiffing" our VCR. I grew up in the 1980s during the crack era. Crack was everywhere. When I went to school, I would see crack vials all over the schoolyard. Everywhere you went, you saw crack, whether you used it or not; it was very prevalent. And I saw the effects crack had in my neighborhood in Brooklyn. I would hear the gunshots at night. So there were shoot-outs going on. I saw somebody being stabbed, you know, at a very early age. Some of the things that were going on in New York at the time, it was really like a crazy *Wild Wild West* type of energy. You never knew what you were going to see the next day. Every day it was like, man, I can't believe that this just happened. I can recall seeing a guy running down the middle of the street on Pitkin Avenue in Brooklyn with a helicopter chasing him. I presume it probably was drug related. Imagine: To see a helicopter chasing a guy running on foot as fast as he could down the street. Every day there seemed to be a new precedent set for ignorance and violence. I remember we lived a block away from the Cypress Hills housing project in Brooklyn. I heard about entire families getting thrown off the roof of the housing project due to drug money debts. This was just common—seeing the ambulances and police cars on a daily basis just flying down the street. That was the kind of environment I grew up in. I remember being in the third grade. I had a friend named Naeem, who lived in the same housing development in the Bronx as me. He had an older brother that both of us looked up to. One evening Naeem's older brother and his best friend were standing behind my building when there was a drive-by shooting. Naeem's brother made it out alive, but his brother's best friend was killed right outside of my window. I remember looking out the window and seeing him slumped over on a bench with a bullet to the head. Years later I remember still seeing the blood trail.

My parents always wanted to have a little bit better for their kids than they had for themselves. So they ultimately ended up moving us up to the Bronx. There are people who say that the Bronx is a scary place. There were bad things that were going on in the Bronx then as well; however, it was a step up from my experience in Brooklyn.

How did your parents guide you through such hostile surroundings outside of your home?

My mom was, and still is, very strict in her parenting style. She was definitely focused and strict with me when it came to education and making sure that my schoolwork was done. Luckily I had a natural curiosity for learning. That curiosity for learning was something that my mom helped me cultivate as well as my dad. My dad was also rather gifted when it came to schoolwork. He didn't always make the right decisions, as far as . . . staying in school, but nonetheless he was very gifted. I remember my dad taking me to the library as early as probably six years old and going through astronomy books with me, a subject I was very interested in at an early age.

In addition to your parents' involvement in your life, did you have mentors?

I definitely had people to look up to, like my grandfather. My grandfather ended up moving down to Florida when I was nine or ten years old. But typically my sister and I would go to Florida and spend the summers with our grandfather. My great grandmother was involved in my life a lot too. She lived in the projects in the south Bronx. Last year she passed away. With her it was a time that not only me but my siblings could escape from the negativity of the drug and crack culture of New York City. I had family members who succumbed to the crack epidemic. There were people in my own family who, my parents told me, "Okay, watch your pockets when you are around Such and Such." And, "I don't want you to be around Such and Such when we are not there." These are the kinds of things that you are hearing about friends of the family and people even in your own family. You learn to grow a *healthy suspicion* as a New Yorker in this type of environment. You become very skeptical of people and suspicious of authority. And so this is the type of environment that I was raised in.

Despite the craziness of the times and the drug culture threatening to harm your childhood, you prevailed. What were some of your favorite childhood memories that still made you rise?

My fondest memory of my childhood was of my father bringing me to a park behind the Cypress Hills housing project and teaching me how to play baseball. I probably was three or four years old at the time. It was special for me, especially because we didn't get a lot of quality time together. But I can remember, specifically, him taking me out to this park, giving me a bat, and passing the ball to me. Also another childhood memory: I can remember my dad teaching me how to ride a bike. I never had training wheels. My dad would say to me, "If you fall down, you get back up. We are going to do this until you get it correct."

So you then left the inner city to go to a prestigious boarding school in Connecticut for your education. How did that decision come about, and how was the educational experience different than the education you received in New York City?

The boarding school idea came about when I was in sixth grade in New York. I was already part of a talented and gifted program in middle school. A lot of the kids in my program were obviously overachievers and earned exceptional grades. Many people viewed us throughout the school as nerds. Even though we were wearing the same clothes as everybody else, watched the same TV shows, joked about the same things, they still considered our class as the nerd class. Somehow in that "nerd class" I found out about other students' academic interests, including going off to boarding school. So I started doing my own investigation and learned about a program called Prep for Prep that some of my fellow students were a part of. What Prep for Prep did was prepare you and give you additional coursework on top of your public school curriculum, with the goal of getting [you] into preparatory schools. I was fascinated by this. I felt that I was capable academically of not needing the additional coursework that Prep for Prep provided. I believed that I could do it on my own. I was an avid reader and a top performer in my class, even beyond those students who were in the Prep for Prep program. So I made the decision that I wanted to go to boarding school, because I thought it was a place that I would be able to fully challenge my academic capabilities. On top of that, I thought, I would not have to deal with the negative street culture on the streets of New York that tells me I am a nerd, and because I am a nerd and I like to learn, I am perceived as a lesser being and therefore somebody who should be picked on. The idea, then, of me extracting myself from my current environment to go to a place where people love to learn and intellectualism is encouraged, and at the same time a place where I could learn more about how the real world operated, was very attractive to me.

I knew that, even though boarding school was kind of a bubble and I would be immersing myself in an environment that I was not comfortable with, and where I would be the minority, it would be reflective of greater society and the challenges that I would face throughout life. I had discussions with my mom when I was in sixth grade about attending boarding school. She indicated that "we would see." Eighth grade came, and I started filling out applications and made it happen!

You are incredible and were shining at such a young age already. There are adults who don't have that kind of rigorous and objective internal discussion and will to turn a dream into a reality.

When you actually attended the boarding school, what was that experience like for you?

For me I loved the entire experience of boarding school. For my fellow classmates of color, everyone had a different take on it. Like I said, coming from the Bronx, where I am the majority and am used to seeing black and Hispanic people everywhere on a daily basis, to being one of six black males in my class—and that was most likely the largest number of young black men that they had enrolled in the freshmen class, when I started, for quite some time—was incredible. So basically I go from being one of thousands to one of a handful of black male students in this high school, which is located in Watertown, Connecticut. And within the town at large there were very few, if any at all, black and Hispanic people. Hence, some of my classmates of color, who came from other parts of New York City and other parts of the country, went into culture shock. I on the other hand looked at it as a new challenge and a new experience.

At this boarding school I was able to learn about the conversations middle-class and upper-middle-class white Americans have on a regular basis. You know, this was foreign territory for me. So I felt like a sponge in this environment. I was absorbing how things worked in their world. I discovered that there were generations of students who had gone to this boarding school or another boarding school somewhere in New England and married each other and continued this generational wealth and tradition within their families. I observed and *participated* in this culture. I wanted to understand how this worked so that I could implement some of the same strategies that would make my black community successful for generations.

Would you say that you soared in this new environment at the boarding school because you were not dealing with the stresses of the street culture and crime?

I think so. There were different stresses now. I had to deal with the stress of people not understanding my experience. At the same time I never felt that I was physically in danger, which is a huge difference. Whereas in New York City every day you had to have your eyes peeled open, because you never knew when your life may be physically at risk. Removing that burden of survival was a totally different experience for me. So any stress related to the random ignorance that I might experience from some of my Caucasian brothers and sisters was minimal compared to the stress of just getting to school and coming home in one piece.

So what did you do about dating at this boarding school? You are in high school at this point.

Right. That was unique. When I entered high school, I was very small physically. I didn't really hit my growth spurt until I was sixteen. I do recall, even prior to going to high school, the first girl that I dated was Puerto Rican. She and I were good friends in New York City. In the city there was not much of a difference between Hispanic and black. It was looked upon as natural for Hispanics and blacks to date. So there were not too many questions about me dating a Puerto Rican girl and her dating a black guy in New York.

When I got to boarding school in Connecticut, I remember my first crush being a white girl. This was the first time that I had a crush on a white girl. Her name was Meredith. I remember thinking to myself, How do I approach this girl? We were completely different: I was black and not wealthy; she was white and rich. I had no idea how to navigate those differences. Finally after some time I mustered up the courage to hint to her that I was somewhat interested. She pushed back on it or did not want to have a relationship with me. To this day I am not sure what the reason was why she didn't date me: whether it was because I was not physically mature or if it was because of my skin color or my income bracket. I'll never know. But what I do remember is being rebuffed by the first white woman that I was ever attracted to. And for me or any guy who is rejected, it can be damaging to your ego. So moving forward I then consciously thought about that experience with any woman I was interested in. At that point in my mind, it was, "Well, this is not something that is even possible for me, so I am not even going to look at this population in terms of people I may be capable of dating." That option was removed from me early on, in ninth grade. And I never thought about broaching that situation again. I can't say that since then I was not attracted to other white women. I was, but I did not consider dating white women or even attempt to approach them in that fashion.

The next landmark on your map was Nashville, Tennessee, where you attended Vanderbilt University, a private liberal arts college. Why did you choose to go to Vanderbilt?

I was at the boarding school in Connecticut. I did not see a lot of faces that looked like mine for four years. At this point I was, like, Now that I got this experience at the boarding school and I see how things operate, I want to go somewhere where there are a lot of *my* faces. I had, especially during my high school years, grown a great appreciation for my African American culture. So I was especially looking for other *black intellectuals* too. In addition I wanted to go somewhere I could have a good time, be amongst my peers, and feel accepted in the community, including when I entered a room or a place. In a nutshell it was very important to me that I attend a college or university that was academically challenging but also had the social infrastructure where I could relax and be myself on more of a permanent basis.

And I also knew that I didn't want to be in New England anymore because I had been up in the mountains of Connecticut for a while, and the climate was very cold. That's when I knew that I had to go to school in the South.

I applied to all of the best colleges and universities in the South. I went down for a visit to Vanderbilt. They had a Minority Student Recruitment Weekend for potential students, which I participated in. I remember getting picked up from the airport in a bus. There was a kid from Washington, D.C., attending the same event. We were just chatting with each other, saying, "Man, we know that we are not going to school in Nashville, but they paid for us to come and visit this school, so why not check it out?!" So we were laughing about Nashville being kind of country and backwards. These were the perceptions we had at that time of Nashville, not having visited this place yet.

So what did you discover, once you arrived on Vanderbilt University's campus?

To make a long story short, when we arrived, the campus was amazing and beautiful. From Vanderbilt's standards maybe 6 percent of the student population was black. But for me 6 percent of six thousand students was an exponential increase of black people. In the boarding school I attended in Connecticut, there were about five hundred students in total, and about twenty-five to thirty of the students were black and/or Hispanic. I love those guys/girls I went to boarding school with to this day. Three of my closest boarding school friends were in my wedding. So you know we are still very tight. However, by making the decision to attend Vanderbilt, I was blessed to develop more good relationships with students, particularly students of color, who turned into friends.

What did you study?

I actually arrived at Vanderbilt as a biomedical engineering major. I was always curious about science as a little kid. As I said earlier, from the moment I could read, I would beg my dad to take me to the library. I would study science and biology in the library and loved it. Though, after my freshman year, I ended up switching my major to economics. The reason being, while I still love science to this day, I realized after struggling academically during my freshman year that my strengths as a scholar were not in the areas of chemistry or calculus or most of the subjects that engineering students are required to take. I ended up becoming an economics major simply because it sounded like a major that would make me a lot of money; and if I made a lot of money, then I could help my family and friends with their economic situations.

Did you enjoy studying economics?

I can't say that I loved studying economics, but I was determined to complete the degree, and that is what I did.

I was awed by the black Greek culture, not only at Vanderbilt University but also the black Greek culture that was kind of shared throughout the city of Nashville. I didn't know at the time that Nashville was home to Tennessee State University and Fisk University [a predominately African American university]. I was fascinated with Fisk because I had studied W. E. B. Du Bois, his literature, and his work as a sociologist and avid thinker, and he earned his bachelor's degree there.

So just the incredible heritage, culture, and legacy of W. E. B. Du Bois, and the many other black leaders that went to Fisk, was astounding to me. I had not even considered, prior to attending Vanderbilt, that Fisk was five minutes from there. So I had Tennessee State University, Vanderbilt, Fisk University, Belmont University, all within a couple of minutes of driving. So it was easy to fall in love with Vanderbilt and the location, once I learned all of this.

Okay, you were living and studying in the heart of black American history. So what did that do for you as a young black man?

At this point I realized that something was going to have to happen for me in Nashville that I could use to completely change the environment that I saw growing up, not only for people in New York but for people that I met from other parts of the country who went through very similar experiences that I did. I felt that Nashville was the magic place where I was going to get this enlightenment that would allow me to change things for the better. Fortunately it was. I met people there who literally changed my life. Some of them have become my business partners.

Let's talk about your professional career. You are the executive director of the Black Male Empowerment Institute and also cofounder of dN|BE Apparel. Your experiences both educationally and professionally have taken you a lot of places, including up the corporate ladder. Why did you choose to put your energy, talent,

resources, and time behind the Black Male Empowerment Institute and dN|BE Apparel? Walk me through the mission, the targeted audience, and the impact.

Right after graduation one of my fraternity brothers, Tre, and I got together and collaborated on a business plan. In college he always had some kind of connection to making t-shirts and jackets. For him it was a side hustle throughout college for making extra money. But once we graduated from college, we realized that we both had valuable and marketable skill sets. One of Tre's skills was to create t-shirts and jackets. Mine was coming up with unique ideas. And so we looked at a few of our other friends and identified their strengths. That's when we decided to start up a t-shirt business.

The business was not designed to simply sell a whole lot of t-shirts that didn't mean anything. We wanted to do something that catered to our belief system and uplifted the black community. We were looking to combine all of our natural curiosities and academic strengths for this endeavor. So we started this clothing company called dangerous-NEGRO. We knew that it would be controversial because of its name.

Yes, it is an eyebrow-raising name. How did you come up with it?

At Vanderbilt there was this particular black studies class that Tre actually took. In this class they went into depth about the lives of A. Philip Randolph [an activist in the civil rights and U.S. labor movements] and Dr. Martin Luther King Jr.

Both men were publicly called "the most dangerous Negro in America" at two different points in American history. In 1919 A. Philip Randolph was trying to integrate the military. He was also one of the first proponents of labor unions. Essentially he did a lot that agitated local, state, and federal government. So President Woodrow Wilson went on the radio and publicly declared that A. Philip Randolph was the most dangerous Negro in America.

Fast-forward to the civil rights movement. FBI Director J. Edgar Hoover had a vendetta against Dr. King. Every opportunity he had to paint Dr. King as a negative figure, he did so. So J. Edgar Hoover sent William C. Sullivan, who was with the FBI's Domestic Intelligence Division, to the March on Washington to write up a report on what he saw.

Sullivan didn't believe that there was anything wrong with what Dr. King was doing. He actually respected Dr. King. But because Sullivan's paycheck was coming from the FBI and J. Edgar Hoover, he went ahead and wrote this report anyway, describing Dr. King as the most dangerous Negro in America.

Going with that trend of the dangerous Negro, not being the drug dealers that I saw growing up in New York City or the gangbangers that my business partner had to deal with growing up in Louisville, Kentucky, we realized that the dangerous Negroes are the A. Philip Randolphs of the world, the Martin Kings of the world, black men who were courageous enough to stand up for what was right when it was unpopular. That's where we got our idea for the name of our clothing line. On top of that, we believed that people were going to pay attention to what we were doing. People would be curious. And people would stare at some of our shirts with the name on it and ask us, "What the hell were you thinking, putting *that* on a shirt?" That then gave us an opportunity . . . to start a conversation with somebody. Through word of mouth our message and our t-shirt business were spreading. People would start talking and then would go home and say, "I saw a dude today who was wearing this t-shirt that said 'dangerousNEGRO' on it. Can you believe it?" The next thing you know, we had people e-mailing us, stating that they heard about our company and asking where could they purchase a "dangerousNEGRO" t-shirt. It then kind of had a snowball effect from there.

What products are in your clothing line?

We sell urbanwear: t-shirts, jackets, hoodies, and hats. We still operate dangerousNEGRO years after its inception as a well-oiled machine.[5] It also allows us the opportunity to explore other interests that we have.

The natural progression for me was to do something hands-on. The clothing line is one vehicle that I can use to uplift people in their life, but I wanted to physically go out and talk to other young black men, who I consider in similar positions that I was in growing up. So I developed a workshop where I can impart my wisdom to youth, emphasizing the lessons that I learned in my own journey: what kept me motivated in each situation and stage in my life, and what keeps me motivated today. Through these types of workshops came the idea behind the Black Male Empowerment Institute.

On my way home today, I was listening to the news and they discussed black-on-black homicides that are affecting our youth all across cities today. Clearly this type of crime is a problem that needs to be addressed. Do you think that the realities impacting the youth are slightly better now compared to when you were growing up? Are the realities different in comparison?

From what I am seeing in the present day, unfortunately, I haven't seen things getting much better in terms of homicides. What I do think has changed in the black community is that we are no longer in the height of that crack epidemic. That is different.

I have talked to my little cousins and have heard from them stories of their friends that they have seen being murdered and the friends of their friends who have been murdered. You continuously hear about it. Unfortunately, for whatever reason, this is news, and this is what you hear about black men when you turn the TV on and watch the news broadcasts. In some instances it is an overexaggeration of reality. But in many instances, like in Chicago, where I have business partners, it seems more black men are dying in Chicago than in Afghanistan or Iraq. We do have a problem. I am hoping that some of the ideas that I have can stem some of these problems.

What do you think is the core of the problem?

I think that this goes all the way back hundreds of years ago to American slavery and the Reconstruction period. These periods in history have given some young black men a *nihilistic* mentality, where they find no value for not only their life but the lives of others. Ingrained in today's culture, you see these kinds of behaviors, where you have twelve-, thirteen-, fourteen-year-old kids killing each other. They are not even old enough to value life. There are so many different factors that go into the core problem. There are profit structures, like the prison-industrial complex policy, that have deep and lasting implications on black people, black men in particular.

Also I think that, for youth, there are negative influences that are mirrored and magnified by some elements of hip-hop culture. I want to be clear that mainstream hip-hop is not the cause of the problem but more so a symptom of how we have been led astray. All in all there are probably twenty or thirty ingredients that account for what we are seeing today.

What do you think is part of the solution to this epic problem?

The only solution in my mind to reaching these kids and defeating this nihilistic mentality is by helping them believe in themselves before they endanger themselves or other people.

Where does hip-hop fit in the discussion of empowerment? Is it a relevant form of expression right now?

I think the mistake we made over the last decade or two is that our elders, and people who many of us view as leaders in the black community, have specifically *attacked* hip-hop culture. And when you attack hip-hop culture in a certain way, it is an *attack* on black youth. Hip-hop culture is something that many of us were born into. It wasn't something that you necessarily decided to be a part of. If you grew up in New York City, you were born into hip-hop culture. So any type of criticism of that is going to alienate that segment of the population, causing them to put their wall up. And then you really can't get through to them. *Positive change has to come from within hip-hop culture.* I consider myself a part of hip-hop culture.

How would you define hip-hop culture?

Hip-hop culture is a way of dressing yourself, of communicating. It is not just the music. The music is the messenger, but it is not the entirety of it. It is how you walk, how you talk, how you dance. It encompasses so many aspects of your life. It is what you wear on your feet. What kind of sneakers do you have on? It is so much.

It's deep.

Right. So somebody coming from outside of hip-hop culture, like an elder in the community blasting folks for doing something wrong and stupid, the response is then to automatically turn your ears off. And in your mind you're thinking, "You are old. You have no idea what it is like for me growing up, whatever you say is irrelevant." The problem then continuously gets worse. That's why you need to work *within* hip-hop culture to alter the message for the better. Sadly what I am seeing now is that there are a lot of negative messages on the radio—this is true. The reasons for that are not because of a supply or demand kind of thing, like they would like you to believe. As someone who started a record label with an independent artist who was a Grammy Award winner, I have seen how this process works. It is all about money. You have the radio stations, [of] which there are only a few major players in the market: Radio One and Clear Channel, [which] own a majority of black radio stations across the country. . . . They are not going to play necessarily what sounds good or what people think is uplifting. They kind of force-feed what you are going to hear. Fast-forward to the economic recession: We are at the point where radio stations and record labels are losing tremendous amounts of money because of declining sales, and therefore we are starting to see more organic artists coming up through the ranks via social media and the Internet to speak on more positive topics and be more creative with their music. Hip-hop is cyclical. Now we are back at a point where creativity is paramount, and sounding like other people is not cool anymore. That is the one positive that I see going on.

You have indicated that you consider yourself part of the hip-hop culture. What positive messages are you sending to the youth within the hip-hop arena?

I specifically target my message to young black men. But young black men and young black women for the past two decades have been hit with this stream of gang culture and materialism. Since I understand that reality, I am able to use it in my messages. I know that materialism is about *bling*, it is about money, it is about who has an expensive car, and who can afford to buy x-y-z. That being said, my question to black youth is, How do you control your own destiny in being able to obtain and accomplish those things?

One of the best pieces of advice that I have received came from my uncle Dwayne. He told me from an early age that nobody is going to pay you like you can pay yourself.

Now I am connecting the dots. The advice from your uncle is what helped you make the decision of choosing an entrepreneurial route versus corporate America?

Precisely. I went into corporate America right out of college. At that time I had not figured out my professional path yet. I didn't know where I was going to fit in terms of generating income for myself other than within corporate America. Still, I kept on recalling my uncle's frustration with having to work for other people and remembered him telling me, "Nobody is going to pay you like you can pay yourself." I attribute the change in my trajectory to that simple message and having an entrepreneurial mind-set as a young black man. When my course shifted, my life changed for the better.

I take that same belief I hold for myself and share it with youth around the country. My goal is to counter the beliefs many of these youth are conditioned to believe within the structure of the hip-hop culture. For instance hip-hop culture sends the message "You want to have a Bentley. You want to have Louis Vuitton accessories. You want to be able to buy $500 champagne like P. Diddy." I understand that for many youth that is the message that they have been hearing for the past fifteen to twenty years, so I am not going to argue with them on those points. Instead I ask each one of them to reassess in their mind how they can take charge of their own life and create a solid plan on how they are going to attain those things that they want. I emphasize that the only way to achieve that goal is by controlling their destiny and by having an entrepreneurial mind-set. And once these young people realize that they are the master of their fate, it starts to change the way they think about their priorities. They then ask themselves, "So now that I am in control and doing positive and healthy things in my life, is it really important for me to drink $500 worth of champagne?" The response to that should be "No, it's not smart!"

That certainly sounds like a persuasive argument for young people to hear.

Now you have a mind shifter. A new message that says, "I am in more control of what happens to me today, tomorrow, and next year." When you take more responsibility of your choices in life, you begin to realize that this is just entertainment. So going out to buy a $1,000 pair of Gucci loafers is simply stupid! Why? Because now I am an entrepreneur, or now at least I have an entrepreneurial mind-set within corporate America, and I value every dollar that I take in, and I have a plan for what I am going to do with this dollar once I have enough saved up. At the end of the day the mind-set shift starts with the entrepreneurial thought process.

You have made it a priority to also invest time, expertise, and energy into the interracial or transracial adoption community. You have traveled to Denver, Colorado, to attend the African Caribbean Heritage Camp to work with white parents who have or are planning on adopting black and biracial children. Why is your investment in this particular demographic group important to you?

I was invited to participate at the African Caribbean Heritage Camp for adoptive families in Colorado a few years ago. I actually did not know a lot about transracial adoption before then. The times I have attended the camp, I delivered a keynote address much like the material we are talking about here. Once I spent time and listened to the parents, I realized that these are people who love their children and are going to great lengths to understand where their children fit culturally. Many of the parents recognized that even though they loved their kids, there were some obvious racial differences that they could not ignore. They also recognized that it was important for their children to feel comfortable in their surroundings too.

The biggest question they posed to me was, What can we do to ensure that our children have the best possible future? I have seen these parents investing so much love and attention into their children. Also I have been to Africa before—Ethiopia, Kenya, and Tanzania. I have seen the conditions of many of the children over there. For instance, when I was at the market in Tanzania, there was a kid, maybe seven or eight years old, who was begging for money. Half of the kids are telling me not to give him money because he was strung out on glue. I saw some crazy stuff. And here it is, that back in the States there are people giving kids who came from unfortunate circumstances an opportunity to live the American dream. I fully support that. And so I wanted to make sure that I could give my time, resources, and thoughts to these parents in order that the lives and the futures of their children would thrive.

What words of advice did you give to the youth who attended the camp? I ask that because it is a gold-star opportunity for transracial adopted black boys and girls to have access to an African American role model like you.

For them I had to walk both sides of the fence, because obviously they can't escape the fact that they are black young men and women.

Too, they are living, many of them, in remote environments where they may or may not see anybody who looks like them. But on top of that, even if there are people who look like them, they probably don't have a similar family experience. So in connecting with this group, I found that my experience at boarding school was a common denominator. I know firsthand what it is like to be one of few in an environment that many black men and women don't find themselves in. I know what it feels like, seemingly being thousands of miles away from where you originated and being with these people who are totally different but still needing to fit in with the community and family around you. So I shared with these young men and women my story. I also told them that everybody has unique experiences, but the key is that they have to use everything that has happened in their life to equate to something more positive. I encouraged each of them to look at their personality strengths, as well as their academic and cultural experience strengths, and combine those traits with what makes them curious about how the world operates and use all of that for the good.

Just listening to your story I can't even imagine some of the things that you have gone through. It is amazing to me how you have been able to take your experiences, some very painful experiences, and objectively analyze them and find solutions that not only help you but also contribute to society for the better. To me that is brilliance.

I think that it is an accepted premise in the transracial adoption world (at least I hope it is) that it is beneficial to connect with people that share similar racial and ethnic backgrounds as their children. But how do you exactly approach it as a discipline outside of a culture camp? And this is one of the primary reasons why I am working on this project. How do we, living and part of transracial adoptive families, connect to a Demetrius Walker—an esteemed and accomplished person who has wisdom that is vital for our families but in many cases sadly is separated by an invisible wall filled with assumptions, societal stereotypes, fear, and uncertainty?

I think it is very important for transracial adoptive families to extend their network base by connecting to people in the African American community. One of the things that breaks my heart, that I hear from white folks that I know, even here in my neighborhood, is, "We don't

see race. That does not matter to us." Whether you are black, Hispanic, or Asian, you don't see race? Really? Let's be realistic. If you
try to pretend that race does not matter, therein lies the problem. I
understand that many of these folks want to treat everybody equally.
That is good. But it is also important to *respect* that there are going to
be differences. We are also at a point in the United States where we
have not progressed to be truly color blind. So I think, first and foremost, white adoptive parents should recognize that their child of color
is going to have different experiences than them because of their different racial and ethnic background. Two, I think that it is important for
transracial adoptive parents to understand that their children are going
to be naturally curious about those differences, and pretending that
they don't exist is going to do a lot of damage to the child and to them.

I think that it is beneficial for these families to be intentional in
finding mentors. Personally I have had mentors throughout my life,
more so once I got into college. I have had people in my life like
Michael, a big marketing director. Just being able to e-mail him because we were not in the same city was advantageous. It is like having
a virtual mentor. We are so connected in the digital age. So if there
aren't any black, Asian, or Hispanic people for these adoptive parents'
kids to interact with, or for them to interact with, you have Facebook,
you have Twitter, you have e-mail. There are multitudes of ways you
can connect to people, including those of color, to share and obtain
good advice.

One of the eye-opening realities for me is probably an obvious
one to you. In the community where my husband and I live in
Michigan, the population is heavily Caucasian. One thing that almost makes me crazy with my husband is that in our community,
which we have been living in well over a decade, he still drives like
he is a visitor in his own community. He drives at a snail's pace.
No offense to snails. I'm talking ten, twelve, sixteen miles per hour.
Then my brother, who is white, comes to town, and you would think
that he owns the town. He is speeding down the streets with a sense
of privilege, much like, I would argue, most of the Caucasian residents in this town do. I operate somewhere between my brother
and my husband. But my point is that there is a different feel from

living in my white adoptive family and now living with my African American husband.

Another scenario is [that] I like doing my Home Depot projects, and every now and then I have my husband help me. So early on in my marriage, I used to say to my husband, "Honey, can you run to Home Depot with me?" The next thing I know, I am waiting in his car for him for what seems like a very long time. I go back into the house, and I hear the shower running! And he had already taken a shower earlier in the day. It got really bad when he was ironing his jeans. He has relaxed a bit since then. When I asked him what he was doing, he told me that he didn't want to be followed in the store. I get it, now. I have seen situations where we have picked up a twelve-dollar item from the mall, and everybody else who is white goes through the line without any problems, and then my husband comes up with a twelve-dollar item, and they say, "We want two forms of ID." My mouth drops because I was not used to that. And you have to address this stuff immediately.

I did not see my white family members being second-guessed, followed, or thought to be invisible when waiting for services to be rendered. There is a different reality, racially speaking. As a transracial adoptee I had to mature into understanding these different realities and nuances and to find solutions as to what a healthy response would be in these types of scenarios when dealing with the public. It is different being black in America and especially being a black male. I see it now. It angers me and frustrates me.

It is a lot of the subtle things that, if you are a white male or even a white female, you probably wouldn't notice the fact that the black guy in front of you in a line has to show his ID, and no other person in that line had the same requirement.

Sitting in a restaurant and hearing my husband say he is invisible is hard for me to hear. Now he handles his business and things get addressed. However, when I hear him say that he feels invisible, I want to talk to the manager immediately. For instance we start at a certain amount for tips at restaurants. I think that it is about 25 percent. If I even hear my husband say that he feels like he is invisible, we are now down to 2 percent. If the issue does not get resolved in that sitting, I'm writing a letter or talking with the owner or manager of that establishment. It's like I've had to figure out how to advocate for my husband and myself. For me it is important that I show him that, Look, I have our back, honey just like he has my back. If my husband remains visible, then I am not going to frequent that place. Like I said, most things get resolved in a positive way but it's exhausting. I'll be honest with you: it's *exhausting*.

I hear you. It can be exhausting. I remember being in Marquette, Michigan. I was there a few years ago. One of the relatively few black families that live there brought me up to speed. Very similar to what you were saying. People think that racism only still lives in the South. That's a myth. Hearing this family's experiences in Marquette, it was very obvious that racism was alive up North. When I got off the airplane, it was like people there had not seen a black guy in person before. I *felt* all eyes on me everywhere I went, like I was suspicious. The very subtle things that happen nowadays against minority groups can easily get overlooked because these acts can be so subtle. In the forties, fifties, and sixties, when folks were growing up, you could read about overt racism that was inflicted on people, where folks would just tell you in your face that "We are not serving any niggers here!" It's now covert, which can be worse because it is harder to put your finger on exactly what happened.

There are so many transracial adoptive parents who are trying to get this and are trying to prepare their black daughters, and sons in particular, for this reality. But when you are growing up in an environment where you believe that all police officers are your friends, or you think that the person down the street is safe because he goes to the same place of worship as you do, it is very hard as parents to think any differently because that is the world in which they live. Yet these parents still have the desire to prepare their children for what they may experience in this at times harsh world because of the color of their child's skin but how? How have you and your wife walked the tightrope of parenting now that you have a son?

The moment I found out that we were having a son, every experience that I've had as a black man hit me like a rock. I told myself that I have to make sure that I do everything in my power to ensure that my son doesn't have to experience the same things that I did, in terms of having to be in fear of his life or being picked on for being academically gifted. I wanted to make sure that whole cycle stopped. Realistically, yes, my son is probably going to have to deal with covert racism. It wouldn't even make sense for me to believe that he is going to get to eighteen years of age and not have some type of experience where he feels like he is being treated differently or unequally compared to his white friends or even Asian or Hispanic friends. That is just the reality of the United States at this point. But the fact that I believe that I will be able to prepare him for it, as a result of the multitude of my experiences, is huge. Going to not only white institutions of learning but also growing up in a predominately black community has certainly prepared me to teach my son how to overcome any obstacle that may come up for him because of his race. I am definitely excited about fatherhood. I want to make sure that society is more, just so that he doesn't have to go through as many of those experiences as I did, but I also realize that he does have to be prepared for them when they do come up.

How do you prepare your child, exactly?

It's funny that you asked that because a few months ago my wife and I got into a discussion. My wife was concerned that I would explain the world to our son in a "you against them" kind of way. I needed to help her realize that, no, that is not what my outlook of the world is, and that is not my plan to raise our child, to constantly be pessimistic about humanity. The message that our son will get from me is not to settle for mediocrity in anything, whether it comes to academics or how you are treated by other people. Everything needs to be at the highest level that it can be. If our son feels that he is in a situation where he is being treated in a less than stellar manner than his peers, I will teach him to identify that and figure out why he believes it to be so and then come and talk with me about what the potential solution might be to solve the problem. That is my parenting style and how I am going to move forward. My wife was concerned that I was going to imbue in our son some kind of "angry black male" attitude — "F—the police, and white people can't tell me anything," et cetera. That is definitely not the case!

Before we end I want to say that I think right now, in present-day America, we are still at a primitive mind-set when it comes to the human race. We are going to look back a couple of hundred years from now and say, "What were we thinking? We were cave men and women!" Rhonda, we still have these irrational preconceived notions about people based on skin color. I believe that it is everybody's job to make sure that on a daily basis we are progressing beyond that type of mentality. The only way that we can do that is for people to be able to genuinely connect with people of other races, cultures, and heritages and share their experiences so that we can grow as a human race—not as black people, white people, Asian people, and Hispanic people but as a human race—in order that we realize that we are all one despite our differences. At the end of the day I ask myself, "Demetrius Walker: What did I learn about myself, my people, and my country today?" I try to do that self-reflection daily. I would encourage others to do the same. If you go to bed and wake up the same person as you were the previous day, then what are you really living for?

Demetrius, thank you.

Conclusion

IN THEIR VOICES: BLACK AMERICANS ON TRANSRACIAL ADOPTION
was written from a place of love and support for fostered and adopted
children of color raised in white homes, white adoptive parents, nonadopted siblings, extended family members, and the ever-growing
transracial adoption community in the United States. My intention is
that this book will reach policy makers, researchers and practitioners
in the fields of social work and clinical therapy, and communities of
color as well as the broader society. Adoption workers and the transracial adoption community have given minimal attention to recruiting
and listening to the insightful voices of black Americans on the adoption of black and biracial children by white parents. Even progressive
adoption agencies and transracial adoptive families that understand
the importance to their families of making connections with the black
community have found this difficult to accomplish because of the lack
of know-how, access, and urgency. This book is my effort to make the
process of integrating transracial adoptive families with people of color
easier by tapping the voices of black Americans and including them
in the complicated discussion of why love *and* race matter, especially
when raising children across racial and cultural lines. By no means do
the stories told by the participants in this book reflect the experiences
of all black Americans. But their stories, taken together, do reflect certain experiences common to African Americans, and virtually all have
expressed the need to prepare young black and biracial transracial
adoptees for the likelihood that they, too, will have these experiences.

I hope that readers have come to realize, based on the interviews
presented throughout these pages, that in the twenty-first century it remains crucial for the development of healthy self-esteem and identity

by black and biracial transracial adoptees for them to regularly see and interact with people who look like them. As a transracial adoptee and ally of transracial adoptive families, I believe it is valuable for black and biracial transracial adoptees to know about their racial and ethnic history and to learn how to navigate comfortably in mainstream society and in communities of color across socioeconomic, professional, generational, and geographic borders.

Further, I believe that for the transracial adoptive family as a whole to move comfortably in different circles, these families must build cultural skills and literacies in their adoptee's racial and ethnic community/ies of origin. These refined skill sets will allow the family as a unit to understand, and show compassion to, one another, as well as participate in the struggles, activities, interests, and physical and emotional journeys of every one of its members on a more heightened and engaged level. For too long the transracial adoption community in general has not gone beyond the white world in its attempts to seek answers for its children of color, which has left them isolated and without the desperately needed experiences or wisdom found in the communities from which these beautiful children originated.

I have made the case that a social and geographic distance remains between communities of color and transracial adoptive families with white parents, despite increasing efforts by transracial adoptive families to identify themselves as multiracial, and that this distance means these children and their families do not get the help they need. Transracial adoption can be a beneficial and *bold* way to build a family. That is why I argue that the practice of transracial adoption, and the policies that support it, must embrace the adopted child's historical, cultural, and racial background: those characteristics make up a significant part of the child's identity.

Here are some examples of my own cultural confusion. My husband is African American, and after we married, I was shocked at the extra care he gave to ironing his clothes and making sure that his shoes always were polished. I tended to be less attentive to my dress, especially on Saturdays. One day he ironed his shirt and jeans just to go to Home Depot with me to pick up some tools and light fixtures. I thought that was a bit excessive. I also could not understand why we always had to be at our destination twenty to thirty minutes early whenever we were going somewhere together, whether it was to church, meet friends, or attend some event. And I was completely baffled when he became annoyed if I did not schedule my hair appointments regularly (they take three hours and a lot of money). These interviews caused me to revisit events in my own life that had been obscured by my color-blind upbringing and led me to a deeper understanding of, and historical perspective on, what I had actually experienced. Just being black in America—accomplishing basic tasks in public—can be exhausting. In this country black people still find a cloud of suspicion or concern overhead as they go about their lives. African Americans like my interviewees—and my husband—do what they can to reduce some of that suspicion by dressing well, speaking properly, behaving respectfully, arriving on time, following the rules, maintaining the care of their hair and skin, and so on. No one wants to be followed in a store or find themselves in altercations with the police or others in authority. Still, even black Americans who do all these things have no guarantee they will be treated fairly.

Yet, like me—and I left home more than twenty years ago—most transracial adoptees of color continue to grow up in a bubble of white privilege, attitudes, and experiences and apart from people of color. Research shows transracially adoptive families with white parents interact with mostly white family members, attend predominately white places of learning and worship, live in predominately white neighborhoods, and have predominately white friends. A common theme expressed by young black and biracial adult adoptees in *In Their Own Voices* (Simon & Roorda, 2000) is that their parents do not see color. They "accept us for who we are as people," as all parents should. But the problem comes when we, as transracial adoptees, open the door and walk out into the real world, where we are judged by the color of our skin. While this color-blind mind-set may come from a place of good intentions, it ignores the distinct history and realities of race in America. For many transracial adoptees who participated in *In Their Own Voices*, white culture and attitudes taught in their home and communities became the norm, the determiner of what is good and valid, leaving no room for them (or their family) to embrace diversity.

The result is that the transracial adoptee learns to want to be white and to dislike whatever makes them look different, including their hair, skin, eyes, and racial and ethnic heritage.

When I left the bubble of my white family and ventured out into society as a young black woman, my world changed. I no longer had the shelter of my white parents and their privileges. It was a rude awakening to realize that black Americans, including black and biracial transracial adoptees like me, are constantly assessed—on the street and in the classroom, boardroom, and workplace—and often are judged to be second rate because of the color of our skin and the painful history tied to it.

As I was struggling with my own racial identity as a young adult transracial adoptee, one of the first bits of advice that I received from my African American mentors is to *know* that you are black, a key point made by participants in this book. It is important that, as transracial adoptees of color, we have a healthy black identity and an awareness of our strengths and weaknesses so that when we find ourselves being judged—by society, our local communities, ourselves, or even our own adoptive families—we can stand firm on who we are, where we came from. That is why the interviewees who are parents and grandparents focus a great deal on instilling in their offspring firm values that will help guide and support them to become strong, centered, and confident individuals with exceptional purpose.

The parents and grandparents I interviewed also give their children the unambiguous message that they are black in America, which means they are inheriting challenges and struggles around race and identity that they must learn to navigate. These parents are intentional about initiating conversations with their children about race and culture, and as families they are tightly connected to the struggle, the history, and the experiences of being black in America. As Tabitha said of her and her husband's approach to raising their two children, "We are raising them on purpose and with purpose." She and her husband regard immersion in African American culture important to the development of their children's racial identity; equally important is ensuring that their children are routinely exposed to African Americans who are excelling in their professions and giving back to the community. They believe that a strong comprehension of black history is vital to their children's formation.

One way that Mahisha Dellinger and her husband expose their children to African Americans who excel in their professions is by ensuring that their daughters see black dentists and pediatricians. Mahisha, ever mindful of the appalling results of the Clark and Clark doll study, works especially hard to instill in her girls positive messages of self-worth. Her company makes a line of quality hair care products for people of mixed ethnicities and with different hair textures, and she uses the products to reinforce the message of the importance of healthy self-esteem. She says, "Self-esteem is important for girls of color, women of color, and hair maintenance and health is a huge part of that." She encourages transracial adoptive parents to pour a lot of energy, time, and resources into strengthening their child's self-esteem, ideally before they become teens, so that they will have a foundation for making good choices about dating, friendships, and education.

Parenting boys in the post–civil rights era is especially challenging, forcing parents to consider how society views their black sons. Shilease Hofmann and her husband saw their own teenage sons in Trayvon Martin, the seventeen-year-old Floridian shot to death by a neighborhood watch volunteer in 2012. Shilease and her husband thought they had counseled their sons effectively about how to address authority appropriately and not be harmed, but "Trayvon Martin did what I would have told my children to do." His death, Shilease said, "reinforced . . . my beliefs that you always have to be vigilant and you always have to be aware, because the rules can change on you."

Unfortunately such powerful words and sound parenting advice are often muted in a color-blind world. The black community knows from bitter experience always to be alert to white America's level of concern toward black people. That is an awareness that white parents, especially of black boys, need to acquire. When white adoptive parents do not introduce their children of color to their history, and fail to seek out mentors and pursue relationships with people color, these parents may be depriving their children, especially their sons, of information that is crucial both to their identity and to learning to safeguard themselves as they move about in society at large.

I wrote this book in the belief that if white transracial adoptive parents recognize the value of learning about the historical, racial, and ethnic experiences of black people in this country, they will realize that they have a vested interest in knowing and caring about the issues and concerns important to black America. In addition I believe that when transracial adoptive parents regularly interact with people of color, these parents will gain a comfort level in talking with their children about issues of race. I strongly believe that the skill set transracial adoptive parents acquire will better equip them to protect their children of color from the impact of racial insults by enabling them to instill in their children countermessages that are positive and that reinforce their child's self-worth and the adoptive family's worth as a multiracial-multicultural unit.

Good role models. Healthy self-esteem. The life-saving value of vigilance and good manners. These are the reasons why black Americans and white adoptive parents who are entrusted with children of color should become proactive in developing sustainable relationships with each other. We now know, through transracial adoption research, oral histories from transracial adoptees, and the testimony of African Americans, that the realities of black and biracial transracial adoptees merge with the realities and experiences of black and brown America as these adoptees move out of their childhood homes and communities. Society does not ask these transracial adoptees whether they were raised in a white family, nor does it care. Left to face that harsh truth alone, transracial adoptees are often ill prepared to figure out how to navigate in society with dark skin even as they are becoming distressed that their adoptive families lacked the understanding and depth to draw on the assistance of black people for the benefit of the transracial adoptive family.

All the participants I interviewed for this book are supportive of transracial adoption, especially if it means that the many available children who are languishing in the U.S. foster care system (a disproportionate number of whom are children of color) will be placed in loving, permanent, and secure homes. The interviewees recognize that children can grow roots and build a strong foundation in good families of all combinations. However, they expect white transracial adoptive parents to grasp the importance of embracing their family's connection to the black community, its diversity, culture, and history. That the people I interviewed vulnerably shared their stories and gave their time, love, and knowledge to transracial adoptive families is a testament to the interviewees' sincere desire for these families to establish relationships with other African Americans to ensure the well-being of black and biracial adoptees living in white families.

One group that could be instrumental in introducing transracial adoptive families to the black community is black social workers. As a transracial adoptee I had to work through the hurt I felt at the hands of both a foster care system that too easily assumed my destiny based on the color of my skin and my age and the National Association of Black Social Workers, which also projected a dim future for me. I felt that the NABSW's 1972 statement opposing transracial adoption left me, other transracial adoptees, and our families with little or no guidance and support in navigating society's roadblocks and pitfalls. I have long been a firm believer that transracial adoptive families need the NABSW and the broader black community, and now I have the courage and experience to push both communities to establish meaningful connections.

I am incredibly enriched by each participant in this book. W. Wilson Goode Sr., who ministers to children and their incarcerated parents; Vershawn A. Young, who found a means to integrate black language in academia; Demetrius Walker, who inspires young members of the hip-hop culture to learn about black history and intellectual empowerment; and others in this book who demonstrate that as, they have risen up the economic ladder, they have not forgotten who they are, where they came from, and the responsibility they have to give back to their community. That will to promote advantage, opportunity, and guidance in their communities is what they bring to the table when talking to black and biracial transracial adoptees and their families.

According to Chester Jackson, a crucial step for white parents who are considering fostering and adopting black and/or biracial children is to "believe that you *can* foster and adopt these amazing children and that these children can have a bright future." Chelsey Hines is unyielding in her view that once parents believe that they can foster and adopt children, they must actually *invest* and *participate* in their child's life. Families, particularly transracial adoptive families, need added support from their adoption agencies. White parents who adopt black and biracial children need a strong network, and I am convinced that postadoption services need to more effectively prepare transracial adoptive families for this experience.

As I speak around the country, a key step that white transracial adoptive families struggle with is actually building relationships with black people, which includes finding a role model or mentor for their child. I know that is not an easy task. Many of the transracial adoptive families I have met want to be respectful of the black community and do not want to appear desperate. I hope this book will provide common ground for both groups to build relationships with each other with much more clarity and comfort—and the assistance of the NABSW. Henry Allen suggests that transracial adoptive parents establish networks that reflect a range of people, including members of their child's ethnic community. W. Wilson Goode Sr. suggests that white adoptive parents humble themselves and ask the black community for help. He does caution that they may encounter a backlash but urges them to persist. According to Goode, a great way for transracial adoptees to connect with black people is by joining black fraternities and sororities at colleges and universities or even by spending time in the home of a black family overnight or for a weekend. Other interviewees suggested participating in black churches and attending local black cultural events.

In an effort to help make the suggestions offered by those in this book more manageable for transracial adoptive parents, the appendix provides a strategic multicultural adoption plan for the long-term enrichment of each family member, particularly the transracial adoptee. The goal of this plan is for the adoptive family to become knowledgeable about and comfortable with the adopted child's racial/ethnic heritage and adoption experiences. The entire family's involvement in learning about and understanding the developmental path of transracially adopted children will give these children greater support in their efforts to develop healthy racial identities and senses of self. The hope, of course, is that, with the engaged support of the adoptive family and those in communities of color, transracial adoptees ultimately will be in a better position to flourish and lead centered and meaningful lives.

Afterword

FEDERAL ADOPTION POLICY, as embodied in the 1994 Multiethnic
Placement Act (MEPA) and the 1996 Interethnic Adoption Act (IEPA),
needs to be adjusted to address the inadequacies that leave so many
children languishing in the U.S. foster care system. Although both
measures were designed to move more children, a disproportionate
number of whom are children of color, into permanent homes as
quickly as possible, both measures have had an adverse, albeit unintended, effect. Neither measure requires agencies—whether public
child welfare agencies or private agencies under contract to them to
place children—to have expertise in preparing or training potential
adoptive parents to care for the cultural and racial needs of children of
color, nor does either law provide incentives to adoption agencies that
hire professionals of color, despite the demographics of the children
these agencies are serving. Moreover, neither measure includes clear
guidelines on how adoption agencies can institute targeted outreach
and educational efforts in communities of color for the purposes of
recruiting potential adoptive parents. As a result, when adoption professionals place children of color with white adoptive parents, they
do so with minimal attention to the cultural and physical needs of
the child, which leaves these children to fend for themselves in their
adoptive homes.

Because MEPA and IEPA take a color-blind approach to placement, adoption agencies fear they will be breaking federal law if they
prepare white transracial adoptive parents for meeting the racial and
cultural needs of the children of color they will be raising.[1] Doing so
requires specific parenting skills and connections to these children's
ethnic communities of origin. Adoption agencies need to be freed of

any legal repercussions if they require their staff to learn how to do this. Parents deserve to know how best to raise their children and have the support network to do so. Some may argue that adding requirements to current transracial adoption policy will slow down placements and/ or face legal challenges, but I believe that it actually will give potential parents the confidence and awareness that they need to succeed in raising their child instead of feeling helpless and overwhelmed after the fact—or instead of rejecting domestic transracial adoption in favor of international adoption because they don't know how to deal with the cultural and historical issues.

Further, before the 2008 release of the Evan B. Donaldson report "Finding Families for African American Children: The Role of Race and Law in Adoption from Foster Care" (Smith, McRoy et al., 2008), it seems to have occurred only to me, other transracial adoptees, and precious few others that the color-blind policy of the U.S. child welfare system is irresponsible and unethical because it essentially ignores the persistence of racial discrimination, an everyday fact for communities of color, and minimizes the uniqueness, challenges, and benefits that each child brings to a new family. The child welfare system should make it a priority to provide services and/or financial support to families and communities trying to raise children in challenging circumstances. I truly believe that whether children are placed with relatives, same-race couples, or transracial parents, public and private adoption agencies and their staffs must figure out how best to meet the needs of these children with compassion, cultural understanding, inclusiveness, innovative thinking, and with the support and clarity of good adoption policy.

Finally, I want to emphasize that while this book focuses largely on black and biracial children raised in white adoptive homes, the suggestions provided here are relevant to transracial adoptive families of all combinations. Transracial adoption includes international adoptions—of children from Korea, Ethiopia, Latin America, India, Nepal, Haiti, and many other countries. Thus Americans adopting from Korea need to learn Korean history and culture and figure out how to introduce their families to members of the Korean American community, just as American adoptive parents will need to learn the history and culture of Ethiopia or Thailand and befriend members of the Ethiopian American or South Asian American communities. My hope is that researchers, parents, adoptees, policy makers, therapists, and social work professionals continue to ensure that the discussion and study of transracial adoption is a priority so that we can increase our understandings of how best to meet the racial, multicultural, and emotional needs of children in transracial adoptive settings.

Multicultural Adoption Plan

Strengthening the Heart and Mind of the Adoptive Parent:
Preparing to Embrace Your Child of Color

As white parents, the successful adoption of children of color requires
you to be willing to experience the close encounters with racism that
your children—and you as parents—will have and to be prepared to
talk to your children about them. Ultimately you will need to examine
your own identities as white people, going beyond the idea of raising
a child of color in a white family to reach a new understanding of
yourselves and your children as members of a multiracial family (Tatum, 1997, p. 190). And now that you have read *In Their Voices: Black
Americans on Transracial Adoption*, you have taken another step in
moving beyond a color-blind way of thinking to an awareness that will
strengthen your multiracial family.

Generations of your family will be affected by your decision to
adopt transracially. In order to make the experience smoother for all
involved, what follows are step-by-step guidelines that will help you,
as white adoptive parents, to prepare for the added responsibilities of
raising black and biracial children to become confident and centered
adults who are able to find balance in their multiracial-multicultural
existence and adoption story. These guidelines are based on the findings in this book and from two decades of listening to adult adoptees
of color, white adoptive parents, and nonadopted siblings.

*Think carefully about whether you are willing and able to take on the
responsibility of raising a child transracially.*

- Understand that because of the history of the United States, racial discrimination remains a reality, experienced by virtually all black people and other people of color at some point in their lives. Choosing to raise a child of color transracially means you will need to learn how to advocate for your child's best interests at home, in the community, and in school— ensuring that he is also safe psychologically. Because of race, your child will not always be treated fairly or be seen by others as capable or worthy.
- Recognize that your child will grow into a woman or man of color. Connecting your child to supportive black people (and other minorities) will strengthen your child's racial identity and self-esteem.
- Commit to raising your adopted child of color to adulthood with the goal of maintaining a lasting and respectful relationship, even if your child ultimately decides to closely identify with the African American community (and/or other communities of color) and its issues or chooses to marry a person of color from a different socioeconomic background.

Ask yourself what your views are of your adopted child's ethnic community/ies of origin.

Do you tend to feel superior, inferior, or equal to your adopted child's ethnic community? Whatever your views, your child will see the truth. Therefore, if you are not already there, you need to change your thinking so that you see value in your child's ethnic community of origin and will want to form relationships with people who look like your child. Even if at first you are not entirely comfortable associating with people who share your child's ethnic or cultural heritage, you can start to become comfortable by building social connections in your place of residence. We now know, from research and personal accounts by adult transracial adoptees, that developing a healthy racial identity is key to your child's self-esteem. Here are a few examples of what you can do, as early as possible, to make your child's ethnic background part of your family's identity:

- Include artwork or artifacts in your home that reflect your adopted child's ethnic background.

- Ensure that your child has black dolls or action figures and regularly sees positive black or brown characters in books, movies, and in other media.
- Introduce your family to the traditional foods of African American culture and other cultures, both within the United States and from around the world. (Some of my favorite African American foods are greens, black-eyed peas, grits, cornbread, and sweet potato pie.)
- Learn about your child's hair and skin care needs and seek out products that meet the specific needs of your child of color. (African American hairdressers and barbers will be wonderfully helpful in this regard.)

Continuously build a reservoir of knowledge of your child's ethnic and/ or cultural heritage and the subject of adoption.

- Read! Read! Read! Become educated about racial issues, the history of African Americans in this country, and the sometimes difficult losses that are also a part of many adoptees' story.
- Prepare to share your child's adoption story with her. Be sure to use age-appropriate language that honors the child and her need to know the truth. Revisit the story over time as your child's questions may change and develop. Children are likely to ask, "Where do I come from?" "Who am I?" "Where do I belong?" And they are likely to want more specificity from you as they mature. For example, the results of a DNA test would mean nothing to a four-year-old but would mean a lot to a fourteen-year-old.
- Participate in a local reading group made up of transracial adoptive parents and people of color that focuses on books about transracial adoption and the black experience. Three of my favorite books that can lead to great conversations are *The Warmth of Other Suns: The Epic Story of America's Great Migration* by Isabel Wilkerson; *Jesus Land: A Memoir* by Julia Scheeres; and *From Fear to Love: Parenting Difficult Adopted Children* by B. Bryan Post.
- Visit African American art and history museums or exhibits in your state or in your travels to other places. You might want to document your adventures by taking pictures, recording oral histories, or by

making a life book about your adopted child's adoption story and experiences.

- Join the Transracial Adoption Facebook group and use the opportunities it affords to chat with transracial adoptees (of all combinations), many of whom are professionals in their own right and have given transracial adoption a great deal of thought. This group also consists of birth parents, people of color, adoptive parents, and non-adopted siblings. Other great resources are conferences, seminars, or camps organized by such groups as Bridge Communications; the North American Council on Adoptable Children; Pact Adoption Family Camp in California; Umoja: A Black Heritage Experience in Wisconsin; the Ethiopian Heritage Camp in Virginia; and the Colorado Heritage Camps, including the African Caribbean Heritage Camp.

Develop smart support systems for you and your family, and take steps to limit contact with anyone you suspect will be hurtful or less than accepting.

- Assess personal and professional relationships and resources within your community that can help you in your efforts to raise your child of color and support your multiracial-multicultural family.
- Identify anyone in your inner circle who is likely to be critical of your family. You should think seriously about severely curtailing any contact that such a person or people have with other members of your family. Transracial adoption is a wonderful journey, but it is fraught with pockets of emotional land mines, patches of racial insults, and bumps of exhaustion, confusion, and anxiety. You want people in your inner circle who will offer you kindness, a listening ear, compassion, wisdom, and encouragement.
- Seek out new, positive relationships with people—especially people of color—who are supportive of you and your family.

Consider whether you regularly encounter African Americans in your community, your place of worship, and in your place of business.

The way to build safe, nurturing environments for your child (and family) is by ensuring that family members regularly encounter people who look like them.

- As you go about your day, do you see African Americans in the grocery store, your exercise class, at the local library, or right down the hall in a nearby office or cubicle? If so, these are wonderful opportunities to introduce yourself. Make a connection with your smile and wit.
- Have you established any genuine relationships with African Americans and other people of color? For example, have you taken the next steps and invited these folks over for dinner, set up play dates with their children, or visited them at their home?

It is important that you have African American friends and acquaintances who share your socioeconomic background because they will offer your child of color familiar and comfortable role models; the result will be that your child will see that he can achieve good and noble things. If such role models simply are not available in your neighborhood, consider moving into a predominately black or multicultural neighborhood so that your child is not the only person of color (or one of very few) in your neighborhood, schools, or community.

Create tangible connections to the black community.

- Attend a black church. If you are religious, you might even want to *join* a black church. Your minister, priest, or rabbi can introduce you to black clergy in your community.
- Make an effort to frequent black (and other minority) businesses. For example, when caring for your child of color's hair, instead of doing it by yourself, connect with barbers and stylists in the black community. Remember that barber shops and beauty salons are important social gathering places in the black community and provide an opportunity for you and your family to create meaningful relationships with people who look like your child while ensuring that

your child's hair is properly maintained. Simply passing the time of day with black dry cleaners as you hand over your clothes or as the butcher of color packages your order is another way for your child to learn how black culture works and is different from the white culture.

- Locate black pediatricians, dentists, and other professionals for your child; they will be knowledgeable about your child's specific health and wellness needs while also acting as great role models.

Once you commit to participating in activities in the black community, you will quickly gain a comfort level that will encourage you to expand your connections with the community. Simply by doing so you will be showing your child how to navigate effectively within the black community and other communities of color. Your newfound skills and knowledge will help you better hear your child and advocate for him at school and in your community. These skills will also help you and your family achieve a broader and more integrated worldview. Other means of multiplying your connections within the black community include

- Developing personal friendships and even finding godparents and mentors for your child. The relationships that you develop may become lifelong.
- Learning about your new friends' joys, struggles, and experiences, many of which will be unlike anything within your personal experience. You will see on an intimate level how your friends of color address within their families racial insults and discrimination and how they move forward.
- Using your privileges to open doors of opportunity for people of color in the workplace and elsewhere. Speak up against racial injustices that occur within your sphere of influence. Support adoption policy that is inclusive of communities of color.

Within the pages of *In Their Voices: Black Americans on Transracial Adoption*, you have met black women and men who show what it means to be vulnerable, courageous, and giving to a community that is different than theirs but shares common ground. The participants' investment in the transracial adoptive community and other communities is valuable and should not be minimized. By their incredible example and frank discussions they have shown how white adoptive parents, transracial adoptees, nonadopted siblings, and extended adoptive family members can break down racial and cultural barriers and develop meaningful relationships with people in communities of color for the advancement of transracial adoption.

I would like to close with a personal example of how a relationship between a transracial adoptive family and an African American family can blossom through work, love, and commitment. In 1973, shortly after my adoptive family moved to the Washington, D.C., area, we joined a Christian Reformed church. I was three years old. The church was predominately white, but within its membership were black families from the community and several transracial adoptive families.

One of the black members, Ms. Myrtle, who was also the organist-pianist, saw me sitting in the pews with a white family. As she told me years later, she looked over the top of the organ and saw my runny nose, my ashy skin, and dry, apparently uncombed, hair. After the service she approached my parents and firmly told them that she did not believe that a black child should be raised in a white home. Then she added, "Since you chose to adopt her, it looks like I am going to raise Rhonda with you." My father, a tall man with blond hair and blue eyes, said that was probably the first time that he ever said "yes, ma'am" to anyone. After that, Ms. Myrtle became my godmother and worked closely with my mom and dad to nurture and love me. From her constant involvement in my life, my parents and siblings gained a special and respectful relationship with her and her family. We shared regular meals together at each other's homes, we laughed and cried together, and we grew together. When I faltered—had an identity crisis, failed to focus on my education, or behaved badly—my godmother would wrap her arms around me, look into my eyes, and inspire me to get back on track and remember who I was and what my destiny was. My godmother's expectations of me where high and unwavering.

I will always remember watching *The Color Purple* and *The Sound of Music* with her while eating chocolates and popcorn, occasions that always seemed to brighten my life in subsequent days. I will always be appreciative of my adoptive parents and siblings for opening our lives to Ms. Myrtle and her family. My relationship with them became the first of many priceless and enriching relationships with friends and mentors from the black community.

In the mid-2000s, as my godmother was struggling with health issues and had difficulty driving, it was my dad's turn to give back. Until she died in 2006, he would pick her up at her home and drive her to and from choir rehearsal, where she found joy, and he made sure that he was a constant support system. Four years ago, when my brother, Chris, got married, his best man was Myrtle's son. The relationship our families shared changed all our lives for the better. We loved more deeply, thought more keenly, and acted with more compassion in every aspect of our lives.

Good luck on your journey!

Notes

Introduction: Moving Beyond the Controversy of the Transracial Adoption of Black and Biracial Children

1. In the Clark and Clark Doll Test, which played a significant role in the Supreme Court ruling in *Brown v. Board of Education* (1954), psychologists presented black children aged three to seven with two dolls that were identical, except that one was black and one was white. They then asked the children which doll they preferred to play with, which doll was "bad," which was "good," and which looked most like the child. Many designated the black doll as bad and almost half said they looked like the white doll. Children who attended segregated schools were more likely to deem the white doll the nice one. The Supreme Court's decision cited the Clarks' research and noted: "To separate [African American children] from others of similar age and qualifications solely because of their race generates a feeling of inferiority as to their status in the community that may affect their hearts and minds in a way unlikely ever to be undone" (Cherry, n.d.; NAACP, 2014).

Part I. Jim Crow Era (1877–1954)

1. The term *Jim Crow* comes from a character of that name created by a white comic, Thomas Dartmouth Rice, who performed a popular song-and-dance show in which he became a caricature of a black slave. He darkened his face, exaggerated his lips, played the fool, and spoke in distorted imitation of African American dialect. This negative and degrading imagery later became the symbol of the post-Reconstruction era (Jim Crow Museum, n.d.).

Part II. Civil Rights Era (1955–72)

1. According to Asante, "Eurocentric ideology . . . masquerades as a universal view in the fields of intercultural communication, rhetoric, philosophy, linguistics, psychology, education, anthropology, and history. Yet the critique [Afrocentricity] is radical only in

the sense that it suggests a turnabout, an alternative perspective on phenomena. It is about taking the globe and turning it over so that we see all the possibilities of a world where Africa, for example, is subject and not object. Such a posture is necessary and rewarding for both Africans and Europeans. The inability to 'see' from several angles is perhaps the one common weakness in provincial scholarship" (Asante, 1997, p. 1).

2. Cotillions, or debutante balls, in fact were common social events among the upper crust in the North as well and date to the mid-eighteenth century in one form or another both above and below the Mason-Dixon line (Lewis, 2012; Kendall, 2002).

Part III. Post–Civil Rights Era (1973–Present)

1. In the 1967 *Loving* decision (*Loving v. Virginia*, 388 U.S. 1), the Supreme Court ruled unconstitutional the state law prohibiting marriage by people of different races, declaring it in violation of the due process and equal protection clauses of the Fourteenth Amendment.

2. According to the U.S. State Department, which is the U.S. central authority for international adoptions, the Hague Convention on Intercountry Adoption, signed by the United States in 1994, requires parents to take "at least" ten hours of training. "Such mandatory training addresses a wide range of topics, including the intercountry adoption process, developmental risk factors associated with children from the expected country of origin, and attachment disorders. The training also prepares you for the adoption of a particular child, when possible" (U.S. State Department, 2006, p. 16). The State of Colorado, for example, requires twenty-four hours of parent training, including "parenting a child of a different culture or racial background, long term implications from infancy through adulthood" ("Adoption Training Classes," n.d.).

3. Alex and Nicole are pseudonyms. Chelsey, the oldest, is three years older than her brother and five years older than her sister.

4. Chelsey offered this clarification in a subsequent conversation: "I have been incarcerated on and off in my young adult years for different things," adding that her first experience with jail was "for two months when I was fifteen or sixteen for theft and breaking and entering."

5. Walker said the company's full name remains dangerousNEGRO Black Empowerment Apparel. dN|BE, as the company is more widely known, is simply "easier to fit on designs," he explained.

Afterword

1. According to Kris Faasse, adoption services director at Bethany Christian Services in Grand Rapids, Michigan, "Federal law says there can't be race-specific resources. It would prevent me from creating some sort of race-specific education or resource because we're required to offer it to all families" (McKendry 2013).

References

Alexander, R. Jr., & Curtis, C. M. (1996). A review of empirical research involving the transracial adoption of African American children. *Journal of Black Psychology*, 22(2), 223–235.

Altstein, H. (2006, January 29). Race need not be an issue in adoption: More matches possible if we stop talking about race. *Houston Chronicle*. Retrieved http://www.chron.com/opinion/outlook/article/Race-need-not-be-an-issue-in-adoption-1854438.php.

Andrews, W. L., et al. (1992). *African American literature: Voices in a tradition*. Austin: Holt, Rinehart and Winston.

Asante, M. K. (1997). *The Afrocentric idea*. Rev. ed. Philadelphia: Temple University Press, 1997.

Baden, A. L., & Steward, R. J. (2000). A framework for use with racially and culturally integrated families: The cultural-racial identity model as applied to transracial adoption. *Journal of Social Distress and the Homeless*, 9(4), 309–337.

Bertelsen, P. (dir.). (2001). *Outside Looking In: Transracial Adoption in America*. Documentary film. New York: Big Mouth Productions.

Bertrand, M., & Mullainathan, S. (2004). Are Emily and Greg more employable than Lakisha and Jamal? A field experiment on labor market discrimination. *American Economic Review*, 94(4). Retrieved from http://public.econ.duke.edu/~hfi4/teaching/povertydisc/readings/bertrand-mullainathan2004.pdf.

Bloom, H. (2004). *The Harlem Renaissance*. Broomall, PA: Chelsea House.

Burke, C. (2013, December 31). MSNBC panel mocks photo of Romney holding adopted black grandson. *Newsmax*. Retrieved from http://www.newsmax.com/Newsfront/mitt-romney-race-msnbc-media/2013/12/30/id/544475/.

Chandler, D. (2012, August 28). Teen Emmett Till victim of kidnapping, brutal murder on this day in 1955. *NewsOne for Black America*. Retrieved from http://newsone.com/2032853/emmett-till-story/.

Chestang, L. (1972). The dilemma of biracial adoption. *Social Work*, 17, 100–105.

Davis, F. J. (1991). *Who is black?* University Park: Pennsylvania State University Press.

Evans, M. (1992). Contemporary poetry. In Andrews et al., *African American literature* (pp. 643–649).

Fenster, J. (2002). Transracial adoption in black and white: A survey of social worker attitudes. *Adoption Quarterly*, 5(4), 33–58.

Fisher, A. P. (2003). Still "not quite as good as having your own"? Toward a sociology of adoption. *Annual Review of Sociology*, 29, 335–361.

Ghatt, J. (2014, January 8). Romney, Perry and the politics of transracial adoption. *Washington Times*. Retrieved from http://communities.washingtontimes.com/neighbor hood/politics-raising-children/2014/jan/8/romneyperry-controversy-politics-transracial-adopt/.

Herman, E. (2012, February 24). Transracial adoptions. The Adoption History Project, Department of History, University of Oregon. Retrieved from http://pages.uoregon.edu/adoption/topics/transracialadoption.htm.

Hoard, D. C. (dir.). (1998). *Struggle for identity: Issues in transracial adoption*. Video. Ithaca, NY: PhotoSynthesis Productions. DVD release May 2007.

Holland, J. J. (2014, April 3). National Urban League State of Black America 2014 report says minorities lossing economic ground. *Huffington Post*. Retrieved from http://www.huffingtonpost.com/2014/04/03/national-urban-league-state-of-black-america_n_5083025.html.

Hollinger, J. H., & the ABA Center on Children and the Law. (1998). *A guide to the Multiethnic Placement Act of 1994 as amended by the Interethnic Adoption Provisions of 1996*. Retrieved from http://www.americanbar.org/content/dam/aba/administrative/child_law/GuidetoMultiethnicPlacementAct.authcheckdam.pdf.

Hollingsworth, L. D. (1997). Effect of transracial/transethnic adoption on children's racial and ethnic identity and self-esteem: A meta-analytic review. *Marriage and Family Review*, 25(1), 99–130.

Householder, M. (2012, April 19). New Michigan museum showcases racist artifacts. *Associated Press*, on the website of the Jim Crow Museum of Racist Memorabilia, http://www.ferris.edu/htmls/news/jimcrow/more.htm.

Hughes, L. (1992). I, too. In Andrews et al., *African American Literature* (p. 326).

Identity formation in adolescence. (2002, November). *Facts and findings*. Retrieved from http://www.actforyouth.net/resources/rf/rf_identityformation_1102.pdf.

Independence Hall Association. (2008–14). A new civil rights movement: Rosa Parks and the Montgomery bus boycott. *U.S. history*. Retrieved from http://www.ushistory.org/us/54b.asp.

Ingram, B. (1956, November 14). Supreme Court outlaws bus segregation. *Montgomery Advertiser*. Retrieved from http://www.montgomeryboycott.com/supreme-court-outlaws-bus-segregation/.

John, J. (2005). *Black baby white hands: A view from the crib*. 2d ed. Silver Spring, MD: Soul Water Rising.

Kennedy, R. (2003). *Interracial intimacies: Sex, marriage, identity, and adoption*. New York: Pantheon.

King, M. L. (1992). I have a dream. In Andrews et al., *African American Literature* (pp. 616–619).

Kreider, R. M., & Raleigh, E. (2011, April). *Contexts of racial socialization: Are transracial adoptive families more like multiracial or white monoracial families?* Paper presented at the Population Association of America meetings, Washington, DC.

Leadership Conference. (2001). Civil rights chronology. *CivilRights.org.* Retrieved from http://www.civilrights.org/resources/civilrights101/chronology.html.

Lemann, N. (2013, January–February). Deconstructing Reconstruction. *Washington Monthly.* Retrieved from http://www.washingtonmonthly.com/magazine/january _february_2013/features/deconstructing_reconstruction042046.php?page=all.

Macaulay, J., & Macaulay, S. (1978). Adoption for black children: A case study of expert discretion. *Research in Law and Sociology, 1,* 265–318.

McRoy, R., Zurcher, L. A., Lauderdale, M. L., & Anderson, R. N. (1982). Self-esteem and racial identity in transracial and inracial adoptees. *Social Work, 27,* 522–526.

McRoy, R., Zurcher, L. A., Lauderdale, M. L., & Anderson, R. N. (1984). The identity of transracial adoptees. *Social Case Work, 65,* 34–39.

NAACP. (2000). *Thirty years of lynching in the United States: 1889–1918.* New York: Oxford University Press.

NAACP. (2009–2014). *Criminal justice fact sheet.* Retrieved from http://www.naacp .org/pages/criminal-justice-fact-sheet.

Phillips, J. (2006, May). Reconstruction in Mississippi, 1865–1876. *HistoryNow.* Retrieved from http://mshistorynow.mdah.state.ms.us/articles/204/reconstruction-in -mississippi-1865–1876.

Phinney, J. (1990). Ethnic identity in adolescents and adults: A review of research. *Psychological Bulletin, 108,* 499–514.

Reid-Merritt, P. (2010). *Righteous self determination: The black social work movement in America.* Baltimore: Imprint Editions.

Samuels, G. (2009). Being raised by white people: Navigating racial difference among adopted multiracial adults. *Journal of Marriage and Family, 71*(1), 80–94.

Shireman, J. F., & Johnson, P. R. (1986). A longitudinal study of black adoptions: Single parent, transracial, and traditional. *Social Work, 31,* 172–176.

Simon, R. J., & Roorda, R. M. (2000). *In their own voices: Transracial adoptees tell their stories.* New York: Columbia University Press.

Simon, R. J., & Roorda, R. M. (2007). *In their parents' voices: Reflections on raising transracial adoptees.* New York: Columbia University Press.

Simon, R. J., & Roorda, R. M. (2009). *In their siblings' voices: White non-adopted siblings talk about their experiences being raised with black and biracial brothers and sisters.* New York: Columbia University Press.

Simon, R., Altstein, H., & Melli, M. (1994). *The case for transracial adoption.* Washington, DC: American University Press.

Smith, D. (2013, March 31). Raising culturally responsive black children in white adoptive homes: Uncovering the importance of code-switching in the battlefield of racial identity development. *Huffington Post.* Retrieved from http://www.huffingtonpost.com/darron-t-smith-phd/adopted-black-children_b_2550751.html.

Smith, D., Jacobson, K., & Juàrez, B. (2011). *White parents, black children: Experiencing transracial adoption.* Lanham, MD: Rowman & Littlefield.

Smith, N. S., & Hjelm, R. T. (2007, June). Transracial adoption and the Multiethnic Placement Act. *Issue brief.* Retrieved from http://thehill.com/images/stories/white papers/pdf/MEPA_Final_IB.pdf.

Smith, S., McRoy, R., Freundlich, M., & Kroll, J. (2008, May). *Finding families for African American children: The role of race and law in adoption from foster care.* Report for the Evan B. Donaldson Adoption Institute. Retrieved from http://66.227.70.18/advocacy/findingfamilies.htm.

Tatum, B. (1997). *"Why are all the black kids sitting together in the cafeteria?"* New York: Basic Books.

Townsend, J. T. (1995). Reclaiming self-determination: A call for intraracial adoption. *Duke Journal of Gender Law & Policy, 2*(1), 173–190.

Turner, S., & Taylor, J. (1996). Underexplored issues in transracial adoption. *Journal of Black Psychology, 22*(2), 262–265.

Vandivere, S., Malm, K., & Radel, L. (2009). *Adoption USA: A chartbook based on the 2007 National Survey of Adoptive Parents.* Washington, DC: U.S. Department of Health and Human Services. Retrieved from http://aspe.hhs.gov/hsp/09/NSAP/chartbook/index.pdf.

U.S. Department of Health and Human Services. Children's Bureau. (2013, November). *The AFCARS report.* Retrieved from http://www.acf.hhs.gov/sites/default/files/cb/afcarsreport20.pdf.

Wilkerson, I. (2010). *The Warmth of Other Suns: The Epic Story of America's Great Migration.* New York: Random House.

Wright, G. (2013, February 13). The stunning economic impact of the civil rights movement. *BloombergView.* Retrieved from http://www.bloombergview.com/articles/2013-02-13/the-stunning-economic-impact-of-the-civil-rights-movement.

Zastrow, C. (1977). *Outcome of black children: White parents, transracial adoptions.* San Francisco: R & E Research Associates.